Death of a Rebel

Death of a Rebel

The Charlie Fenton Story

Scott Donaldson

FAIRLEIGH DICKINSON UNIVERSITY PRESS
Madison · Teaneck

Published by Fairleigh Dickinson University Press
Co-published with The Rowman & Littlefield Publishing Group, Inc.
4501 Forbes Boulevard, Suite 200, Lanham, Maryland 20706
www.rowman.com

10 Thornbury Road, Plymouth PL6 7PP, United Kingdom

British Library Cataloguing in Publication Information Available

Library of Congress Cataloging-in-Publication Data

The hardback edition of this book was previously cataloged by the Library of Congress as follows:

Donaldson, Scott, 1928–
Death of a rebel : the Charlie Fenton story / Scott Donaldson.
  p. cm.
  Includes bibliographical references.
  1. Fenton, Charles A. 2. Biographers—United States—Biography. 3. College teachers—United States—Biography. 4. Authors, American—20th century—Biography. 5. Yale University—Faculty—Biography. I. Title.
PS29.F46D43 2012
810.9—dc23 [B]

2011034585

ISBN 978-1-61147-493-0 (cloth : alk. paper)
ISBN 978-1-61147-624-8 (pbk. : alk. paper)
ISBN 978-1-61147-494-7 (electronic)

™ The paper used in this publication meets the minimum requirements of American National Standard for Information Sciences—Permanence of Paper for Printed Library Materials, ANSI/NISO Z39.48-1992.

Printed in the United States of America

This is for mentors and students everywhere, among them Merrill Skaggs, who showed me the way before departing, and Vivie Donaldson, who continues to make books and many happy things possible.

Contents

Acknowledgments

The Fenton family has been extraordinary generous in helping me write this biography of Charlie Fenton. His son Andy (Charles Andrews Fenton, Jr.) opened doors to a number of sources, and provided his own insights. He and Charlie's brother Dave retrieved and sent invaluable letters, manuscripts, and photographs. Wendy Nielsen and Richard D. Grant, Fenton's stepchildren, contributed memories of the man who was their father from 1944 to 1960. Everyone in the family, up to and including grandchildren, has been helpful. They all want to see Charlie Fenton's life commemorated, as do many of his students and colleagues both at Yale and Duke. Never in fifty years at the task have I encountered such enthusiastic cooperation.

Among these sources—an alphabetical list hardly does them justice—were Virginia (Ginger Price) Barber, Judith S. Baughman, Matthew J. Bruccoli, Louis J. Budd, Dr. John C. Carson, Stuart Chase, Marshall Coleman, Joel Colton, William W. Combs, William Deresiewicz, Gwendolyn R. Fenton, Frank Gado, Maxwell Grant, Tom Greening, Lewis Jones, Alice Kaplan, J. Gerald Kennedy, Herbert Kretzmer, Sybil Kretzmer, Heidi M. Kunz, Peter Matthiessen, Peter Matson, Joanne (Marshall) Mauldin, Donald McQuade, Malcolm Mitchell, Paul Nielsen, Penny Nielsen, Reynolds Price, Edwin Sauter, Jr., Debbie Shepherd, Cal Skaggs, Merrill (Maguire) Skaggs, Gaddis Smith, James Stevenson, Michael True, James L.W. West III, Mary (Church) Williams, and Mary Ann Wimsatt.

Merrill Skaggs and Matt Bruccoli, both of whom pursued distinguished careers shaped by their contact with Charlie Fenton, died within the last few years. The best source of all, Fenton's mentor Norman Holmes Pearson, died in 1975, his invaluable testimony emerging in papers he left behind. Additional important correspondents, also deceased, include Gale Carrithers,

Malcolm Cowley, Leonard W. Doob, Chester Kerr, and Mark Schorer. Still other letters documenting this book came from Ashbel Brice, William P. Fidler, A. Whitney Griswold, DeLaney Kiphuth, Russell Lynes, George Winchester Stone, Jr., and Glenway Wescott.

For access to such communications I thank the following institutions and archivists (arranged alphabetically): David Farrell at the Bancroft Library, University of California; Jay Parini and Danielle Rougeau at Middlebury College (Bread Loaf); Sara Selen Berghausen and Kim Sims, Duke University Archives; Will Hansen at the Perkins Library, Duke University; Diane Ray at the Estates Division, Durham (NC) Courthouse; Marshall Coleman at Eaglebrook School; Susan Wrynn at the Hemingway Collection; John F. Kennedy Library, Boston; Patricia J. Albright at Mount Holyoke College Archives; Helen Long at the Newberry Library, Chicago; Sandra Spanier and LaVerne Maginnis at the Hemingway Letters Project, Pennsylvania State University; Major Brendan Bond, Historian, at Air Force Heritage and History, Winnipeg, Canada, and Mike Abbotts at Library and Archives Canada, Ottawa; Margaret Kimball at Stanford University Archives; Alison Gilchrist at the Taft School; Stephen C. Jones and Natalia Sciarini at the Beinecke Library, and William Massa at the Sterling Library, Yale University.

Introduction

"His life was a movie"

—James Stevenson

"Charlie's two years in the South—a screenplay"

—Paul Nielsen

A few minutes after 5 A.M. on the morning of Thursday, July 21, 1960, Charles Andrews Fenton leaped to his death from the top floor of the tallest hotel in Durham, North Carolina. The story went out on the wire services, and the *New York Times* ran the UPI account the following day.

> DURHAM (UPI)—A Duke University professor and prize-winning novelist plunged to his death Thursday from the 12th floor of the Washington Duke Hotel.
>
> Coroner D.R. Perry ruled the death of Dr. Charles A. Fenton, 41, a suicide. His body landed on a sidewalk beside the hotel. Officers said a screen was removed from a hall window in the hotel. They theorized Fenton jumped from the window about 5 A.M. A hotel clerk said Fenton checked into the hotel about 8 P.M. Wednesday night and was given a room on the eighth floor. He said the man checked out early this morning but returned to the hotel when his automobile would not start.
>
> A member of the Duke faculty for two years, Fenton won the 20th Century Fox—Doubleday Award for a war novel entitled "You'll Get No Promotion." Fenton, a specialist in 20th century American literature, wrote Stephen Vincent Benet's biography while holding a Guggenheim Fellowship during 1957–58. His "Selected [Letters] of Stephen Vincent Benet" is scheduled for printing next October.

1

The writer-teacher received a $6,000 fellowship last May from the American Council of Learned Societies and planned to use it to complete his fifth book— "The Last Great Cause: Spain 1936–39." Fenton also wrote "The Apprenticeship of Ernest Hemingway: The Early Years."

A graduate of Yale University, Fenton served with the Royal Canadian Air Force during World War II. He was married and the father of three children. ("Author Leaps")

This story emphasized Fenton's several accomplishments—his books on Hemingway and Benét, his grants, his work-in-progress on the Spanish Civil War. Here, surely, was a man with everything to live for, a brilliant career ahead of him. So it seemed to Paul Harvey, who commented on the suicide in his nationwide radio show. "Page Three—Durham, North Carolina," he began. "Charles Fenton, prize-winning novelist and re/cip/i/ent" [uttered slowly] "of a pres/tig/i/ous Guggenheim award, jumped to oblivion today." [Pause.] "Jumped from the 12th floor of the Washington Duke hotel. Only 41. Funny" [long pause] "how those who have everything . . . don't seem to know how to enjoy it."

Neither the wire service story nor Paul Harvey's patronizing remarks caught anything of the magical aura that hovered about Fenton. But his students knew, the students he'd taught with such brilliance at Yale and later at Duke. I was one of those, and remember hearing the news with an overwhelming sense of what was lost, and at the same time without entire surprise. In my limited experience—I was a decade younger than Charlie—it seemed that only the most promising people I knew had committed suicide: a head boy at my country day school, an older and popular tennis partner. I suppose I regarded the act with a sense of romance, as if killing oneself were a kind of magnificent gesture that could not be ignored. The hypochondriac declared "I told you I was sick" on his tombstone. The suicide left no one in doubt.

Before long, word began to circulate on the academic grapevine that Fenton had been in love with one of his students and his marriage had fallen apart, investing his death with emotional force. Had he died for passion, or for thwarted passion? "Men have died from time to time, and worms have eaten them, but not for love," Shakespeare's Rosalind tells Orlando in *As You Like It* (IV, I, 110). But that was the judgment of an intelligent lover, an entirely admirable but pragmatic, even prudent, woman. Fenton had not been a prudent man, and I did not want to be one either. Still, I put his death in the back of my mind, having a life to lead—a life in many ways shaped by what I'd learned from Charlie Fenton.

Nearly half a century hurried by before the question that had been haunting me all those years began to insist on an answer. *What in the name of heaven had driven this charismatic man to kill himself?* The trigger was a long article I was writing about Hemingway's battle against biographers. One of those was Charles A. Fenton himself, whose *The Apprenticeship of Ernest Hemingway: The Early Years* (1954) was one of the first and best books on that great writer. He had begun working on Hemingway when I knew him at Yale, and for that reason was compelled to direct my senior thesis on Hemingway's short stories. For Fenton Hemingway was the Master.

Revisiting Fenton's book on Hemingway—and the disputatious letters they exchanged—brought him vividly back to mind: the tall handsome youthful teacher with telltale frown lines on his brow. I decided to find out whatever I could about his life, and to try to understand how it was with him at the end. For the previous forty years I had been teaching American literature and writing literary biographies of twentieth century American writers: in so doing practicing a profession that Charlie Fenton had more or less handed down to me. I loved the work, and owed it to his memory to tell his story as well as I could.

In connection with the Hemingway-Fenton piece, I called his widow Gwendy on May 14, 2007. She had specific memories about Charlie's correspondence with Ernest Hemingway, undertaken during the process of writing his book. "First [Hemingway] wrote nasty letters, and then he sent pleasant ones," she said. "He even offered to send Andy [the Fentons' son] a present from Africa." That was interesting, but what really got my attention were Gwendy's comments about Charlie himself. She spoke of his WorldWar II service as a tail gunner in the R.A.F., and of coming back from the war with a drinking problem. "He was a real drunk," she said, and she'd helped him through the process of recovery. Then, she added, with a trace of resentment, he had become "a big shot" as a college professor, at Yale and Duke.

Without bringing up the suicide directly, I asked if Charlie had been troubled by depression. Gwendy did not especially think so, although, she said, "he used to have spells every so often." She volunteered the information that Norman Holmes Pearson had been Andy's godfather, and said that her daughter Wendy had been in Durham at the time of her husband's death. She'd give Wendy my number, she said, and would ask her to call me. I did not speak to Gwendy again, and she died four months later. But eventually I did talk to Wendy and her brother Richie (the two children from Gwendy's previous marriage who grew up with Charlie Fenton as their father), and communicated at length by telephone and e-mail and regular mail with Andy, the only child of Charlie and Gwendy's union, and with Charlie's younger brother Dave. I'd just finished my seventh biography, on the poet Edwin Arlington Robinson, and without realizing that it was happening, the compulsion that animates those who take vicarious pleasure in exploring the lives of superior beings took possession of me. Knowing a little—"a real drunk" postwar, Gwendy said, and "a big shot" later—I resolved to find out more.

Chapter 1

First Sighting

About a hundred of us, mostly juniors and seniors, turned out for Charlie Fenton's inaugural talk in Yale's Daily Themes course on a Thursday morning in October 1949. This course offered literary Yalies a chance to test themselves as writers. Five times a week, we were required to produce 250–300 words of copy: not themes at all, really, but fragments of fiction, anecdotes, sketches, descriptions, scenes. These had to be placed in an outdoor box by 7:00 A.M. every weekday. The workload was light, but after a while the daily deadline weighed heavily. At least one student still had a nightmare-dream about the deadline 60 years later, in which he wakes in a panic and rushes across campus to drop his contribution in the box with seconds to spare. I took the course with two of my roommates, and some of our effusions were composed late at night after beery outings at Mory's.

It fell to a cadre of four to read these "themes" and in one-on-one conferences suggest how they might be improved. Three of the four were well-established professors. The fourth was Fenton, a young instructor who'd only earned his master's degree the previous spring. Once a week we met as a group to hear one of these mentors illustrate by example the five Daily Themes slogans, or rubrics, containing as Professor Richard Sewall (later the biographer of Emily Dickinson) put it in Keatsian, "all ye know on earth, and all ye need to know."

Daily Themes (or English 77) was first offered as early as 1907, and except for a brief period when funds ran dry, has been taught ever since at Yale (Engle 16). Originally, and again in the twenty-first century, the five rules were inflated to nine. But nine seems entirely too many, so only Sewall's big five are listed below.

1. Individualize by specific detail.
2. Vivify by range of appeal.
3. Characterize by speech and gesture.
4. Clarify by point of view.
5. Unify by a single impression.

Well, there stood Charles A. Fenton before us that October morning. He wore the academic uniform: gray trousers, tweed jacket, striped tie, very Brooks Brothers. But in no other way did he resemble the typical Yale professor. Curly-haired and slightly sardonic, he looked five years younger than his actual thirty. We took to him as more like one of us than his colleagues in the English department. Except that he was different, and the difference appealed to us too. The class of 1950, Yale's largest, accommodated a sizable number of World War II veterans, and soon we heard that Fenton left Yale during his sophomore year in 1940 to join the Royal Canadian Air Force, that he served as a tail gunner flying combat missions, that he was shot down at least once but managed to survive. We also gathered that he'd worked on metropolitan newspapers, that he'd won a prize for a novel (or part of a novel) about the war, and that he was embarking on a book about Ernest Hemingway.

In short he had done and was doing the things we ourselves yearned to do. We admired that, and admired the way he carried himself with the side-of-the-mouth offhand wit and irreverent stance of the hardened warrior and newspaperman. Young as he was, he'd been around barracks and city rooms long enough to acquire a free and easy skepticism that made him dubious about almost all received wisdom and distrustful of anyone who dispensed it.

For his talk, Fenton chose to read from a characteristically non-canonical story, James Thurber's 1941 "You Could Look It Up." Thurber told his tale through the voice of a tough-talking trainer traveling with a major league baseball team. What we could look up, the trainer said, was the time that Squawks Magrew, manager of the team, sent a cigar-chomping midget won-derfully named Pearl du Monville up to bat in an important game, feeling sure that the opposing pitcher would be unable to locate the tiny strike zone and the little guy would get a base on balls. The midget came to the plate with strict instructions to crouch, making the pitcher's task even more difficult, and under no circumstances to lift the bat off his shoulder. Everything would have worked out as planned, except that Pearl developed delusions of grandeur and decided to take a whack at the ball. Unfortunately he connected, hitting a dribbler and being easily thrown out. At which point the exasperated manager Magrew raced onto the field, cornered du Monville, and launched *him* into center field (565).

In quoting from the ungrammatical but savvy trainer, Fenton may have been demonstrating rubric three, "Characterize by speech and gesture" or rubric four, "Clarify by point of view." It hardly mattered. Fenton obviously enjoyed telling us the story, and his auditors had a fine time listening to a yarn so delightful in its improbability. Or not so improbable after all, for less than two years later, on Sunday, 19 August 1951, maverick owner Bill Veeck of the St. Louis Browns sent midget Eddie Gaedel, 3 feet 7 inches tall and weighing 65 pounds, up to bat against the Detroit Tigers in the second game of a doubleheader. Gaedel walked on four pitches.

That was the first I saw of Charlie Fenton, but not the last, for he was assigned the duty of supervising my senior thesis on Hemingway's short stories and thereby hangs a cautionary tale it's past time for me to admit to.

It wasn't easy persuading the powers-that-be in the Yale English department that I should write a thesis on Hemingway. He was too American, too contemporary, too publicly famous for their taste. Shaking off signs of disapproval, I plunged ahead in the fall of 1949, smattering a few articles about Hemingway in the Sterling library and submitting a long term paper on his stories to Norman Holmes Pearson. One of the two scholars who lectured to hundreds of us in the only American literature survey course then offered at Yale, Pearson, like Fenton, broke the professorial mold. A hunchback, a linguist, a brilliant man, he'd parachuted into France behind the German lines during the war for the OSS and sent back vital information about the enemy. After the war he taught at Yale and functioned as a recruiter of likely undergraduates for the CIA. He was witty, charming, friendly, and nobody's fool. Pearson liked my term paper, perhaps because it ran three times longer than anyone else's, and awarded it a grade of 95.

At this stage, giddy with success, I tried to swindle the department by resubmitting the term paper as my senior thesis to Fenton—a project for which I'd already received a reduced course load. The best thing possible then happened. My deception was uncovered, as it had to be if only because (as I was too innocent a criminal to know) Pearson was Fenton's principal mentor among the faculty. As a consequence I received a grade of 75 on the thesis—80 was passing—and did not graduate with my class in June. Nothing much was communicated to me about the reasons for this failure beyond Fenton's calling me "a trimmer," a phrase forever lodged in my mind. I was allowed to rewrite the thesis and in that connection traveled back east in the summer of 1950 for a consultation with Charlie Fenton at his house in Madison, Connecticut. Second time around, the thesis passed, barely, and I got my degree.

When I saw him in Madison, Fenton was well on his way to becoming a legendary figure on the Yale campus. Andrew Patten's laudatory article in the 6 December 1950 *Yale Daily News* described him as "a new bright light among bright lights in the English department" and touched briefly on his youthful misadventures. Fenton was far from "just another guy in gray flannels," Patten wrote, even if "[o]nly some of the rumors of his exploits [were] true." The article presented a summary of his war experiences and his post-war career, and captured some of his wit as well.

After service in the RCAF in England, Fenton returned to the States in 1944, married Gwendolyn Grant (née Ross) in the fall, and went to work first as a reporter for the *New Haven Register* and then at the Yale News Bureau. In June 1945 he got word that a novel he'd written—called *But We Had Fun*, not "You'll Get No Promotion," the title of one of his stories—won the $4,000 Doubleday, Doran-Twentieth Century Fox New Writers Contest among 1,100 entrants ("Doubleday"). At that stage, Fenton quit his job and started revising the novel to suit the requirements of both Doubleday and Fox. As he related the story to the *Yale Daily News*, "I finished the novel. I liked it, my agent liked it, Doubleday liked it—Fox didn't. I rewrote it. Still Fox didn't like it. I got sore, they got sore, and the manuscript is still a dog around New York" (Patten).

Fenton next landed a position on the editorial staff of *Life* in New York, another short-term engagement. "There's a perennial 'Skull and Bones' atmosphere around that place," Fenton explained. "You have to pay [Henry] Luce too big a price to earn his money. If you want to get anywhere you have to move with the crowd, live in Westchester County, and work like hell" (Patten). Fenton was not prepared to conform to these corporate expectations. With the encouragement of Pearson he came back to Yale in the summer of 1947, earned his B.A. 15 months later, his M.A. in 1949, and launched into the research on Hemingway that was to do double duty as his 1953 doctoral dissertation and (once the Ph.D. stink had been rubbed away) as *The Apprenticeship of Ernest Hemingway*, the well-received first book published in 1954.

Patten's *Yale Daily News* account omitted some of the more fantastic parts of the story. He duly reported that Fenton entered Yale in the fall of 1937 after graduating from Taft School *cum laude*, and left in the spring of 1938. And that after a stint as a copy boy on the *Boston Herald* he returned to Yale for the 1940 spring semester and lasted this time until November of that year. At that time Fenton was a party boy and a drinker, a rebel determined to break any rules that limited his pursuit of wine and women. As Patten dryly put it, "any resemblance between the studious English teacher of today and Charlie Fenton [of 1937–1940] was pure imagination." But Patten did not go into the reasons behind Fenton's first two abortive ventures in higher education, or into his checkered military career.

According to family members, former students, and Fenton himself, he was kicked out of Yale in the spring of 1938 for entertaining a girl in his room. On this occasion, as Charlie told the story, the campus police caught him and the girl *in flagrante delicto* and commanded him to "pull out, and get out." Then he was nearly expelled a second time for violating the solemnity of Yale's Tap Day. Each spring aspiring juniors assembled in Branford College courtyard where an exclusive ninety of them would be tapped for membership in Yale's secret societies: fifteen for each of six such societies, of which the most famous was of course Skull and Bones. As his comment about Luce's *Time-Life* empire suggests, Fenton regarded the self-importance and ceremonial trappings of Bones with scorn. To disrupt the sanctity of Tap Day, he wandered about Branford courtyard randomly tapping candidates on the shoulder. "Go to your room," he muttered, following the ritual, "Skull and Bones." As many as 20 young men were temporarily uplifted—and subsequently disappointed—in this way (Ham 173–76). Officials of Skull and Bones, learning of Fenton's treachery, protested to the college administration, and he was under close scrutiny from then on.

The Tap Day episode occurred in May 1940.After spending the summer as a camp counselor, Fenton returned to Yale in the fall, occupying a single room in Calhoun College. During that fall, he spent much of his time veering between New Haven and New York in a haze of alcohol and sex. Then he left precipitously and without formally withdrawing to enlist in the Royal Canadian Air Force in November 1940, more than a year in advance of the United States entry into World War II. He had worn out his welcome at Yale, and he did not want to miss the war.

Chapter 2

Bomber Boy

Fenton, C.A.
R 77443, RCAF

On 21 November, Fenton presented himself to the RCAF in Montreal as a candidate for pilot training. The next day, Arnold Whitridge, master of Calhoun College at Yale, wrote a damning letter of recommendation to the commanding officer at the recruiting center. Fenton, then 21, was "an intelligent boy," Whitridge acknowledged, and quite able to keep up with the academic work at Yale, but had "preferred to amuse himself" instead. He described Fenton as "extremely unstable" and concluded with a devastating sentence the Canadian authorities highlighted: "It is possible, of course, that he will make a good officer, but I should not myself like to see him in any position of responsibility." Despite this warning, the RCAF admitted Fenton and shipped him off to Brandon, Manitoba, where he passed a rigorous four-hour medical exam. That accomplishment, together with his educational background, qualified him for nine months to a year of pilot training. This was what he'd joined up for. He was "very happy."

Before Christmas 1940 he was shipped to Saskatoon, Saskatchewan for routine military indoctrination, including long stretches on guard duty. Then at Regina, two hundred miles south of Saskatoon, he attended Initial Training School: classes, theory of flight, simulated ground flying in Link trainers, and a medical recheck. Charlie was excited about the opportunity, and could hardly wait to start flying. If everything went well, he wrote his parents, he would have his commission by late summer. If he performed poorly or had disciplinary trouble, he would be remustered as a gunner: "a nightmare, as the average lifetime of a gunner in action is two and one-half minutes."

He passed his classes at Regina, and was transferred to Windsor Mills, Quebec, for 70 hours of flying and 11 courses at Elementary Flying School. About a third of the men flunked out, he wrote home, and even if he passed, there would be another school to follow. He'd "certainly picked the most harrowing way of saving democracy. One pitfall after another." He'd never lived through such full days as at Windsor Mills, he added, and for a time he was "frankly terrified" in the air, but eventually he felt he'd "got the damned machine beaten" and started to really enjoy flying. Before long, he told his parents in May 1941, he hoped to ship across the Atlantic as a fighter pilot.

Soon thereafter, and not at all uncharacteristically, Charlie Fenton screwed up. Letting his fierce disdain for entitlements prevail, he went up on a routine training flight and ostentatiously buzzed the officers' club pool. Or so he later maintained, although the RCAF records state that he washed out "because of misconduct": specifically, going AWOL for three days—the first of five such actions on his service record. That breach of discipline cost him his pilot's wings and his commission. Waiting for reassignment early in July, he was punished for drunkenness. Next he was sent to Air Observer School in Chatham, New Brunswick, to be trained as a navigator. He failed that course too, probably because of minimal mathematical skills. In the aftermath, Charlie again went absent without leave for two days in late October. He would not be confined by rules and regulations. Finally, just as he'd feared, the RCAF reassigned him to Gunnery School. Six months later he arrived in England in that precarious role. Upon arrival, he wrote his family, he tried unsuccessfully to persuade the RAF to reinstate him as a pilot. To press his case he volunteered to fly gliders carrying commando troops, but to no avail. He went through a gunnery course at an Operational Training Unit and then was assigned as a tail gunner to RAF's Squadron 7, stationed near Cambridge. He would rather have been a pilot, but Charlie understood that gunners were needed and did his best to become disciplined and professional during the missions that followed.

At precisely that time—the spring of 1942—the British Bomber Command was about to embark on a massive campaign of "area bombing," a euphemism for saturation attacks from the air on German cities. The objective, as Prime Minister Winston Churchill saw it, was to demoralize the German people. From the beginning of the war Churchill had little faith in the "precision" attacks on isolated military and industrial targets his Air Staff was advocating. His doubts were confirmed by a report of August 1941, analyzing the results of the previous two months' raids. The report found that only one third of the bombs had come within five miles of their targets, and in the Ruhr, where the anti-aircraft was heaviest, only one tenth came that close (Hastings 108).

These results did not deter Churchill from elevating his Bomber Command to its prime place in the war effort. With improved navigation on its way, the accuracy of the bombers would improve over time. Meanwhile, he wanted his planes to spread devastation as widely as possible against civilians. "[S]evere, ruthless bombing of Germany on an ever-increasing scale," Churchill was convinced, would not only cripple the enemy's war effort, including U-boat and aircraft production, but also "create conditions intolerable to the mass of German population." He thought of the bomber offensive as comparable to the siege artillery of previous wars, an onslaught that would break down morale by spreading wholesale devastation. Only in that way, he believed, could the German war-will be broken, and the groundwork laid for a success-ful mass invasion of the continent. Churchill wanted to put off that dangerous undertaking as long as possible (Hastings 116, 119, 123, 139).

By the end of 1941 the prospects for victory were growing brighter. The Germans had invaded Russia in June, converting the Soviet Union into an ally, and the Nazis were discovering that—despite inflicting terrible losses—they could not blitz the Russians into surrender. Then, with the Japanese attack on Pearl Harbor on December 7, the vast resources of the United States were enlisted in the war.

The RAF Bomber Command itself was making substantial improvements. Four-engine heavy bombers, Stirlings and Halifaxes, were replacing their two-engine predecessors, and the first of the four-engine Lancasters—by far the best of the lot—were beginning to roll off the assembly lines. A new electronic navigation system, called Gee, was developed to help these air-craft find their targets and return to their bases. And a fresh corps of airmen, "romantic young idealists" from the United Kingdom, its colonial outposts in Canada, New Zealand, and Australia, and allied nations like Poland and Norway, were ready after operational training to fly these airplanes (Hastings 154–55, 142; Bishop 86–91).

On Valentine's Day 1942 the Air Ministry issued a directive removing all restraints on bombing policy. Previously it was mandated that bombardment should be confined to military objectives, with no intentional attacks on civil-ian populations. But with the advent of unrestricted air warfare, these rules no longer applied to German, Italian, and Japanese territory. The Bomber Com-mand set out to destroy entire cities—houses, apartment buildings, schools, and hospitals included—and so to demoralize the enemy. Few of the airmen flying these missions were troubled by the terrible damage they were inflicting. They were too busy trying to do their job while evading the anti-aircraft batteries and night fighters to feel any sympathy for women and children below. Nor were the British people much disturbed, for they well remembered what the Luft-waffe had done to their cities during the 1940 Blitz. The Bomber Command lost about 56,000 airmen during the war, but to those in authority such losses seemed a reasonable price to pay as measured against, say, the millions of Rus-sians dead on the Eastern front (Hastings 133, 170, 140).

Restricted by wartime censorship, Charlie Fenton could not say much in letters about his part in the operations of 1942. During his first weeks there, he wrote his parents about daily life in wartime England. It was cold in his quarters without central heating, he reported, and the English had "the God damnedest diet." The food improved, though, after "they threw us a kipper for the fourth consecutive breakfast" and Fenton and his mates rioted in the sergeants' mess. He got along well with the English except for "that old school tie business," which he disdained, and on the whole had a very good time. On frequent trips to London he revisited sites his parents had introduced him to a decade earlier.

Charlie Fenton, born in 1919, grew up in an atmosphere of privilege. Daniel, his father, swept through Yale, graduating at 19, and after teaching at Princeton and Yale took his doctorate as a classicist. He married Dorothy Russell, from a prominent Staten Island family. High Episcopalians, her parents objected to her union with the Catholic Fenton, and for two years cut off communication with the young couple. It helped that Daniel Fenton was not a particularly observant Catholic—Charles and his only sibling David, 11 years his junior, were brought up in the Episcopal church—and that he proved resourceful enough to convert his scholarly skills into a career as an executive with Fisk Tire and Rubber. In his capacity as head of the firm's international division, Fenton took his wife and young son to London several times. One year they had a flat in St. James's Place, only 30 feet or so from what had by 1942 become a lavish speakeasy. As an airman Charlie went back there, and to Green Park where he and his mother used to walk among the sheep and the prams—both gone, he reported, under wartime duress—and to the Savoy hotel, where his father had once bought him a shampoo in the barber shop: a costly indulgence that Flight Sergeant Fenton repeated. In earlier days his father had taken him to see John Gielgud in *Richard II*; in wartime Charlie went by himself to see Gielgud in *Macbeth*. His parents had introduced him to horseback riding—as a boy he'd brought home equestrian trophies—and this expensive habit, too, he was able to replicate in England, riding to hounds on at least one weekend.

After the depression of the early 1930s, the largesse of Fisk Rubber no longer sustained the Fenton family. The company, famous for its "Time to Re-Tire" advertisements showing a young boy with a candle on his way to bed, lapsed into receivership in 1933. Daniel Fenton lost his job, and to keep his head above water became a master at the Taft School in Watertown, Connecticut. This demoralizing transition relegated him to teaching Latin to the sons of those who still had money and the sort of lifestyle to which he and his family had previously been accustomed. He was very good at the work, a successful if somewhat forbidding teacher remembered as "Dapper Dan" for

Dorothy and Daniel Fenton with son Charles, en route to England, ca. 1930. Fenton Family Photo

his impeccable appearance. Dorothy Fenton carried on the correspondence with Sergeant Fenton in England, but in his letters home Charlie often called up happy memories of his father. Daniel may have come down in the world, but not in the eyes of his son. Charles (as his proper mother insisted he sign himself, although to the rest of the world he was Charlie) felt a strong bond to his father.

Fenton's surviving fiction about the war—three stories written immediately after his service and a short novel called *The Long Summer* he wrote from a more analytical stance 15 years later, in 1958—provides a far more vivid picture of his life as a tail gunner in the RAF than he set down in letters. He and his crewmates, he wrote in the novel, "imagined themselves as worldly" airmen, but were really only boys arrested "in a state of frozen adolescence." Each English bomber crew of seven, averaging 21 years of age, tended to be stratified along social and economic lines. So consistent was this pattern that in British novels about the air war, the authors regularly assigned an Oxbridge "graduate to the pilot's cabin, an alumnus of a provincial university to the navigator's bench, a white collar worker to the wireless operator's key, a cockney to the turret." Such divisions were less marked among Canadian and American crews, but Charlie Fenton, flying as a tail gunner, represented something of an anomaly, being better educated and from a more genteel, background than most of his mates, including the pilot and navigator (*Long Summer* 11, 197).

The task of the tail (or rear) gunner was particularly onerous. As Max Hastings described it in his *Bomber Command* (1979),

> the rear gunner faced the loneliest and coldest night of all. Gazing back into the darkness . . . he often felt that he inhabited a different planet from the tight little cluster of aircrew so far forward in the cockpit. Even after electrically heated suits were introduced, they often broke down. Many gunners cut away their turret doors to dispel the nightmare of being trapped when the aircraft was hit— they were wedged impossibly tightly in their flying gear. It was difficult even to move to clear jammed guns with their rubber hammers. There was no chance of wearing a parachute—it was stowed beside them. Some carried a hatchet to give themselves a forlorn chance of hacking their way out of a wreck. The cold was intensified by the removal of a square of Perspex to provide a central "clear view panel" of the night sky. (160–61)

The .303 caliber gun the gunner manned offered flimsy defense against night fighters. His principal duty, and that of the other two gunners, was to serve as a lookout, alerting the pilot and navigator to enemy aircraft and bursts of flak. "If they saw the Germans first," Hastings wrote, "they could survive. If they did not, they were probably dead men" (164).

No matter how alert and disciplined the gunner and other airmen were, they faced daunting odds against survival. The goal was to get through 30 missions, at which time they would be relieved of further flying duty. The Air Ministry expected a loss of five per cent on each trip, and there were times when the toll ran higher. You didn't have to be a mathematician to work out the odds (Hastings 156). "It was interesting how it worked," the narrator in one of Fenton's stories reflected. "For the first five trips it never occurred to you that you might be killed. For the next ten it never occurred to you that you wouldn't . . . But after that was the worst period, when you began to think you had a chance of beating the percentage."

A French Canadian flight sergeant in Fenton's squadron, who was invariably well-fixed for money after fleecing the others in the payday poker games, took a brutally frank position when approached for a loan of a pound or two. "How do I know when you'll get the chop?" he inquired coldly. "Every night we send twelve kites out. Every morning we get back nine, maybe ten. You figure the percentage." The sergeant may have exaggerated the loss-rate, but none of the bomber boys needed his reminder about the odds (*Long Summer* 52, 11*). There were few things they gave more thought to, as they lost friends and comrades and wondered if it would be their turn next.

"The war was unnatural," Fenton reflected in *The Long Summer*, "because it was a sequence of dramatic events—enlistment, sleeping in barracks, learning a momentarily interesting trade, new towns, first tail, troop ships, a million different dramatic events—and there were so many of these events, all of which they had been trained by teachers and churchmen and parents to regard as unnatural, and they imagined that they wished they were home": back in God's country "eating ice cream or their mom's apple pie, or riding in a 1936 rumble seat from the local movie to the local roller-skating rink" (27).

Along with more sexual opportunities—"first tail"—the war produced more drinking. Fenton addressed that issue as well. "Drunkenness is often confused with manhood, frequently by males older than we were in 1942.If there was one thing we aspired to be mistaken for, it was men. Q.E.D. If you were drunk, you were a man. It had been that way since recruit depot [in Canada], where we staggered about the wet canteen in the evenings singing 'I've Got Sixpence' and 'Bless Them All.'" As his service record shows, Charlie did more than his share of the staggering. Among his mates he encountered every kind of drinker: "some of them good drunks, entertaining and resourceful and self sufficient, others bad drunks who started fights and insulted officers and pawed ill-chosen girls. And, finally, a handful who might not have become alcoholics did indeed become so because of the license and sanctity of the uniform, because of the opportunities, because of the general climate, because of some weakness, but they were very few and I believe most of them would have become rummies had they worked in a war plant or driven a milk truck for the duration" (*Long Summer* 181–82).

As an American trained with a Canadian unit to fight alongside the English in the RAF, Fenton occupied an unusual position in Squadron 7. An influx of his fellow Americans began to arrive in England shortly after he did, inspiring the widespread joke that the only thing wrong with the Americans was that they were "overpaid, overfed, oversexed, and over here" (*Long Summer* 21). Somewhat to his surprise, Charlie felt no particular kinship with these new troops. Even their voices sounded oddly foreign to his ears. In the early morning, after returning from night raids over Germany, Fenton and his comrades could see the Flying Fortresses of the United States Army Air Force taking off on the murderous daylight missions their generals insisted upon, flying very high and in perfect formation. Then around eleven o'clock they came back, the formations broken and half of them smoking and losing altitude. The Fortresses really took their lumps that summer, and the sight of them limping home was, somewhat perversely, good for the RAF's morale (*Long Summer* 41–42).

If anything, Fenton felt closer to the Canadians than the English. He was especially put off by the English habit of "understating each other all over the place." In one of the Cambridge pubs that the fliers frequented, he heard two of them talking. "Had a rather shaky do last night, old boy," one of them murmured, after coming home with hydraulics gone and one wing hit. "You must have been a bit browned off," his friend said, leading him on. A Canadian, listening, banged his glass mug on the bar. "Browned off?" he shouted. "The son of a bitch was scared shitless" (*Long Summer* 28).

Still, the English cause was Fenton's own, and he was always glad to see the countryside below upon coming back from deep raids into Germany. A rhapsodic passage in *The Long Summer* described one such return trip.

We had climbed steadily after leaving the target, the skipper bringing us into and through and above the chill dampness of thick cloud and then flying the final two hundred miles homeward in the splendid vastness above the cloud, the dampness of the cloud changed now to a clear, icy heaviness which reduced our air speed but the black vastness around and above us seeming a serene haven, the moon obscured now by drifting cumulus and a few hundred feet below us the sweet denseness of the cloud we had climbed through and into whose shelter the skipper would dive headlong if German fighters should appear. And gradually, then swiftly, I could see the cracking of the horizon back beyond where we had been, the bands of light preceding the sun, the horizon multi-streaked now with the promise of this new day's splendors, and then, when the navigator told the skipper to lower through the cloud, for an instant the upper rim of the sun itself was visible, then nothing but the swirling dampness of the cloud, moist, chill, this morning a fresh lotion that dissolved the fatigue just as the jarring air pockets refreshed the body because there was no flak-like menace in their jar, only a kind of heavenly escalator that jarred us downward to England. (165)

That was after a milk run, a piece of cake, "a raid on Mannheim defended by two men and a dog" as one official put it during the pre-flight briefing: an easy trip with light ack-ack or none at all. There were not many missions like that after the RAF Bomber Command, under the leadership of Sir Arthur Harris, initiated its program of massive thousand-bomber raids in May 1942.

As the new Air Officer Commanding-in-Chief, Harris abandoned the previous practice of splitting up his forces and sending them out to bomb two or three different targets. Instead he aimed for concentration, dispatching all available aircraft against but one city at a time. "The primary object of your operations," Harris was instructed when he took over, "should now be focused on the morale of the enemy civil population and in particular, on the industrial workers." The aiming-points, he understood, were "to be the built-up areas, *not*, for instance, the dockyards or aircraft factories" (Bishop 89). His mission was to pulverize German cities through saturation bombing, and with a keen sense of the publicity it would generate, Harris decided to send a thousand bombers to attack a single German city in a single night.

On the clear moonlit Saturday night-Sunday morning of May 30–31, 1942, 1,047 aircraft raided Cologne, Germany's third largest city. Using incendiaries as well as high explosive bombs, they set Cologne ablaze, rendering many thousands homeless and traumatizing the city much as the Luftwaffe had traumatized Coventry eighteen months earlier (Bishop 98–99). Cologne, the city closest to the bomber bases, had already been bombed 58 times, and was to be struck again repeatedly. Other massive raids in the summer of 1942 wrought destruction on other German industrial centers such as Hamburg, Essen, Düsseldorf, and Bremen, and once or twice the bombers ranged as far as Berlin and Frankfurt. So many aircraft were involved that, as Fenton wrote in *The Long Summer*, the bulk of them encountered relatively little flak. But the schedule was a heavy one. Squadron 7 flew "whenever there was clearish weather and a good moon, and sometimes it seemed that summer as if the weather was always good and the moon always full." The trips were long, five or six hours, and during one week—this was a rarity—Charlie and his mates flew five missions in six nights. Soon the men were exhausted and ardently awaiting leave, but nobody got much leave (*Long Summer* 20, 27).

Fenton's novel dealt sardonically with the launching of the Pathfinder Force late that summer. Pathfinder was designed to improve accuracy from the air, for in addition to its saturation bombing the Air Ministry sought to strike and disable industrial targets. The idea was to send a small advance unit ahead of the main striking force, dropping flares to mark the target for the other bombers to follow (Bishop 100–01). An Air Commodore was dispatched to present this plan to Fenton's squadron. With all the men assembled, the Commanding Officer (C.O.) opened the proceedings. "As you know, there is a stand-down tonight," he told them. "Very duff weather, worse luck."

"That [message] was for the Air Commodore. That was to let the Air Commodore know that he, the C.O., liked nothing better than to lead his gallant Squadron into the Ruhr. We were going to hear some rare and moving eloquence this day." When the Commodore rose to speak, he managed to get the group's attention. The bombers were not doing as much damage as they should have, he said, and provided them with a concrete example. The example was Cologne itself, as heavily bombed as any single area in Germany. It was widely believed that the major air strikes of the spring and summer had virtually eliminated Cologne as a productive industrial area. But, the Air Commodore announced, "we are now informed that at no time has Cologne been removed from industrial activity for longer than six days."

That revelation drew a gasp from the crews. "Three times that summer we had left Cologne burning. It had been burning so well that on the way back to England you could see the fires from the Dutch coast." They'd reported to the intelligence officers that the city was in flames. Aerial photographs taken the next day by high-altitude Mosquitoes confirmed those reports. And now they were told that "Jerry had gotten the city back on its feet within six days each time." It was hard to believe.

> We had lost twenty-one aircraft on the Squadron since May. Twenty-one times seven was a hundred and forty-seven. Often they had a co-pilot with them. But call it a hundred and forty-seven men. That was what we had lost that summer, just one squadron, and all the time we had thought we were sticking it to Jerry and shortening the war and all those other inspirational things we read in the *Daily Express* and heard from the intelligence officers — all that time we had really been committing no more than a series of nuisance raids. On a large scale, no doubt, but nuisance raids all the same. It was proper to gasp. Gasping was appropriate under the circumstances.

The solution, the Air Commodore went on, was to dispatch an advance force of some forty bombers, flying low and arriving perhaps twenty minutes ahead of the main force, dropping their flares in a circle around the railroad yards or the tank factories and then getting the hell out of there. Such an operation, the Air Commodore said, required captains and crews of the greatest skill and courage, and he had come there that morning to let them know that their squadron had been chosen as initial members of the Pathfinder Force. "Welcome to Pathfinder," he concluded, and despite knowing better some of the men applauded.

As it worked out, to survive Pathfinder trips the captains and crews needed considerable luck as well as skill and courage. Fenton described how it was in *The Long Summer*. "If we got across France without being picked up by the fighters, or without the target being anticipated by the radar, we dove in quickly and dropped the flares accurately and got out without exceptional losses. Other times, if the target was leaked, or if they guessed the target from our course over France, the losses were high and when the flare run was made across the target you would see the Stirlings and Halifaxes and Lancasters blowing up very suddenly . . . because they had been flying straight and level and at that height the flak was very quick and accurate."

Afterwards the Air Ministry sent out telegrams to families that their son or husband or brother was missing in action. They might more accurately had wired the survivors, Fenton commented, that the "missing" airman could reliably be presumed to have "been either fragmented, decapitated, or, as happened to many, perhaps had choked in his own blood, had at any rate been destroyed at approximately four thousand feet along with six friends, a four engine aircraft, seven tons of bombs, a number of undropped flares, and other expensive and valuable equipment." If enough telegrams of that sort were sent to large numbers of people, he speculated, the war might magically and abruptly have ended. But to expect those in authority to be so brutally frank, Fenton added in a damning indictment, was naïve and unrealistic, because it

left out of consideration such basic factors as national pride, martial commitments, obligations to one's allies, cultural esprit, the sanctity of diplomatic treaties, the search for new consumer markets, the requirements of a credit economy, the indisputable superiority of certain political ideologies to all other political ideologies, and other imponderables whose cosmic significance one was blinded from grasping because of limited perspective. (79, 84–85, 89–90, 118–19)

As the seemingly endless summer of 1942 wore on, Fenton and many of his fellow airmen grew increasingly "windy": English parlance for liable to lose one's nerve in combat. They were constantly reminded of the percentages as they lost aircraft and companions in almost every operation. Charlie's crew suffered several close calls. Once their bomber, damaged by the anti-aircraft fire over Germany, drifted helplessly into the North Sea on the return trip. The men managed to survive the ditching, but spent three days on a rubber life raft before being rescued. It was "rather awkward," Charlie told his parents, succumbing to British understatement ("Alumni Notes"). Another time, he was slightly wounded in the foot by shrapnel. Still, he knew he was lucky. Of the forty men he started training with back in Canada, only five came back from England alive.

The worst trip of all came late that summer, one that Fenton described both in "You'll Get No Promotion," a story published in *Penguin Parade*

Tail gunner Charlie Fenton, second from right, with his crewmates at RAF Squadron 7.
Fenton Family Photo

in spring 1944, its title drawn from the chorus of the popular British Army song "Bless Them All" that ran "You'll get no promotion/ This side of the ocean," and in *The Long Summer*. It was one of the last missions he flew, and the target was Frankfurt. To get there, their slow-moving Stirling had to fly past Mainz, and the new navigator—the old one having been killed—failed to chart the evasive route needed to avoid the searchlights and anti-aircraft batteries concentrated there.

The first they knew about slipping off course came with "the dull, throaty noise of flak" bursting. Then the blue master light came on below, and Fenton yelled "Lights, lights, turn starboard, hard," and the pilot flung the aircraft to the right, but it was too late. "Fifty lights had flicked on them. They became one solid white flame. You could feel their heat." Within seconds flak was exploding all around them, and their bomber took a hit amidships. They had been "coned," and it took eight minutes to get through the twenty-five miles of searchlights below. Later Fenton remembered half-standing up in his rear gunner's turret,

head hitting the Plexiglas roof, firing stupidly down the cones of light, the turret bright now, like a fluorescent-lit room, cursing angrily over and over mother fuckingbastardlysonofabitching lights, the flak synchronized with the lights and the lights and the lights and the lights holding us there while the ground guns got the range, and then finally the pilot outracing the lights in an absolutely straight down dive and wondering if the wings would come off when he pulled out of it, or if he could pull out of it at all, the pain in your ears, yelling the way we'd been taught to keep the drums from breaking, and then coming out of the dive, not sharply and majestically as in a movie, but weakly, uncertainly, the whole plane shaking and so low now that the flak was bursting above them.

By the time they flew out of the cone, the mid upper gunner was dead and the flight engineer knocked out cold. As their plane limped home, the skipper cut the starboard outer engine to keep it from exploding. German fighter planes set off flares as they approached the English Channel, and to make it across safely they came down to eighty feet and slid across the water. When finally they landed, one of the crew brought around rations. Fenton dropped all of his in the oil on the floor of his turret and laid his head on the butts of his guns. It was his 23rd trip.

"That was the night I stopped belonging to the air force," he wrote. "I did not know it then, but it must have happened during the eight minutes, and from then on I was somebody else. I was not really a sergeant in the air force any more" (*Long Summer* 65–68, "*No Promotion*" 152–55).

He and his mates continued to go through the motions, though. They heard about a squadron in Yorkshire where everybody got windy. When the Bomber Command ordered a full complement on the line for that night's operations, the Yorkshire C.O. signaled back that all his aircraft were unserviceable. Then, instead of doing the trip, the airmen would get drunk together. They heard about another crew that took off on a mission, flew the course for about 20 minutes, veered north and stooged around for 3 hours, dropped their bombs in the North Sea, and then came back, where the pilot bluffed his way through interrogation. That worked for about 4 trips, and then somebody in Scotland picked them up on the radar and they were all shipped off to the guardhouse, or the "glasshouse," as the British called it (*Long Summer* 38–39).

Nobody in Squadron 7 actually refused to fly, though they thought about it often. Many went on sick parade regularly, pleading spurious backaches, nightmares that prevented them from sleeping, loss of memory, kidneys that were uncontrollable—"all the sanctified symptoms of combat fatigue by which the Medical Officer could occasionally be persuaded to certify an airman as eligible for rest or even, most wondrous, suitable to be grounded for the duration without susceptibility to a lack of moral fibre charge and with retention of present rank and all emoluments" (*Long Summer* 123). Fenton himself had nightmares and kidney trouble, but the Medical Officer cut him no slack. When he soiled the King's mattresses, his pay was docked.

By September, as he wrote in *The Long Summer*, "only an official communiqué" could have described the unit's morale as high. There was more drunkenness in the Mess, "no longer the rather kittenish, high school boozing of the spring" (when Charlie himself had been court-martialed for drunkenness) but instead men passed out cold on the sofa in mid-afternoon. They were survivors, but they had seen their friends killed or wounded, bearing physical and psychological scars. Among them Fenton recalled "the ones who burned up, and you would see them six months later with the new skin on the face and hands, and . . . the ones they hosed out of the turrets, and the ones who had both legs amputated, and the ones who cracked up and sometimes they would start crying in the Mess . . . [and] the ones they had to send to the rest camps in Scotland, and the others whom they labeled 'lack of moral fibre' and busted down from sergeant and sent to other squadrons as waiters in the Officers' Mess" (35–36, 25).

Above all the men needed leave. As Charlie expressed it, "he wanted to walk through St. James's Park, watch the couples, sit in a cool bar; he wanted to get away from the eternal talk of gen and prangs and good types and popsies. He wanted time to read again, and write the stories his mind was full of. He wanted to hear a good band and get drunk the way he used to, not hopelessly and alone, but with laughs and friends and the knowledge of a good tomorrow. He wanted to be able to plan his life a week ahead, not just for a few hours" (*"No Promotion"* 149). He wanted, in other words, to live like a civilian. When he finally did get leave, seven days was not nearly enough, and he went AWOL for the month from 21 October to 22 November. On December 2 he was busted from Flight Sergeant to Airman Second Class—the lowest rank in the RCAF—stripped of his flying badge, and assigned to General Duties.

Naturally enough, he did not tell his parents these events in his letters home. Instead he wrote them that he'd spent a month in the hospital—the month he actually spent AWOL—because he "was getting nervy." In a 19 December 1942 letter, Fenton further reported that he'd been grounded for "probably three months, at least," that he was in good health and enjoying himself, and that he was stationed south of London in Suffolk, with a congenial job in which he was his own boss. He was "immensely pleased to be grounded," Fenton admitted, even if it to say so sounded "very much like treason." But he'd done "36 trips" by then, which was "quite enough." His luck could not last indefinitely.

What he did not say was that, actually, he was preparing to opt out of the war—that both officially and unofficially he was no longer "a sergeant in the air force." Early in 1943 he went "on the trot," joining the 60,000 other "absentees" at large in the United Kingdom. For more than seven months, from March to September 1943, Fenton evaded capture by the Service Police. He could not have done it without the love and protection of a woman.

Always attractive to women, Fenton found himself much in demand in wartime England, where most eligible men were in the service and away from home. Wherever he went, he wrote his mother, women posed "a real problem." There were thousands of them about, "all very patriotic, and all crazy to get married." Some of his comrades had already been trapped. To avoid a similar fate, he would have to be "very shifty."

Despite that resolve, Fenton almost did get married, not once but twice. The first instance involved a whirlwind affair with a young actress he met shortly after being demoted. His parents would be "appalled to learn," he wrote them late in December 1942, that he'd come as close to marriage as paying three pounds for a license. He'd only escaped the altar when the actress "tearfully decided at the last minute that [he] was a bounder and her career was more important."

The other and more important relationship was with an Englishwoman named Betty Lyon. She was attractive, well-bred, well-educated, somewhat older than Fenton, and married to a husband in the service whom she was seeking to divorce. The way they met more or less summed up the way things were between them. Probably it happened following an alcoholic visit to Charlie's favorite watering hole.

> The women spoke in the accents of every class and locale, of Yorkshire and the East End and Mayfair and Devon. Had there been no war they would have been in the south of France, or waiting on tables in Birmingham, or in school, or tending their children in Tunbridge Wells, or working in a factory, or farming in South Africa, or, a few of them, drinking in this pub on Wardour Street at noon of an autumn day.
>
> There were women whose husbands were in the desert with Monty, and others whose husbands were in Scotland, and a few whose husbands were in London, but rarely, unless they were newly married, were these latter accompanied by their husbands. Their husbands were overseas or confined to camp, or dead or incompatible or adulterous like themselves, or merely tiresome, so particularly tiresome now that all women were desirable. (*Long Summer* 189)

Charlie was drinking excessively in those days, and whether on leave or over-staying leave spent most of his time in bars. Alcohol pervades the 1957 novel, *Fish Flying Through Air,* that Roswell G. (Roddy) Ham wrote to memorialize him. A wartime comrade who also served with the RAF, and the son of the president of Mount Holyoke College, Ham's otherwise undistinguished book testified to Charlie Fenton's capacity to arouse the interest and admiration of nearly everyone who knew him.

In the novel (published in paperback under the alternate title *Till the Rafters Ring*) Ham tracked Fenton's life—under the fictional name of George McGough—from various prep school misadventures through the Tap Day episode at Yale and his desertion from the RCAF in London to his civilian years after the war. The tone is semi-worshipful throughout with regard to McGough, a debonair and wise-talking fellow forever rebelling against authority and often paying for his misdeeds, thereby failing to observe the eleventh commandment that "Thou Shalt Not Be Found Out." The teenage McGough-Fenton is described as tall for his age, with a large head squared away in front, wide-set dark gray eyes, and "a wide mouth with a sardonic quirk at each end." He looked "singularly like an ancient bust of Zeus," Ham wrote, with an overall expression that was "cynical, amused, and savagely intelligent" (17).

McGough is something of a rakehell, with a powerful sex appeal and a strong susceptibility to liquor. One week at Yale, for instance, he was taken drunk for 168 hours. According to Ham, McGough usually attributed his binges to one unconvincing cause or another. He'd received a long letter and small check from his mother. He'd seen one of his professors entering the library in riding habit. It was Friday or Tuesday, the first or last days of the long weekends they took in New York, where they were majoring in Benny Goodman. And so on.

Fish Flying Through Air includes a section about the amiable and attractive "Lucia," a fictional recreation of Betty Lyon. She first encounters Fenton passed out in a gutter in Soho. ("A blackness enveloped me," he explained.) Despite the unpromising circumstances, he looked "so sweet and angelic as he lay there"—actually like a child in a cradle—that she thought, "I must help him." And help him she did. She took him home with her, and during much of the following year Fenton lived in her flat at 16 Glebe Place in Chelsea, well off the beaten track for most servicemen on leave. She took excellent care of him, finding a doctor to treat his ills, encouraging his writing, and helping him hide from the RCAF's Service Police. If he was "on the trot," well, that was "a jolly good thing" for her, too (196, 198). It gave them more time together, and she made the most of it. She was almost desperately in love with Charlie, eager to marry him, to have his child.

It is not entirely clear how many missions over Germany Fenton flew as he battled the bomber boy odds against survival. The RCAF records provide no figures, but strongly suggest that he made his tail gunner flights during the period between 5 August and 21 October 1942. He made 36 trips, he told his parents, but that may have been an exaggeration. Perhaps there were 23, the number used both in "You'll Get No Promotion" and in Ham's novel. As the on-the-trot George McGough tells the narrator in *Fish Flying Through Air*,

"Forty-six times I crossed that Dutch coast. Never again, Cock. Never again. The King and I have severed relations." "Forty-six Ops," I gasped. "No wonder— "He stopped me. "You couldn't be expected to understand, Cock. Twenty-three Ops. You got to cross the coast coming back." (195)

However many missions there may have been, Fenton felt that he'd had his war, and was through with it. Reading between the lines of his letters home, it is clear that he abandoned the air force with some calculation. On 9 March 1943 he wrote his parents thanking them for "the second 15 pounds" he'd asked them to send. He was stationed in London, he told them, wearing civilian clothes, "[d]oing practically nothing and living with friends." A month later his parents forwarded "all [his] money": the RCAF allowance they'd been receiving since he enlisted. He was staying in London because, he dubiously reported, there were "no barracks for us at the moment." For 221 days 15 hours 54 minutes he managed to evade the Service Police. To throw them off the scent, he and Betty regularly took separate buses or taxis, and he would get off some distance from her flat and make his way there by back streets. Eventually, he knew, he would be caught and do hard time in the glasshouse.

Fenton did not idle away his time while on the trot. From prep school days on, he'd wanted to be a writer. Even during training in Canada, he'd been turning out stories. "It's good to have something else to write of besides college boys," he told his mother. Wartime England and the combat missions fueled his imagination, and during his seven months with Betty Lyon in 1943 he worked hard on his writing. On September 5, he reported on his progress in a letter to his parents. He'd finished a novel that was at a typing agency to be retyped and bound. One copy was going to a contest sponsored by Macmillan, and another to Bodley Head, the British publishers. (Apparently, nothing came of these submissions). *Penguin Parade* had accepted his "You'll Get No Promotion," and sent him "a check for *30* guineas!" A "very precious left wing magazine" had taken another story. "As you can see," Fenton said, "I am much more concerned with my own career than with the war, now that I am off flying." Once he stopped flying bombing runs, he became in effect a civilian, pursuing the career he'd long imagined for himself. In the early fall of 1943, he sounded extremely optimistic about the future. Editors were becoming familiar with his name and his work, he wrote home. By the end of the war he hoped to be "economically solvent" as a writer: an ambitious goal that proved to be beyond his reach.

When he wasn't writing, Fenton advanced his literary education with the assistance of the books he asked his mother to send him along with socks and soap and toothpaste, pipe tobacco and American cigarettes, and the

New Yorker. He read not only the latest work of William Saroyan and John O'Hara and Stephen Vincent Benét and Somerset Maugham, but also—more ambitiously—Dante's *Inferno* and Tolstoy's *War and Peace*, Eliot's *The Waste Land* and the dialogues of Plato. As early as his school days at Taft, Charlie had thought of himself as a literary lad. He wrote a column called "The Review" for the *Papyrus*, the school newspaper, in which he evaluated contemporary fiction and poetry and drama. In 1936, for example, he made favorable comments on Margaret Mitchell's *Gone with the Wind* and Robert Frost's *A Further Range*, and speculated that an era could best be judged by the literature it produced (Shepherd).To encourage this bent in her aviator son, his mother faithfully sent him the books he requested. In March 1943 three books arrived, one of them the *Men at War* anthology introduced by Hemingway. The introduction, which dealt at some length with conquering fear under fire, was "very interesting but pure bull," Fenton thought. He told his parents he was considering writing a short story in rebuttal to be called "Dear Mr. Hemingway."

He did not do so, but eight years later, by way of introducing himself to Ernest Hemingway as a fellow writer, Charlie told the great man about his novel that had won the $4000 prize in 1945."Hollywood and Doubleday money. . . . Was a lousy novel, so it never got published, though I kept the money. Was really very funny, in a sort of sad way, since the novel dealt with an English glasshouse (i.e. stockade) with which I'd had intimate contact, and the killing of a prisoner by the sergeant-major. Hollywood people wanted the narrator to meet the serg.-maj.'s daughter (a creature of their imagination not mine), and round off the tale in that brisk way. Jesus." Both Fenton's straight-forward prose style and his voluntary enlistment in the war owed a good deal to Hemingway's example.

In mid-September he got word that the Service Police were on his trail and turned himself in, thereby shortening the subsequent sentence from 121 to 90 days at the Darland Detention Barracks. Actually, he was released on 19 November, after serving but 60 days. Darland was not as notorious as the glasshouse at Aldershot, where "field punishment" was regularly meted out to deserters: "four hours tied to the wheel, pack drill every hour all through the night, guards handpicked for brutality from Royal Army regulars" (*Long Summer* 207). Still, those were 60 extremely tough days Charlie spent in detention, and he turned the experience to fictional account in his prize-winning 40,000-word draft of a novel.

Fenton did not mention his confinement at Darland in letters to his parents. Neither did Betty Lyon, whose first letter to Charlie's mother was written on 12 November 1943, a week before he was released. Instead she presented a cheerful account of his health, his writing, and future prospects. Charlie stayed with her "whenever he had leave," she said, and she looked after his books and things. She'd taken him to see a specialist, who was treating him both for asthma and thyroid trouble, and Charlie was feeling much better. He'd been doing a lot of writing with some success, and Betty believed that one day he'd be "a great writer." He'd cut down on his drinking, and during time on leave he worked at his desk all day and they went to movies or plays at night. It did not seem likely that he would fly any more; in any case, she hoped not. Betty added that she'd got quite used to living in London under wartime conditions, although clothes-rationing posed something of a problem. Mrs. Fenton would be amused, Betty wrote, to see quite stylishly dressed women going about barelegged or with unsightly darns in their stockings. It was an engaging letter, preceded by the gift of a book she'd picked out for the birthday of Charlie's 12-year-old brother David, and served as an overture to the news to come.

Early in February 1944, Fenton wrote his parents that he and Betty were in love and planned to be married. He assured them that the decision was neither hasty nor furtive. He'd known Betty for 18 months, and felt she possessed all the qualities he'd been looking for in a wife. She was very lovely and intelligent. Her brother—Harrow, Cambridge, B.B.C., a captain in the British army— would stand up for them at the wedding. But there were complications. "She is older than I, and has been married before, both factors which may make you a little dubious, but to me they seem more [like] advantages." In conclusion, he implied that Betty had made a new man of him. For the first time, he said, he felt he might make something of his life and talent and everything his parents had given him, "after making such a mess of most things for the last seven years"—a period stretching back to his freshman year at Yale.

Betty Lyon followed with another thoughtful letter to Mrs. Fenton, declaring that she was deeply in love with Charlie, wonderfully happy herself, and confident that she could make him happy. For a long time, she'd been troubled by the difference in their ages (how wide a difference was not made clear) but did not think it mattered any longer. "Perhaps in some ways," she might be able to help him more. Then she confessed that they could not yet be married, for her divorce had not become final. When it did, they would be married quietly at the Chelsea Registrar's Office. Everything would be done properly, and she would send Mrs. Fenton a picture of the two of them and the clipping from the *London Times* announcing their marriage.

Moving rapidly was crucial, however, inasmuch as Charlie had been kept hanging about at a "disposal depot" and might soon be "repatriated," she concluded.

The very next day, 14 February, Fenton wrote home that he was going to be sent back to Canada and probably discharged for "what they call 'functional stress.'" He was trying to delay his departure until Betty's divorce came through, in hopes that they might make the trip together as man and wife. That did not work out. Fenton crossed the Atlantic alone, and although he and Betty Lyon continued to correspond, the ocean between them eroded their commitment to each other.

Retrospectively, it is clear that Charlie Fenton's experience in World War II had a tremendous influence on his writing and his life. He enlisted as a reckless ne'er-do-well, with a boy's idealism and yearning to be involved. He was discharged three years and five months later quite a different person: a young man who'd been through the fire and emerged with a determination to make something of himself. If he was not yet fully grown into manhood and through making "a mess of things," he was at least on his way.

The war left Fenton with certain indelible convictions, chief among them a passionate distrust of authority, as exemplified by the RAF "leaders" who sent airmen out on deadly Pathfinder missions. As his stepson Richie expressed it, Charlie Fenton was thereafter deeply suspicious of "brass": of the motivations, the self-serving behavior, the lightly researched decisions and inadequate intellectual rigor of those in positions of power. Sometimes, their directives led to loss of innocent lives. Often, they resulted in other unpleasant if less drastic consequences. For the rest of his life Charlie Fenton took the side of the oppressed and uncomplaining; he even did some of their complaining for them.

He learned during his months flying bombing raids over Germany that it was impossible to generalize about war. As Tim O'Brien observed in *The Things They Carried*, an account of his experience as an infantryman in Vietnam, the truths were contradictory. "Almost everything is true. Almost nothing is true." War could make a man of you, but it could also make you dead. The very proximity to death brought with it "a corresponding proximity to life. After a firefight, there is always the immense pleasure of aliveness. The trees are alive. The grass, the soil—everything. All around you things are purely living, and you among them, and the aliveness makes you tremble" (80–81). So it was for Charlie Fenton after the harrowing trips over the Ruhr. As Churchill declared, "nothing in life is so exhilarating as to be shot at without result."

Then, too, the war generated bonds of friendship with fellow bomber boys. Among those closest to Fenton were Bill Orndorff and Johnny Caskie, two other American enlistees he'd first met in Canadian training camps. Orndorff parachuted out of his stricken aircraft over Switzerland in late 1942, and was missing for six months. Charlie had given him up for dead when, one day in London, he looked into the mirror behind the bar and saw his friend walking toward him. Caskie had a rough war too, and was discharged as mentally unfit for service. Both men returned to the States in advance of Fenton, and he encouraged them to look up his parents in Watertown.

It was not all bad, then—far from it—yet the most pervasive and lasting effect of Fenton's service in the RAF Bomber Command was trauma. For years he was subject to nightmares as he relived the eight minutes coned over Mainz, the beating at the glasshouse. In a very real sense, his mother believed, he never really survived the war.

Compulsively Charlie Fenton returned to the site of the terror. He wrote fictional accounts about the war in a series of stories, two plays (both lost), and three novels, only one of which has been located. He wrote about it immediately after his time in the air, during the AWOL months of 1943. He wrote about it during the next two years while he was finding out what to do with the rest of his life. And he returned to it a dozen years later in *The Long Summer*, when he tried to recollect the emotions of the time with a measure of equanimity, if not entire tranquility. In addition, he collected and edited *The Best Short Stories of World War II* in 1957. For his two major books of nonfiction, on Ernest Hemingway's apprenticeship as a writer and Stephen Vincent Benét's life and work, he chose subjects with substantial involvement in wars. Hemingway's case was clear enough along those lines: he attended all the wars of his time, and by way of introduction to Hemingway, Fenton made a point of presenting himself as a fellow warrior. Benét's case was somewhat different, for he was not physically fit enough to serve on the front lines. But he came from a military family, and is depicted in Fenton's biography as ruining his health through his extensive efforts as a propagandist during World War II. Both authors were advocates of the Loyalist cause during the Spanish Civil War—the subject for a book Fenton was researching at the time of his own death.

Fenton knew about Hemingway's Jake Barnes declaring in *The Sun Also Rises* that "[y]ou'll lose it if you talk about it," and its implied corollary that you might get rid of your worst troubles that way. But he did not regard fiction about the war as a form of therapy. He simply was obsessed by the subject. Yet in writing stories, as Tim O'Brien reflects in *The Things They Carried*, "you objectify your own experience. You separate it from yourself. You pin down certain truths. You make up others." And by so doing you go back "through a swirl of memories that might otherwise have ended in paralysis or worse" (158). To some extent, then, Fenton may have alleviated his post-traumatic stress by writing fiction, yet even in the pages of the *The Long Summer* he was unable to come to grips on the page with the most shameful wound of all—his *de facto* desertion from the service in 1943.

Chapter 3

The Young Academic

By mid-March 1944 Fenton was in Ottawa and reveling in the luxuries afforded to returning servicemen. It was "like a Hollywood version of Army life," he wrote home. You couldn't spit "without hitting a snack bar or a soda fountain," all the cinemas were free, and hundreds of WAAFs were hovering about. He thanked his parents for wiring Betty Lyon that he had safely crossed the water and told them that he would probably be discharged soon. He was getting some work done on his "new novel," he reported, but the most important thing on his mind was what he could do to support himself. Perhaps he might land a job on the Watertown paper, he speculated. It wouldn't pay much but might work out better financially than going to New York and spending all his salary to live. He may have turned to his parents for assistance, knowing that his military record would work against remunerative employment. He was discharged from the RCAF "for service misconduct" on 11 April 1944, owing to "repeated and serious breaches of discipline." Having enlisted for "the duration" of the war, he'd served for three years and four and a half months, minus nearly eleven months when AWOL or in detention.

As it turned out, the *New Haven Register* hired him as a general assignment reporter at the usual pittance paid news-side employees. Charlie's real goal was to write fiction, though, and on the strength of "You'll Get No Promotion" and his novel(s) in progress he was admitted as a fellow to the Bread Loaf writers' conference in August 1944. There he came in contact with the novelist Wallace Stegner, who was on the faculty, and with a number of other aspiring writers. In his biography of Bernard DeVoto, another Bread Loaf veteran, Stegner describes the "frenziedly, manically literary" atmosphere of the place, with lots of gossiping and drinking going on. In one sketch he recalls the night one of the fellows—unnamed, but manifestly Fenton—"a

33

boy just invalided out of the Royal Air Force after forty-seven bombing missions, lifted somebody else's bottle and hid it under his coat and took it to his room and went to bed with it and to sleep, and how one of the staff, keeping an eye on him, went quietly over after a while and rescued the bottle and pulled the blankets up over the kid and tiptoed out" (120–24).

During the two-week conference Charlie roomed with a still younger lad, the obviously talented and obviously gay 19-year-old Truman Capote. Lest others assume that he and Capote were intimate, Fenton joked about keeping the shower curtain closed and not going to sleep too early. But he was impressed by Capote's talent, and shortly after Bread Loaf visited him in New York, where he was working at *The New Yorker*. Accompanying Charlie on that trip was his fiancée Gwendolyn Ross Grant, the daughter of a New Haven real estate and investment man. The romantic relationship with Betty Lyon had faded away. Letters to and from Betty crossed the water, but before long Fenton transferred his allegiance to Gwendy. They were married in October 1944.

Gwendy was outgoing, personable, athletic, witty, and well-liked by practically everyone. A year Charlie's junior, she'd been brought up in prosperous circumstances, going to dances at the New Haven Lawn Club but had no patience with pretentiousness or snobbery in any form. Her parents sent her first to Mrs. Day's school and then to Briarcliff Junior College where, she liked to say, she learned to walk with a book balanced on her head and to pour tea, but very little else. She left after her freshman year to marry Richard Grant. They had two children—Wendy and Richie—in rapid succession, and then, separated by the war, they divorced. The breakup was extraordinarily amicable. During a phone call Gwendy asked Richard if he knew you had to have grounds to get a divorce. Yes, he'd heard that. Well, what grounds should she choose? None of them sounded quite right to her. Just choose one, he suggested; he wouldn't object. So it was done, and Grant established a trust fund to support Gwendy and the children.

Gwendy hence brought a ready-made family to her second marriage, and considerable financial support as well—support that Fenton needed when he went back to Yale to earn his bachelor's, master's, and doctoral degrees, and that the family continued to need throughout his academic career. Charlie "wasn't a great breadwinner," stepdaughter Wendy recalled. He had a professorial lack of interest in accumulating dollars and "wasn't good at things he wasn't interested in."

Brought up to be a wife, Gwendy had full command of the domestic arts. She was an excellent cook, knitted sweaters, and knew how to make a home. She also played a good game of golf and a better one of bridge. But she was not an intellectual, nor did she much cotton to them. She was comfortable among family and friends in Connecticut, and had no particular desire to see the rest of the world. Her daughter Wendy remembers her as "probably the friendliest person I ever knew," easy to talk to and at the same time sometimes brutally frank in expressing herself. Gwendy "did not lie, and she did not embellish to the point that what she said was not true." She was also a notorious flirt.

In Roddy Ham's novel, Gwendy is depicted as Isabelle Standish and supplied with a mansion on the shore in Westport, a considerable leap in value above her actual domicile. According to Ham, she issued "clear signals of patience and inner amusement," was rather a giving person by nature, and possessed "a degree of emotional maturity." Nice looking if not facially beautiful, she had a good figure, "magnificent" legs, and emitted "loud, clear signals of sexuality." Ham outlines a scene in which Charlie Fenton (George in the novel) demonstrates "[h]umanity, empathy, even jocular affection" for Gwendy/Isabelle's two young children. "And love, by God," for Isabelle. "It was hard to believe" from such a committed reprobate (241–48).

Not that Charlie Fenton had entirely reformed. Gwendy did her best to guide him through the process of recovery, but it was not easy. There were times when he'd start drinking and show no signs of stopping. Like his fictional counterpart George McGough in *Fish Flying Through Air*, Charlie could consume substantial amounts before passing out. Often the drinking was preceded or accompanied by depression. At times he felt suicidal, but made no overt attempt to do away with himself. When one of these black periods struck, Gwendy did her best to talk him through it. Sometimes, afterwards, Charlie could not remember what had happened.

Gwendy grew to dread visits from Charlie's RCAF buddies, Bill Orndorff and John Caskie and Charlie Dow, because they were liable to lead to extended binges. Once in a while she kicked Charlie out of the house. He'd pack up his books and off he'd go, but a few days or a week later she'd relent and take him back. No doubt the drinking contributed to the series of short-term jobs he took, and left, during the 1944–47 period. That, and Fenton's "visceral suspicion of brass": his fierce independence in the face of anyone in a position of authority, an attitude he extended from military and business to academic and political realms.

Meanwhile the war continued to dominate his imagination. During 1946, he completed at least one story and two plays based on his experiences in the RCAF. The story, "Another Language," appeared in *Cross Section 1947*, a literary annual published by Simon and Schuster. The other "language" was that of the Polish airmen flying bombing runs with the RAF. Assigned to join an attack of 750 bombers on Munich, the five planes with Polish crews took advantage of their "full load of petrol" to bomb Berlin instead. Flying dangerously low at 1,000 feet, they survived heavy fire to achieve "jolly good bombing results."

The well-crafted story is told from the point of view of a bewildered and terrified war correspondent who went along on the mission. "But, Christ, man, why did they do it, five aircraft?" he asks the control officer afterwards. "They're Poles," the officer replies: they'd seen Warsaw bombed to death and their families lined up and shot. Berlin, the capital of the Third Reich, symbolized those atrocities to them. They carried with them "a kind of hate" that was difficult for British or Canadians or Americans to understand. When they were chastised for disobeying their orders to accompany the other bombers on the Munich raid, the Poles simply spread their hands and said they couldn't understand English. "Yes," the control officer says thoughtfully, "they definitely speak another language" (78–79).

Fenton also recast his wartime adventures in dramatic form, in a long play called *Members Only* and a short one titled *Happy Valley*. Both plays were among the finalists for the 1947 awards of the Dramatists' Alliance at Stanford University—an unprecedented double, according to Margery Bailey, proctor of the Alliance. Although neither one actually won in its category, Bailey thought enough of Fenton's plays to recommend *Happy Valley* for consideration in the annual collection of Best One-Act Plays. She also tried to interest local theater groups in mounting productions, and had some nibbles but no takers. The problem lay in the topical nature of his plays, she wrote Fenton. "[M]odern directors, readers, and audiences," she explained, "are now in the postwar slump when they refuse to remember what has gone on so recently."

After fighting the fiction market for much of 1945 and 1946, Fenton wound up financially embarrassed and to pay the bills started teaching night school English at the New Haven Junior College of Commerce. Like his father before him he had a gift for teaching, but realized that to get anywhere in the profession he would have to earn the requisite degrees. Learning that his Canadian service might qualify him for support from the G.I. Bill of Rights, Fenton petitioned the RCAF Discharge Review Board to amend his discharge papers. On 22 November 1946 the board complied, eliminating mention of his repeated "misconduct" and supplying as a "reason for discharge" the ambiguous phrase "services terminated," a revision that qualified him for G.I. educational benefits. Fenton enrolled at Yale for the third time and started a rapid rise up the academic ladder—B.A. in 1948, M.A. in 1949, Ph.D. in 1953.

This time Charlie was highly motivated as a student. He needed an occupation, and knew that he was unlikely to support himself and a family as a writer of fiction. He had made a hash of his previous experiences at Yale, and wanted to make up for them. He was following in the footsteps of the father he admired, and who—he knew—would be proud to see him achieve a university career. If he could make a success at Yale first as a graduate student and then as a professor, he would in a way avenge his father's having to settle for teaching Latin and Greek to prep school boys at Taft.

Fenton revealed his own attitude toward prep schools—one of qualified scorn—in his story "You'll Get No Promotion." Charles Mathews, the airman/protagonist, looks back on his education at a "phony prep school" where he was taught "bad manners and what clothes to wear and the superiority of your class. But if you were lucky you had in the four years perhaps one intelligent master, and you discovered Hemingway and Keats and the dusty charm of history books" (150–51). Fenton himself spent four years in prep schools, one at Eaglebrook and three at Taft. Eaglebrook, situated above Deerfield, Mass., was one of the nation's very few pre-preparatory institutions, offering instruction for boys in the sixth to ninth grades. Charlie was sent there for his ninth grade year in 1933–34, a time of upheaval for the Fenton family as his father prepared to readjust from an executive salary at Fisk to a schoolmaster's at Taft.

Charlie was 14 years and 9 months old when he took the IQ tests administered at Eaglebrook in March 1934, with a "mental age" recorded as 17 years and 5 months. His IQ was measured at 122, well above average, and he tested in the 92nd percentile on Independent School tests. His grades did not reflect his promise, however. He completed his year at Eaglebrook with some Bs and Cs, but in final exams flunked beginning Algebra and managed only a D in French. He had not yet learned to apply himself, except in extracurricular areas that interested him.

The headmaster at Eaglebrook, C. Thurston Chase, Jr. (the first of three generations of Chases to lead the school) took a strong interest in the psychological development of his students. Near the end of his career, in 1957, he contributed a long article on the youths he had observed to a volume entitled *Psychotherapy of the Adolescent*. Chase's basic assumption was that the adolescent "is *ipso facto* a somewhat disturbed person who, however 'normal' he might be, requires at least a mild and continuous therapy from parents and teacher." Too often, he observed, we treated these adolescents "as a lost group—clumsy, unattractive, troubled" (186–87). Chase expected and even welcomed a certain amount of rebelliousness from the boys under his charge. He believed that to achieve their own independence and adulthood, they must necessarily "rebel against unreasonable authority, and occasionally against *all* authority" even if such mutinies often had unhappy consequences (207). "All one can know," as F. Scott Fitzgerald summed up his own adolescent years, "is that somewhere between thirteen, boyhood's majority, and seventeen, when one is a sort of counterfeit young man, there is a time when youth fluctuates hourly between one world and another—pushed ceaselessly forward into unprecedented experiences and vainly trying to struggle back to the days when nothing had to be paid for" (Mizener 27).

The adolescent Charlie Fenton rebelled, all right, turning in a mediocre record during his first year at Taft. Chase, who carefully tracked the progress of his students as they proceeded from Eaglebrook to the nation's leading prep schools, was deeply disappointed in his performance, especially as he had recommended the boy to Taft as a scholarship student. Actually, the recommendation was less than glowing. "Charles has a quick mind and should develop as an able student," he wrote headmaster Horace D. Taft in May. "He has a certain haste and carelessness. I believe, however, you will find him a satisfactory candidate for Lower Middle Form [at Taft] next fall." On those fragile grounds, and the rather contradictory results of his grades on the Secondary Education Board examinations in June—good on English and Latin, fair in French, and "passing" in Algebra—Charlie was admitted with the scholarship available to qualified sons of Taft's masters.

Charlie's first year at Taft, located in Watertown, Connecticut, coincided with his father's initial year teaching there. This placed the lad in a somewhat difficult position. He had been pampered much of his life. For example, he spent part of the summer *before* going to Eaglebrook, according to the school newspaper, in Europe and part of it at the sea shore: the sort of summer vacation that only very well-to-do boys might experience. Yet in the fall of 1934 Charlie became the son of a schoolmaster—an honorable occupation, to be sure, but several steps down the social ladder from head of Fisk's export division. In addition, as a faculty child, he may have felt an obligation—analogous to that of the notoriously naughty preacher's kid—to defy the expectation that he should shine in the classroom.

In passing the boy along to Taft, Chase added a caveat. "I hope he will be forced to stand very much on his own feet, and not allowed to [rely] too much on the help of his family." Chase, apparently unaware of the arrival of Charlie's younger brother David in 1930, thought of him as an only child—as indeed he had been for his first 11 years—and hence subject to excessive self-regard.

This attitude emerged repeatedly in Chase's correspondence with Andrew D. McIntosh, dean at Taft, and with headmaster Taft, as they lamented the discouraging grades of Charlie's year as a "middler" at the school. The symptoms governing Charlie's behavior remained much the same as they had the previous year, Chase thought. "Interest in loads of things outside of the classroom [debate and dramatics and the school newspaper, for example] and relying on something—goodness knows what unless it be the Goddess Luck—to pull him through at the last minute." Fenton was "the only one of our boys who is falling down in his secondary school this year," he told McIntosh, and he promised to try to "stir him up" with a letter. "Come, come," he wrote

Schoolboy Fenton with German Shepherd Rex, ca. 1932. Fenton Family Photo

Charlie in December, "is this the way to uphold Eaglebrook tradition?" All nine of his classmates were on the honor rolls of their new schools. Was he going to let the side down?

Upon hearing in June 1935 that Charlie's grades at the end of the year were even less satisfactory than during the fall semester, Chase wrote Horace D. Taft that he was "disgusted" with the boy's showing, for there was no question about his ability. In his letters, the youngster sounded just as "conceited and sure of himself" as he had at Eaglebrook, Chase observed. "Last year, even though he and his parents were separated by some forty miles, we had the problem of a spoiled boy to deal with and it was frequently not easy." Nonetheless Chase wanted to help if he could. Was there some way he could play the "Dutch uncle" to young Fenton?

In a discouraged-sounding reply, Taft pointed out that Charlie's attitude had been "very poor." He was "undoubtedly a spoiled boy," and Taft did not know "how we can get at him." Perhaps with the passage of time, he would mature and show his ability. Taft like Chase was afraid that proximity to family worked against such growth, and the boy's "quite peculiar" situation as well. "I am not sure that it would be a bad thing to send him to some other school, possibly in exchange for the son of some master at that school," he suggested. "I think that a master's boy is under something of a handicap in his father's own school." But given Charlie's attitude and behavior, Taft was afraid the other school would feel he had played a trick on them.

As it turned out, Fenton began to improve as a student with the beginning of his junior (Upper Middle) year at Taft. There were at least two reasons. From the beginning of his stay at Taft, his parents had aimed him toward Yale, he too hoped to go to his father's university, and it dawned on him that he would have to achieve much better grades if he hoped to gain admission. Then too, in the fall of his junior year he moved out of his parents' apartment to room in a dormitory, a development that alleviated what Chase continued to think of as his unfortunate "family situation." It may well have been his father, the superficially stern schoolmaster, who did most of the boy's spoiling. Certainly he orchestrated his son's career at Taft, choosing the right courses to give him the best chance for Yale.

By senior year, for example, Charlie was through with mathematics, after scraping through re-exams in both Algebra and Plane Geometry. He continued his four-year struggle with French, and achieved honors in Latin—under his father's tutelage—and in English and American History. His overall average for senior year, despite a 73 in French, came out to 85. That enabled him to graduate Cum Laude, and to go on to Yale with a scholarship. His IQ, tested again in March 1937, ascended to 134. All of his teachers commented on what a pleasure it was to have Charlie in their class. He played club hockey and golf, did well in debate and dramatics, and—always a reader—wrote ambitious literary reviews for the school newspaper. With the encouragement of his English instructor, who was impressed by Charlie's "keen penetrating mind and unusual powers of expression," he began to think of a career in journalism. In that final year he lived neither with his parents nor in a dormitory. Instead he was one of three seniors chosen to reside in the home of Horace D. Taft himself, the revered and recently retired headmaster and brother to President William Howard Taft.

In his letter of recommendation to Yale, Taft's new headmaster, Paul Cruikshank, sketched out characteristics that defined Charles Fenton for the rest of his life. Fenton "has a fine personality and shows great intellectual promise," Cruikshank wrote. "He is one of the best read boys in his class [and] is mentally more advanced than his age. He is very independent in his thoughts and spirit and this has, at times, brought him into conflict with the school regulations, but not seriously. His integrity is extremely high and during the past two years he has shown great industry and is now one of the ranking scholars of his class." The details of the flights of independence that led him into trouble went unspecified, and no examples were cited of his integrity. So Cruikshank summed up Charlie Fenton at 17 going on 18.

He had come a long way in his last two years at Taft, but not far enough to survive at college without disciplinary restraints. In his first semester, he did well at what he liked—English and History—and made connections with the *Yale Literary Magazine*, but failed Biology. He drank and chased girls, and spent much of his time in New York. When he left to join the RCAF, it was with recollections of high old times at Yale. He remembered "the Smith and Vassar girls in their Saks sweaters, soft and eager and not very bright. The gay divorceés in New York. Dinner at Armando's and the shadowy corners at Number One [Fifth Avenue] and the open trolleys to the football games" ("No Promotion" 151).

When he returned to Yale a decade later in 1947, a war veteran with a wife and family, it was with a resolve to live up to his capabilities. Seasoned by experience, he found that he liked research and teaching, and that he was very good at both of them. In graduate school, Yale evaluated its students on a four-grade scale: Honors/High Pass/Pass/Fail. Fenton received Honors in all of his courses with the exception of a single High Pass. That came from A. Whitney Griswold, who took over as president of Yale in 1951.

His field, Fenton soon established, would be American literature as viewed in the wider context of the nation's social, cultural, and historical development. His mentor and advocate throughout was Norman Holmes Pearson, an enormously popular teacher who recognized a kindred spirit in young Fenton. Malformed at birth, Pearson carried a hunchback and a game leg. At the first meeting of his large American literature class, Pearson would limp across the platform, reassemble himself into a sitting position, and announce that "when God made me, He made me incomplete." *Pause as students stared in embarrassed silence.* "He gave me a terrible memory," Pearson said, "and I probably won't be able to call on most of you by name." *Smiles of relief from the audience, then delight as Pearson delivered his customary sparkling lecture.* Four months later, after the last meeting of the class, the students rose and applauded as Pearson, with a farewell wave of the hand, made his way off the platform.

During World War II Pearson had done yeoman duty as a spy, working behind the German lines in occupied France and escaping suspicion through his command of languages and his misshapen body. Later he turned his considerable intellectual attainments to work as director of counterintelligence for the Office of Strategic Services (OSS), the forerunner organization to the Central Intelligence Agency (CIA). Back at Yale, Pearson helped recruit the best and brightest students for the CIA. In the class of 1950, for example, he steered both William F. Buckley, Jr. and Peter Matthiessen into postgraduate CIA assignments. Unlike them, Charlie Fenton became Pearson's protégé in the academic world—a young man he liked and believed in and did everything possible to support. Pearson monitored his progress both at Yale and in wider literary circles he was well acquainted with. Only ten years Fenton's senior, Pearson served not only as godfather to his son Andy but as a father figure to Charlie himself.

Pearson did not publish much, at least by the rigorous standards of the Yale English department and had to wait an unconscionable length of time for promotions.

He poured much of the energy that made him a master of espionage into his friendships. He "collected people" of talent—among them some of the leading poets of the time, especially including H. D. [Hilda Doolittle], John Gould Fletcher, and W. H. Auden, with whom he edited several poetry anthologies. Something of a maverick in the English department, Pearson staked out a territory for himself as director of the graduate program in American Studies, recruiting and guiding not only American but many overseas students (Winks 310, 316–21). Thus it was that for the summer of 1948 he landed Fenton a teaching position in American Studies at Yale for Foreign Students. Pearson also encouraged Fenton's interest in contemporary writers of fiction, and directed his dissertation on Hemingway.

Along the way to his doctorate, Fenton was given various teaching assignments within the English department. These he performed with great success. Students in English 15, which Fenton taught in the spring semester of 1949 while working on his master's degree, evaluated him in almost incredibly enthusiastic terms. English 15 was Yale's basic English literature course, designed to introduce undergraduates to a few of the major writers across the centuries. The course normally enrolled students with no special competence in literature—the more talented ones were siphoned off into English 25—and in Fenton's section of 40 students there were more Engineering than English majors. For several of these students, he managed to open their eyes to literature for the first time. "The teaching . . . made me interested in a subject which before this year had no attraction for me," a Civil Engineering major commented.

Another student, inspired by the class, switched his major from pre-med to English. "I cannot praise his course enough," this lad wrote. "Fenton is *by far* the best of my teachers." Two students, going further, called Fenton the best teacher they'd ever had.

Others praised Fenton in similar terms: "an *excellent* teacher in all respects," "the teaching in this course is exceptional," "an outstanding stimulating teacher," "an aggressive, dynamic teacher," "my most interesting course," "an excellent instructor who makes every class enjoyable," "an instructor the university should be proud of." Thirty eight of the forty students submitted highly favorable evaluations along these lines. (Two wanted more written work, and less reliance on ten-minute in-class quizzes). Fenton did not earn this praise by any compromise in his grading practices. No one had a grade higher than 80 at the midpoint of his course, and several noted that he gave low marks.

Manifestly, it was Fenton's engaging personality that generated most of these encomiums. He was "a great guy," a "regular" guy who spoke with "almost incredible naturalness" and provided "down to earth" explanations. He was "straightforward," with "a magnetic personality." He could talk to the students on a level they could comprehend. Unlike the usual "king in the class-room," Charlie Fenton did not simply hold forth from the rostrum. He made no pretense of infallibility and invited, even welcomed, dissenting views. This tolerance led to "full participation" and "lively discussions" in class that involved his students in the learning enterprise. Undoubtedly it helped his popularity that Fenton was not quite 30, and youthful looking for this age. But in addition he had mastered the art of communicating his ideas while making "the class feel that he [was] one of them." And often, he was quite funny. As one of his colleagues remarked, "a keener penetration and a sharper wit hadn't been seen around [Yale] for a long time" ("Charles Fenton").

On the strength of such evaluations and his published and unpublished writing, Fenton was assigned to Daily Themes in the fall of 1949 and chosen to lead Yale's fledgling course in creative writing (short stories) in the spring of 1950. Still a lowly instructor, he wrote Wallace Stegner at Stanford—one of the first institutions to develop a graduate program for aspiring fiction writers—for advice on how to teach the writing of fiction. Most of the people at Stanford followed "the practice of working as much as possible from [the student's] manuscript," Stegner told him. What was best was "not to over-teach and let the students lead and then to look at it with an eye to seeing anything of value the manuscript may contain." But nobody could really tell him how to do it, Stegner said. Fenton would have to find out for himself. What he did find out, not only in English 15 and the writing classes but in the course in Twentieth Century American Prose he initiated and even such other out-of-his-field courses as the Age of Chaucer and Romantic Poets, was that he liked teaching, and it was "a hell of a lot more satisfying than anything else" he'd ever done (Patten). He decided to keep doing it.

His work in Daily Themes and the creative writing class introduced Charlie Fenton to several of Yale's most talented undergraduates. These students remember him as "a superb teacher, intense, funny, down to earth, and wholly committed to his subject." Or as "an ideal role model—handsome, laconic, with the whiff of warrior." Or as "a wonderful guy, honest and straightforward, completely approachable," with high standards where writing was concerned. In class he presented his students with the best of examples to emulate. He read the beginning of *A Farewell to Arms* to rows of rapt faces.

In the late summer of that year we lived in a house in a village that looked
across the river and the plain to the mountains. In the bed of the river there were
pebbles and boulders, dry and white in the sun, and the water was clear and
swiftly moving and blue in the channels . . .

"What clarity of vision, what specificity of detail, what perfection!" Ed Sauter, class of 1952, thought. He was drawn to the instructor who spoke the
words and who had thrilled him, after sharply critiquing his writing, by adding, "Keep trying—you have all the potential." Sauter felt he'd been touched
by the hand of a master (Sauter 5–6).

Malcolm Mitchell, '57, took both Daily Themes and Fenton's Short Story
Writing class during his junior year and in senior year earned two credits
for continued story writing under Fenton's direction. Charlie "never let me
get away with anything," Mitchell recalled, repeatedly sending him back to
revise his work. On one of his efforts, Fenton wrote: "What's wrong with
this I'm sure you know yourself. It's not finished." Tough words to take,
but as a critic, Mitchell realized, Fenton was invariably right. Neither Sauter
nor Mitchell became full-time professional writers or accomplished scholar-
teachers, but a number of Fenton's students at Yale were to achieve remarkable success in these fields.

James Stevenson, '51, became one of the nation's most eminent authors
and illustrators, contributing 2,000 cartoons and 80 covers to the *New Yorker*
and producing more than 100 children's books. He took Fenton's writing
class in the spring of 1950, and during his senior year wrote a novel under
Fenton's direction as a Scholar of the House while editing the *Yale Daily
News*. Fenton had "a tremendous influence" on his life, Stevenson recalled.
"I remember him very fondly—his great attitude, his humor, his jaunty presence. What a refreshing guy he was in contrast to the drab eminences of
scholarship around Yale."

In his class, Fenton inspired his students to feel that writing was important
and that it had better be good and not "fancy." In an elegant passage he was
quite proud of, Stevenson elaborated on the pattern of light as it fell on the
kitchen floor. "Isn't this just fine writing?" Fenton wrote in the margin, and
well, yes, Stevenson could see the point of that. A lesson learned: writing was
not a matter of showing off. A somewhat parallel episode involved a "pretentious aspirant to writing" who repeatedly presented shows of erudition in class.
This sort of pretentiousness did not sit well with most of the students, and
infuriated Fenton. One day, after this fellow contradicted him about a passage
from Shakespeare and declared that he should have paid further attention to
its subtext, Fenton made a suggestion. "Why don't you go fuck yourself?" he
asked the student. That outburst could have led to a serious censure from the

administration, but the majority of those in the class were solidly on Fenton's side and saw to it that no complaint was made. Fenton's strongest advocates liked to think of themselves, Stevenson observed, as "part of a wonderful, small, select, and subversive underground dedicated . . . to a certain kind of courage and excellence and impertinence" that their teacher exemplified. He had "star quality," Stevenson thought. "We all wanted to *be* him."

Or at least to emulate him. His coterie knew all about Fenton's melodramatic wartime adventures. They thought of him as a kind of hero, as brave in defying authority as in fighting the enemy. Peter Braestrup, in the same writing class as Stevenson, enlisted in the Marines shortly after graduation. Braestrup would not have volunteered had it not been for his admiration of Fenton, Stevenson thought, and the decision had lasting consequences. Sent to the front in Korea, Braestrup was severely wounded in combat. Later he became a prominent journalist reporting for *Time*, the *New York Herald-Tribune*, the *New York Times*, and—during the Vietnam war—as Saigon bureau chief for the *Washington Post*. Like Fenton, Braestrup swam against the current. He wrote a book about how the media had misreported the Tet offensive in Vietnam, and during his last job—he died in 1997, while serving as Senior Editor and Director of Communications for the Library of Congress—he was known "for his gruff affect, quick wit, and sharp editorial skills."

Yet another member of Fenton's spring 1950 fiction writing class was Peter Matthiessen, author of such major works as *The Snow Leopard* (1979), *At Play in the Fields of the Lord* (1991), and *Shadow Country* (2008). Like many students in the class of 1950, Matthiessen served during World War II before enrolling at Yale. He showed tremendous early promise as a writer, publishing a story in the *Atlantic Monthly* while still an undergraduate. On the strength of that, Fenton arranged for him to return after graduation to teach in Daily Themes and the Short Story writing class during 1950–51. He and Fenton hit it off immediately. He "was my mentor and my pal," as Matthiessen put it, and as pals they did their share of carousing together.

One night, Matthiessen, Stevenson, and Fenton decided to explore New Haven's sewer system. They removed a manhole cover and went down into the dark. "Absolutely drunk" as they were, they took only one flashlight, a couple of cigarette lighters, and a candle with them. Before long, these guttered or burned out, and they wandered for hours in the below-ground labyrinth before finally finding their way out somewhere in North Haven, miles from the Yale campus. Another night, Fenton was observed "tottering around Pierson College" obviously in need of a place to recover. Sympathetic students came to his rescue, depositing the young instructor in one of the college rooms to sleep it off. Such widely rumored incidents may have amused Fenton's youthful admirers, but were regarded as beyond the pale by respectable senior members of the English department. If he were to make his mark in the academic world, he would have to amend his ways.

Gaddis Smith, the Larned professor of history emeritus at Yale and an expert on American foreign relations and maritime history, took the Daily Themes course in the fall of his sophomore year and Fenton's Short Story writing class in the spring. In senior year (1953–54) he was named a Scholar of the House while serving as chairman of the *Yale Daily News,* and like Stevenson before him chose to write a novel under Fenton's direction as his year-long project. As a director Fenton offered occasional perceptive comments but mostly encouragement, Smith recalls. The novel itself was forgettable, making it clear to Smith that his future did not lie in writing fiction. But he carried away from that experience and from the Short Story class an abiding sense that literature was important and that it could be produced by undergraduates, if not necessarily by himself.

Smith vividly recalls the day that Fenton brought Edward Weeks, the eminent editor of the *Atlantic Monthly,* to sit in on his writing class. "Gentlemen," Weeks declared, "most of you are writing better now than you ever will again": with fewer inhibitions, more spontaneously. It was heady news for the students to hear, and the more inspiring coming from a famous editor.

These students of Fenton's were among the most promising undergraduates he encountered at Yale during the postwar period. Several of them, especially in the classes of 1950 and 1951, had served in the military during World War II. A few of them had been officers, placing them in the somewhat anomalous position of taking instruction from a former enlisted man. But rank did not matter to Charlie Fenton, then or ever. And very few of his students had been under fire as fiercely and for as long as Charlie Fenton. According to historian William Manchester, of the 16 million Americans in the armed forces during World War II, fewer than a million actually saw combat (500).

Fenton made friends among the best and brightest of his undergraduates, men like Peter Matthiessen and Jim Stevenson. He spoke to them openly of going AWOL in England, and of doing time in the glasshouse—revelations that he did not share with most of the students who admired him as a teacher very different from the other professors they encountered at Yale.

One of these was Matthew J. Bruccoli, Class of '53, who came to Yale fresh from high school in Brooklyn. Bruccoli first met Fenton during his junior year, a connection that was to be instrumental in shaping his career as a prolific writer-scholar on American literature. At the time, Fenton was sharing an office in Berkeley College with Dale Underwood. Bruccoli stopped by to talk to Underwood, his teacher in a course on Literary Comedy, and was immediately impressed by the books on Fenton's side of the office.

At the time Bruccoli was reading contemporary writers like Budd Schulberg and Ben Hecht, and there on Fenton's bookshelves were Schulberg's

What Makes Sammy Run (1941) and Hecht's *Collected Stories* (1945). Such writers had no purchase at all in university literature classes, and Bruccoli was delighted to find someone on the Yale faculty he could talk to about them, and about F. Scott Fitzgerald and Ernest Hemingway, who at the time were only slightly more acceptable academically. In his courses, too, Fenton defied the conventional wisdom that "respectable literature terminated in 1922," making the study of contemporary American literature a serious endeavor.

In later years Bruccoli was to produce dozens of books on Fitzgerald, and Hemingway, and John O'Hara, and many others. He remembered vividly "the precise moment" when it occurred to him to pursue such a career. In senior year he took Charlie Fenton's writing class and his course in the Twentieth Century American Prose. One day in class, they were discussing Hemingway's "The Light of the World." Fenton said he didn't understand the story. He didn't know about the middleweight boxer Stanley Ketchel (who appears in the story as Steve Ketchel) or about his famous bout with the black heavyweight champion Jack Johnson. Bruccoli was able to tell him about that, and it opened up the story for Fenton. "I felt then," he said, "that if I kept on with that kind of research, maybe I had a future as an American Lit scholar." And indeed, Bruccoli's greatest contribution to the field came through unearthing documentary and factual information to illuminate the work of various writers.

Like other Fenton disciples, Matt Bruccoli was swept away by his teacher's style. "Everything about him was classy," Bruccoli thought. His students adopted "the Limey slang" Fenton brought back from wartime England. When he came to class in a Glen Plaid suit–a departure from the usual gray flannels—his young followers soon started wearing Glen Plaid. Bruccoli made a point of introducing his dates to Fenton. Charlie made the visiting girls feel important, and in that way made his students feel important too. "I adored him," Bruccoli said. "I worshipped him."

Tom Greening, class of '52, came to Yale from a small town in New Jersey, son of a mechanical engineer and expecting to earn his degree in engineering. That changed when an adviser, looking over Greening's aptitude tests, noted his talent for the humanities and steered him toward courses in philosophy, literature, and history. In that way he was introduced to such professors as Norman Holmes Pearson and Pearson's protégé Charles Fenton. In Daily Themes and Fenton's story writing class, Greening came to idealize Fenton, regarding him as "an American mythic hero" who'd volunteered to go to war early, who carried himself with a kind of jauntiness, who was manifestly an iconoclast rebelling against stilted convention in academia and everywhere else during a time when going along with the status quo was increasingly mandated by the culture, and who was widely rumored to be able to outdrink everyone and seduce dozens of women. Greening thought of Fenton as a tough guy, patriotic, dedicated to the craft of writing, a risk taker forever pushing his luck.

The connection to Hemingway formed part of the image that Fenton projected and had a strong appeal to many of his students. As Greening retrospectively realized—he became a prominent practitioner and professor of humanistic-existential psychology and a published poet as well—American life exerted tremendous pressure on young men to achieve mastery, to win the struggle to feel powerful, to try to be somebody. And, not least, to validate these accomplishments by demonstrating them to others. In Hemingway they found an exemplary role model. "In no other writer of our country, perhaps in no other man," as Leonard Kriegel observed, "had America embedded the actual presence of manhood as it had in Ernest Hemingway" (94). He became a public figure, and eventually the media-driven image of the great white hunter, the journalist covering wars in advance of the troops, the world traveler, the boxing fan and race track expert, the bullfight aficionado, the nightclub brawler, the four-times serially married Papa Hemingway almost obliterated that of the writer, though even there, the photographs of the author at work in his Cuban workroom, wearing shorts and his signature beard, and standing up while he typed his daily 1,000 words, projected a memorable image.

In short, Hemingway apparently felt compelled to demonstrate his masculinity to others as well as himself. He was on stage, much of the time, and "many events of his life seemed shaped and governed by an overriding desire to display himself in a tough masculine role." This persistent pattern subjected him to the charge of glorifying "machismo, blood sports, physical violence, and war" (Strychacz 3–4). The public bravado, the manhood-posing explains the still more common charge leveled against him—that he remained an adolescent throughout his life. In the twenty-first century, Hemingway probably does not serve as a role model for many young men, but his example had a significant appeal in the middle of the twentieth century. "Hemingway understood," Kriegel wrote in 1979, "that boys looked forward to the condition of manhood because it was presented to them as something one needed courage to take" (98–99).

Acquiring and demonstrating such courage may well have constituted the single greatest challenge facing young men. In this respect, they sought to emulate Hemingway's repeated willingness, or eagerness, or compulsion to face down fear—his determination to achieve "grace under pressure" in combat most of all but also in the bullring and the African wild. Both Fenton and Hemingway were driven by what Otto Fenichel called "the counter-phobic attitude: cases in which a fear of entering a fight is overcompensated by a counter-phobic tendency to struggle and to compete with everyone on every occasion." Such an attitude was characteristic among those who engaged in dangerous sports (273–74). The fighter tried to defeat his phobia by going back into the ring, the torero once again faced the murderous bull. In an extreme case, the skydiver William H. (Bill) Ottley, Yale class of 1950, stepped out into space more than 4,000 times to parachute to earth. Ottley broke twenty bones on these jumps, and half a dozen more while skiing, flying planes, gliders, and balloons, and riding motorcycles, but survived to tell his classmates about it and to chide them for leading colorless lives ("Skydiving Legend" 19). The suicidologist Edwin Shneidman regarded such blatantly reckless behavior as a form of "indirect suicide," or "subintentional death" (62–63).

Severely wounded in World War I, Hemingway attempted to overcome his trauma by repeatedly placing himself at risk in frightening situations. In the process he suffered an astounding number of injuries to his arms and legs and head. He also managed to impress General Buck Lanham, during the worst of the World War II fighting in the Hürtgenwald, as the bravest man he'd ever known. Greening detected a similar quest for counter-phobic mastery in Charlie Fenton's lifelong pattern of taking chances: breaking all the rules in boyhood, flying life-threatening missions as a bomber boy with the RAF, and defying any and all authority.

Tom Greening, like others among Fenton's students, has continued to be haunted by the ghost of Charlie Fenton over the years and to wonder what led to his tragic end. There may have been a clue in his recollection of a brief encounter at Yale one winter night. Greening was walking across campus between the Sterling Memorial Library and Berkeley College when he saw a man approaching, overcoat collar turned up against the cold but without a hat or scarf, and realized it was Fenton—not the Fenton of usual jaunty presence but somehow looking vulnerable, shorter than his six feet one, less than himself. Out of diffidence Greening did not approach him.

I came to Yale from Blake School, a good country-day school in Minneapolis. I was only 17 upon matriculating there, without any specific plans for the future, and ended up majoring in English with a particular interest in American literature. It never occurred to me that I could be Charlie Fenton's friend, but I admired him unreservedly. In August 1950 I visited Fenton at his home in Madison, Connecticut. That was to have a tremendous effect on my life.

By that time I was 21, and still without a career plan. I'd made a hash of my last semester at Yale, getting into trouble not only through the double-dipping deception with my senior thesis but through an ill-advised liaison. Out of that moral morass I crept home to Minneapolis, and decided to enroll at the University of Minnesota for the fall term. I vaguely hoped to acquire an M.A. in English along the way, but to do so it was necessary to secure an undergraduate diploma. That brought me to Madison and a talk with Charlie Fenton about revising my thesis on Hemingway's short stories.

I drove up from New Haven on a magical summer day, the waters of Long Island Sound sparkling in the sunlight. Charlie took me into his study, cluttered with books and papers. He recommended a couple of sources for me to consult for my revision, but aside from that I do not remember precisely what he said. It was teaching by example. He showed me a paper he'd done for one of the Yale graduate school seminars, remarkable for its clarity and the depth of research that had gone into it, and went back to his own work. Young children scampered by: Wendy and Richie. Gwendy popped in, wondering what Charlie wanted for dinner. She looked older than her husband, I thought, but I envied him for the way she wanted to take care of him. It looked almost ideal, and a thought began to form. *Maybe I can do this*, or even more boldly, *I can do this too.*

I left that day with this idea somewhere in the back of my consciousness. I was no Charlie Fenton, but he was doing the kind of work I might be capable of and living the kind of life I might enjoy. Like Fenton, I was to become first a newspaperman and then a professor of American literature who wrote books and biographies about major twentieth century American authors. I do not think that would have come to pass but for that day in Madison. Roads have many turnings, but some stopping places are more important than others.

Fenton's own writing shifted from fiction to literary criticism and biography as he endeavored to make a place for himself in the academic community. In May 1951, still two years short of his doctorate, he published an article on Herman Melville's "The Bell-Tower" and technology in *American Literature*, the foremost journal in the field. The article closely examined one of Melville's least-studied stories, placing it in the context of the technological revolution that Americans of the mid-nineteenth century both celebrated and feared, and hence following the American Studies approach to literary study that Fenton had been absorbing under the tutelage of Norman Holmes Pearson. Down the road, he was planning to teach others similar lessons. First, though, he had to get his drinking and his married life under control.

He and Gwendy were living in one of only two year-around houses on Gull Rock road in Madison, a quarter of a mile from Long Island Sound and handy to the Madison Beach club. "Summer people" arrived with the warm weather, bringing with them—according to Lewis Jones, whose family belonged among the seasonal visitors—enough adultery to qualify the place as "one big soap opera." The Fentons had no reputation along those lines, but

Charlie and Gwendy, young marrieds. Fenton Family Photo

neither were they getting along wonderfully during Charlie's graduate school (and first teaching assignment) years. He made it a habit to bring outstanding students home for supper, and on their visits both Matthiessen and Stevenson noted ill feeling between husband and wife. "I was very fond of him, and knew he was an unhappy guy," Matthiessen said, a conclusion arrived at after dining with the Fentons. "Their relationship wasn't so great," he observed. To Stevenson, the Fentons' quarreling came as something of a shock. "I was used to seeing husbands and wives being polite to each other," he recalled. "They were not like that at all."

Alcohol had much to do with the periodic unpleasantness at the house on Gull Rock Road, and the students Charlie brought home were willing cocktail companions. Gwendy was not quiet in her disapproval of his drinking, and she had good reason to object. At his worst, her husband would disappear on a three-day binge, and call home from a bar in the companionship of a complaisant fellow-imbibing female. After one New Year's Eve party, the Fentons got into a nasty fight, and in anger Gwendy took off her shoe and clobbered him in the eye. All was calm by the time daughter Wendy came home from an overnight stay with a girl friend. The only sign of trouble was Fenton's black eye.

Charlie's drinking was associated with the occasional black spells that beset him, and when they came along the verbal disputes between husband and wife threatened to become physical. Wendy remembers lying in bed and hearing her parents in a terrible quarrel. She started screaming to stop them, and Charlie took her back to bed and quieted her down. "You don't have to worry," he told her. "Grownups fight sometimes. Everything will be all right." Wendy relied on his reassurance, for he was the only father that she and Richie had growing up. She'd been only four years old, and her brother Richie two and a half, when Gwendy and Charlie married, and for the succeeding fifteen years the children had no contact whatever with their biological father. They thought of Charlie as their father, and—as Richie recollected—"a supportive and sympathetic parent," often humorous, who "always had time for our trivial pubescent and adolescent tribulations."

Then, suddenly, the drinking stopped.

In part, it was Fenton's ambition that caused him to give up the bottle. Even more influential, though, was the arrival of Charles Andrews (Andy) Fenton, Jr. in August 1951. In *Fish Flying Through Air* Roddy Ham connected George McGough's eventual and startling sobriety to the birth of his baby boy (273–75). And in life as in that novel, the Fentons did almost no drinking after Andy was born. Her mother simply "didn't like the taste," daughter Wendy recalls, but it was Charlie "who didn't allow any drinking in the house." He reformed his ways, and immersed himself in work.

He worked so hard, in fact, that he and Gwendy had very little social life. Once in a great while, as Wendy recalls, they played poker with Aunt Alice and Uncle Teddy (Gwendy's brother). There was one memorable day trip with the youngsters to visit FDR's home at Hyde Park, but for the most part they simply didn't go out. When he wasn't on campus, Charlie stayed in his workroom. He had a checkered past to make up for. His younger brother David spent a great deal of time in the Fentons' home during his adolescence, almost all of it with Gwendy. His brother was his hero, but he "was on the typewriter," and it was Gwendy—10 years older—who became David's friend, his confidante, his big sister. They went to the movies together, and David confided in her about his first crushes on girls. He thought of her as "cute, fun, just terrific," and saw nothing of the tension between husband and wife.

The subject of the book that would earn Charlie his doctorate and establish his reputation was Ernest Hemingway, and how he developed into a great writer. Here, too, as with abandoning the bottle, there was a connection to his son's birth. Andy was born on 19 August 1951. The next day, Fenton wrote Hemingway about the project he had in mind.

Chapter 4

Hemingway vs. Fenton

In choosing Ernest Hemingway as the subject of his dissertation and in deciding to focus on his apprenticeship as a writer, Charlie Fenton was venturing into risky academic territory. At Yale as at most American universities, living American writers were rarely admitted into the curriculum, and very few articles and dissertations about their work were being produced. Hemingway was too contemporary to find acceptance in basically conservative English departments, and even worse, he was beginning to become defined more as a celebrity than an author—a development Hemingway himself was acutely aware of.

By the midpoint of the twentieth century, Ernest Hemingway was well on his way to becoming the most famous writer alive. To a considerable degree, he had been complicit in establishing the public persona that generated his fame: that of the manly hard-drinking hard-living warrior and outdoorsman who somehow managed to turn out books when not otherwise occupied. Generally he did not shy away from publicity. Gossip columnists Leonard Lyons and Earl Wilson of the *New York Post* both visited the Hemingways at his Finca Vigia in Cuba, for example. But brief items such as "Lunch at Papa Hemingway's" in the Lyons Den column seemed innocuous enough. Far more troubling to Hemingway were three long, up-close-and-personal articles about him in the popular press, and one forthcoming book about him, all appearing in the early 1950s. These publications, he felt, compromised his privacy and threatened to handicap his future writing.

By late August 1951, when he first heard from Fenton, Hemingway was on his guard against any and all intrusions on his private life. He had been made to look foolish and egotistical in magazine articles by Malcolm Cowley, Lillian Ross, and Sam Boal. He was upset by the hostile reviews of *Across*

the River and Into the Trees, furious about Arthur Mizener's biographical
dismemberment of F. Scott Fitzgerald, and so disturbed by Philip Young's
book-in-progress on him, with its psychological interpretation that much of
his work derived from his World War I wounding in Italy, that he was about
to deny Young the right to use any quotations. Charlie Fenton could hardly
have chosen a worse time to broach the subject of his dissertation with Hemingway. The remarkable thing is that in spite of these reservations the great
men gave him an unusual amount of encouragement through the mails, at
least at the beginning. Later, as the project appeared to veer away from Fenton's declared line of approach—a study of how Hemingway shaped himself
from a journalist into a writer—his anger boiled over.

The story emerges in interesting and at times combative correspondence
between the ambitious young instructor at Yale and the world-famous author
in Cuba. The 20 August 1951 letter from Fenton said that he had hoped to
complete his study without troubling Hemingway, but questions kept spring-
ing up. Before posing those questions, though, Fenton assured Hemingway
that his sole interest was in his literary apprenticeship. What he wanted to do
was to establish how Hemingway became Hemingway: how a boy raised in
the Middle West converted himself into a writer of great accomplishment.
Perhaps others might learn from Hemingway's example, Fenton suggested. In
any case, he declared unequivocally, "I couldn't care less about your private
life, and I have no interest whatsoever in writing your biography."

This was welcome news to Hemingway, and he responded to Fenton's two
questions accordingly. Did his experience as a cub reporter with the *Kansas
City Star* (1917–1918) account for the progress in Hemingway's writing from
the stories he'd written at Oak Park high school (1916–1917) to the fluent
features for the *Toronto Star* newspapers (1920–1923)? "I never considered
journalism as of any permanent value or in any way connected with serious
writing," Hemingway replied on 31 August. "It was a way to earn a living
while I learned to write, and later, to make a living while I wrote." "I hope
this doesn't bore you," Hemingway added. "It bores the shit out of me," by
that remark establishing the cussword raillery that was to punctuate their correspondence (Sotheby).

Fenton's second question had to do with the "John Hadley" pseudonym
Hemingway used in some of his articles from Europe during the early 1920s,
and here he broached a delicate issue. Hemingway signed stories he wrote for
the International News Service (INS) with the John Hadley name, in order to
conceal the fact that he was drawing salary and expenses from that organization as well as from the *Toronto Daily Star,* which employed him as their man
in Europe. There was "some confusion over that period, but I believe that
is covered by the statute of limitations," Hemingway acknowledged. In any
case, he did not consider anything he'd written for the *Star* or INS or Univer-

sal, another Hearst news service he represented at the Lausanne conference, to be part of his permanent work. The first writing he endorsed as his "true work" came with *Three Stories and Ten Poems* in 1923 and the lower-case *in our time* in 1924 (Sotheby).

Hemingway's assertions tended to undermine Fenton's thesis that newspaper reporting played an important role in his development as a writer of fiction. Still, the young Yale instructor must have been pleased to receive so frank and forthcoming a letter from a famous author. In his next communication, Fenton adopted the tough-talking tone Hemingway had invited. "While I have you perhaps on the ropes I'll move in quickly with some more odious questioning," Fenton began his letter of 9 September—the same day that Hemingway wrote forbidding Philip Young permission to quote from his work. Fenton asked for Hemingway's comments on the stories he'd written in high school for the Oak Park *Tabula*. But if he didn't feel like answering, Fenton added, he would understand, for he'd spent a lot of time himself telling undergraduates and colleagues "to go fuck themselves" when they intruded on his private turf.

He'd been reading through Ernest's magazine pieces of the 1930s (material beyond the scope of his study), Fenton said, and recommended that they be collected in a volume. Then he went on to commiserate with Hemingway about the critics' unfavorable reviews of *Across the River and Into the Trees* (1950). The only intelligent evaluations had come from real "pros" like Malcolm Cowley and Granville Hicks. The others were written by "tiresome little fags or embittered scholars." Fenton was not like that at all, he wanted Hemingway to understand. When confronted with the slobs of the literary and academic worlds, he sometimes thought nostalgically "of all the illiterate bastards" he'd soldiered with.

Hemingway replied to this letter on 13 September, objecting to the emphasis on his *Tabula* yarns. "What are you planning to do, boy? Publish all the crap I wrote as a kid trying to learn to write?" That would be like publishing the contents of his wastebasket. It reminded him of Arthur Mizener, whom he excoriated for reproducing laundry lists and "looking for the stigmata of wet dreams on old pyjamas" in his biography of Fitzgerald. Then, as was often the pattern in Hemingway's letters, he followed his belligerent comments by waxing expansive with reminiscences and observations peripheral or totally unrelated to Fenton's queries. In this case, he volunteered information about his boyhood and education. His mother had held him out of school one year to study the cello, an instrument for which he had "absolutely no talent." And in high school he had to try to be an athlete as well as to learn how to write. "At Oak Park if you could play football you had to play it" (Sotheby).

Fenton chose in his September 18 response to tell Hemingway something of his own experience as a tail gunner in the RAF, as an aspiring writer who'd won a substantial prize for an unpublished novel, and as an academic in the process of earning his union card—the doctorate—so that he could continue to "teach, God forbid, creative writing and a course in 20th Century American Prose" at Yale. His interest in Hemingway's writing was strictly "a professional one." What he hoped to do was to demonstrate what Hemingway's style and technique were, and how they were developed. Therefore he had to consider the *Tabula* stories "in a quick, tentative way." He wouldn't reproduce the material, only cite portions of it to document his thesis that "journalism was a lot more important than the critics ha[d] recognized, as a training not only in technique, but in the treatment of material, and, indeed, in the very choice of material." The critical resistance to "themes of violence" in Hemingway's work failed to take into account that his journalistic training made his attraction to such material "almost inevitable." Too much had been made of the influence of Pound and Stein instead, he thought. In closing, Fenton asked if Hemingway would be willing to read his finished manuscript and suggest alterations. He was not "a potential Mizener," Fenton insisted. His own private life was "too engrossing to give [him] time to take on someone else's."

Responding to Fenton's letter on September 23, Hemingway expounded upon his years in Paris with Pound and Stein. Ezra had seen only half a dozen things he wrote, Hemingway said. Gertrude read his early stories and wisely advised him to get out of journalism. Later she became angry at him because Alice [Toklas] was jealous of their being friends and also because Stein felt guilty about learning to write dialogue from him and wanted to exorcise the guilt "by an attack." While on the subject of other writers, Hemingway launched an attack on William Faulkner's recent fiction. "Would like to have a job writing sentences like that in pure shit from contented assholes in Octonawhoopoo County instead of trying to write straight." Since Fenton planned to discuss his style, Hemingway offered a definition of his own. Style, he said, consisted of "the awkwardness and visible mistakes you have been unable to eliminate while making a new thing in prose" (Sotheby).

With Fenton wrapped up in teaching, it was 5 January 1952 before he got back in touch with Hemingway about his apprenticeship project. With customary self-disparagement, he apologized for resuming "the inquisition by the dreary pedant," but could Hemingway tell him "what the hell was the Co-operative Society of America" he'd worked for in Chicago in 1920. How did he get the job? How long was he there? What did he learn writing for and editing the *Co-operative Commonwealth*? Where could Fenton get hold of any issues? He promised not to publish anything he found as "by Ernest Hemingway."

Five days later he sent Hemingway a copy of Herbert Cranston's article, "When Hemingway Earned Half a Cent a Word on 'The Toronto Star'" from the Sunday, 13 January edition of the *New York Herald-Tribune Book Review*. Cranston had been editing the *Toronto Star Weekly* when Hemingway started writing free-lance articles for the paper in 1920. His piece on the young Hemingway was vivid, interesting, and full of factual errors. Hemingway would do better, Fenton assured him, by leaving the Toronto material and all other data on his literary apprenticeship "in the hands of a trustworthy scholar and reformed slob" like himself.

In a brief letter on 12 January, Hemingway provided some background on the *Co-operative Commonwealth*. He got his job as managing editor by answering a want-ad in the *Chicago Tribune*, stayed until it became clear that the organization was "crooked," thought about writing an exposé, "and then decided to just rack it up to experience and the hell with it." As for Cranston, he figured "old Cranny" was entitled to his inaccuracies, inasmuch as he'd been badly treated by the *Toronto Daily Star*, which was about as far as a man could go in being badly treated. Maybe Cranston was poaching on Fenton's preserve, but he shouldn't let it bother him: "think of poor old Cowley who has staked out my whole life of which he knows practically fuck-all nothing." Meanwhile, Hemingway offered, "[i]f you want the true gen on anything else let me know" (*Selected* 719–20).

Emboldened by that offer, Fenton weighed in on 18 January with no fewer than 15 specific questions about Hemingway's experience at the *Kansas City Star*, based on the extensive research he'd been doing on the newspaper. As usual, he accompanied these with apologies. "If you don't balk at this inquisition you're bloody saintlike in your generosity," Fenton said, preceding the three pages of queries; afterwards, he added that he was "appalled at [his] own effrontery" and felt "like a lush baiting some amiable stranger" in a bar. Apologias aside, this time he'd gone too far.

Hemingway, put off by the extent of Fenton's questions, pointed out that answering them would get in the way of his work. He was supposed to be a professional writer. If he didn't write, he didn't get paid. Instead he got this questionnaire from Fenton. "The hell with it for these reasons: I was always going to write about Kansas City myself . . . and if I write all about it to you it is finished and I lose it." He had only so much juice for each day's writing, and he couldn't afford to expend his juice for nothing.

Yet after making this complaint, Hemingway went on to produce a detailed 2,300-word letter about his seven months as a beginning reporter on the *Kansas City Star*. He'd wanted to work there because he thought it was "the best paper in the U.S." He had plenty of stories to tell about it, but would rather write them himself. Actually he already had written a few of those stories that were lost when Hadley had his valise stolen in the Gare de Lyon in Paris. Kansas City was "a tough town from the Union Station to the river,"

Hemingway recalled. He'd encountered some unsavory characters there; one of his closest friends was the municipal doctor who followed the merciful if illegal practice of giving shots to dope addicts. "Oh shoot me just once in the gut, Doc," they'd say. "For pity, Doc" (Bruccoli 296).

Three days later Hemingway supplied more information about the *Kansas City Star*. Reporters were not allowed to read the opposition *Kansas City Post*, nor to fraternize with its employees. Yet if they were beaten on a story by the *Post*, they heard about it immediately from the city desk. Everyone in the news room was expected to read every line of each edition of the *Star*, and was held individually responsible for any errors that went uncorrected. What he learned at the *Star* was discipline, Hemingway said. Later, when he turned to serious fiction, he "had some idea of what discipline should be when self applied" and had become a "one man disciplined outfit."

In another paragraph Hemingway reverted to the issue of what other writers had taught him. In the case of Sherwood Anderson, he'd learned some things from *Winesburg, Ohio* but Anderson's most important lesson came by way of a negative example: Sherwood showed him how not "to be as a man or a writer." He'd been upset when he wrote about wasting his juice in his previous letter, Hemingway admitted, and he still had trouble understanding why Fenton should be doing "all this work" unless the end was really useful. On the other hand, since Fenton sounded like a serious character and they knew certain things in common, he trusted and respected him.

Fenton was heartened by this declaration. That was "a fine letter," he wrote Hemingway on 23 January and went on with an apology in advance about what he was up to in his research—reaching out to other sources. "You're likely to hear from people you've forgotten you knew that a punk in a brooks bros. suit has been poking around asking damn fool questions about style and rhetoric, but don't worry about it," Fenton advised. Hemingway would see anything Fenton wrote about him well in advance of publication, and could tell him then what to do with it, and in the meantime he'd lay off any areas Hemingway designated as out of bounds. He was about to put some questions to Margaret Dixon, one of the teachers who encouraged Hemingway in high school—"questions about how and what she taught, not whether he was unhappy or adjusted or queer for other boys "—but only if that was all right with Hemingway.

Less than two weeks later, Fenton sent Hemingway an offprint of his article on the ambulance service in World War I, a subject he'd decided to explore when he started work on Hemingway's literary apprenticeship. He ended this letter with a crucial mistake. "Incidentally (well not really incidentally)," he inquired, "would you care to give me a very brief note to Mr. Eugene

Youngert, Superintendent of the Oak Park and River Forest High School, authorizing him to send me a transcript of your marks at Oak Park?"

That got Hemingway's back up, and prompted him to begin venting his wrath in letters—either nine or ten, in total—that he wrote and saved, but did not send to Fenton. In the first such letter, written on 21 February 1952, he began cheerfully enough by commenting on Fenton's article on the ambulance service, but turned sarcastic about the high school grades request. Why did Fenton need a letter from him to get the grades? Didn't "they give them out without permission of the accused?" Fenton might write a note for him to sign and send to the principal, Hemingway supposed, but he could not understand what he needed the grades for. Obviously regarding this request as an invasion of privacy, Hemingway launched into an extended diatribe against Arthur Mizener, the "licensed carrion crow of the Ivy League," and "a character named Philip Young" afflicted by conceit and lack of knowledge who'd written a book about how everything in Hemingway stemmed from a traumatic neurosis. He was beginning to suspect that Fenton belonged in the same company. "Probably I am a damned fool to trust you because you were in the RAF and write a plausible letter," Hemingway commented. Mizener had written plausible letters, too, and look what he'd done to Fitzgerald.

On 5 April 1952, in a brief (and also unsent) note, Hemingway returned to the issue of his high school record. He was "touched by [the school's] solidarity in not sending grades without the permission of the graded or de-graded," he said. What had Fenton done about it? Did he get the grades? "Did the principal break down or did [he] have to filch them or was the matter just left in abeyance?" And if he did get the grades, what did he plan to do with them?

Inasmuch as these communications did not reach him, Fenton must have worried about the four months' silence from his famous correspondent. On June 7, however, he breezily brought Hemingway up to date on his progress. He'd just about wrapped up the *Kansas City Star* chapter, with the aid of no fewer than sixteen sources. Toronto would be harder, but he was going up there soon to do further research. Material was accumulating about Oak Park. Bill Smith and Carl Edgar were giving him the straight dope on Horton Bay. A couple of good publishers were interested, including the Yale University Press. In case Hemingway didn't know about them, Fenton told him about the forthcoming books from Young, due out in the summer, and Baker, in the fall. He'd heard from Dave Randall at Scribner's that Hemingway's "new long story" (*The Old Man and the Sea*) was really good: high praise coming from Randall, who was not usually enthusiastic about his work. In closing, Fenton asked Hemingway about the legendary newsman Lionel Moise he'd known in Kansas City. Had Moise helped to shape his writing?

This letter only served to confirm Hemingway's suspicion, born of the query about his Oak Park grades, that Fenton had "shifted from a study of how a man writes to biography." He was concerned about all the trailing around Fenton was doing, asking questions like a F.B.I. investigator of Ernest's friends and enemies, forgotten neighbors and various shits. Such "detective story biographies" threatened to invade his privacy and harm his ability to work. "So," he declared on February 12, "I warn you as of now to cease and desist." Mizener and Young were still much on his mind. Mizener's hatchet job on Fitzgerald made it clear that there was money to be made by literary biographers, Hemingway observed, and he'd made the mistake of taking Young's word that his book was "neither biographical nor psychoanalytical."

Two days later Fenton replied with some heat. Sure there was money in books like Mizener's, but he had no intention of writing an intimate exposé. Besides, Mizener was "a horse's ass" and "a rube, intellectually, socially," as Fenton had discovered fourteen years earlier when taking a class from him at Yale. Oak Park matrons and real estate executives kept offering him material about Hemingway's home life, and Ernest's brother Leicester, asked about newspaper work, presented "an impassioned denunciation" of one of their sisters. "The hell with it," Fenton said. "I don't use that." He'd been urged to extend his project to Hemingway's "marriages, his blunders, etc." But all he was interested in was Hemingway's development as a writer, Fenton insisted. Some one was bound to produce a book on his apprenticeship sooner or later, and Hemingway was "a lot better off having it done by a guy who's a writer, who admires your work immensely, who's in the Ivy League and not the sticks . . . and who doesn't get giddy every time he thinks of the literary life." Early the following week, Fenton said, he would send Hemingway the Kansas City chapter so that he could see for himself what he was up to. This he failed to do, another mistake that led to trouble.

A curious misunderstanding influenced Hemingway's reaction to this letter. In making his case, Fenton asserted that Hemingway should not "get the wind up" where he was concerned. What he meant was that Hemingway should not get angry or disturbed. Hemingway, however, took the idiom to mean that Fenton thought he was becoming "windy" in the British sense: that is, paralyzed by fear. He did not like being called "windy," Hemingway replied on 18 June 1952, and he was bothered by Fenton's research into his Oak Park origins. He'd had "a wonderful novel" to write about Oak Park, Hemingway said, but decided against it because he did not want to hurt living people and thought it wrong for a man to "make money out of his father shooting himself [and] out of his mother who drove him to it." So when Fenton started digging into his family—in fact, Fenton told him he was *not* doing that—Hemingway gave him "the cease and desist."

He moderated that command, however, by agreeing that it was better to have "a straight guy" writing about his work than a crook. He thought of Fenton as a straight guy, but no one liked to be tailed by an "amateur detective no matter how scholarly or straight." He may have made "blunders" in his life, but by the time Fenton was 52 maybe he'd have made some himself. Meanwhile, Fenton should leave his "private life the hell alone." Much of the letter had to do with this directive, yet Hemingway also contributed a fine paragraph on his newspaper days that Fenton could and did make use of. He couldn't remember much about Lionel Moise, Hemingway said, because in newspaper work "you have to learn to forget every day what happened the day before." Reporting was valuable up to the point when it began to forcibly destroy the memory, and a writer had to get out before that happened. It was like experience in war. Going to war was invaluable to a writer, but too much experience could be destructive. Fenton should be able to understand that. If he hadn't served as well and as long as he did in World War II, he'd "probably be writing [himself] instead of teaching writing and riding herd on [Hemingway's] childhood" (*Selected* 764–65).

That last remark struck a nerve. Charlie Fenton had been representing himself to Hemingway as a fellow writer who'd been to war and knew his way around. He apologized for intruding on Hemingway's time and taxing his patience, but he did so in the spirit of a colleague, as one writer to another. So when Hemingway made his apparently innocuous observation about how too much wartime experience might have driven Fenton away from his typewriter and into the classroom, Charlie felt offended and responded angrily. "[D]o not think," he declared, "that by needling me about being a scholar and having once been a writer that you can get at me or shame me." He liked to pay his own way, Fenton said, and after the war he hadn't been able to make a living as a writer. So he'd gone back to Yale, where he was happy with his present setup. Yes, he taught writing courses, and did it as well as it could be done, and liked doing it, because it was easy for him and gave him time for his own work—that is, his writing. He liked to think of himself—then as always—as a writer doing time in the academy. One day, he would be liberated. Right now, he had this dissertation/book to finish.

In this same letter of 9 July 1952, Fenton promised Hemingway that there would be "no invasion of privacy" in the Oak Park chapter. In Toronto, he reported, he'd interviewed novelist Morley Callaghan, a fine, savvy guy who remembered Hemingway with affection and admiration. "You may remember that I offered to send you the Kansas City chapter," Fenton added. Since Hemingway said nothing about it, he hadn't done so. Now, he reported, he'd sold a condensed version of it to *New World Writing*. They paid two-and-a-half cents a word, and Hemingway could read it there in September. In closing Fenton confessed that he'd managed to get hold of galleys of *The Old Man and the Sea*. It was "a bloody fine story," he said, and the critics would have to do some fancy footwork to reverse the negative positions they'd taken after *Across the River and Into the Trees*.

This letter produced three extremely irascible responses, all dated 13 July 1952. In an unsent five-page letter, Hemingway took up the matter of the Kansas City chapter. "You said to write you if anything needs clarifying. This needs clarifying. You wrote me you were sending me your chapter on the K.C. Star. You didn't offer to send it. You wrote you were sending it. Now you write that you have sold a condensed version of it to a magazine which will be out around September and I can see it there. Clarify me that if you don't mind."

Next Hemingway dealt with Fenton's apparent over-sensitivity. He had not "needled" him about being a scholar who was once a writer, nor tried to shame him, nor belittled the teaching of writing. Was Fenton blowing his top in order to escape his obligation to Hemingway for helping him in his research? Or was he simply resentful about washing out as a writer? "There [is] no bitterness like that of a failed writer," Hemingway observed, "except perhaps that of a de-odorized skunk" Why didn't Fenton control his temper, write a straight letter, quit hinting what he could do if he were not a certified Ivy league gent, and keep his promises? Hemingway stipulated a four-step program for Fenton to undertake. (1) Tell *New World Writing* they could not publish his article until Hemingway okayed it. (2) Furnish him with a list of people he'd contacted in Oak Park, Chicago, and Washington, D.C., along with copies of the correspondence that his attorneys could examine for invasion of privacy. And, by the way, explain why he wanted the principal of the Oak Park and River Forest high school to send a transcript of his grades. (3) Supply a similar list for Toronto, and copies of the letters. (4) Cease and desist in his project which had begun as a study in apprenticeship and had reached such proportions that Fenton was receiving offers to write about Hemingway's wives.

The second and third letters of 13 July were, I believe, mailed to Fenton, although Matthew J. Bruccoli in his informative article on the Hemingway-Fenton correspondence maintained that Number Two was not sent. In that one-page communication, Hemingway enclosed a check for $200 and invited Fenton to use the money to come to Cuba for a physical confrontation (Gwendy and Andy Fenton both remembered hearing about this letter). A visit to the Finca Vigia offered several inducements for the scholar, Hemingway pointed out: first-hand information from the subject of his study, a pleasant climate, free meals and drinks, and lodging in the same quarters where Hemingway's children stayed when they were visiting. If he came to Cuba, Fenton could speak to him face to face as he spoke in his letters, and they

Charles Andrews Fenton, winner of the $4,000 prize in the New Writers contest sponsored by Doubleday, Doran and 20th Century Fox, June 1945. Publishers' Weekly

could go down to the tennis court to settle their differences. His fifty-third birthday was July 21, and he would like nothing better as a birthday present than to fight Fenton in "any enclosed space." He did not really expect him to show up, Hemingway said by way of insult. Fenton might write "a rough letter," but he was a "chicken boy" who wouldn't back up his play.

Hemingway's third and shortest letter asked Fenton to tell *New World Writing* that they could not print the *Kansas City Star* material. Fenton had assured him, after all, that nothing would be published until he'd checked it out for facts. He then inquired about Fenton's mental condition. Was he all right in the head? His sudden rages and general truculence were disquieting signs. Hemingway doubted that authorities at Yale would approve of them or of the tone of some of his letters. And why had Fenton started signing himself by his last name only, in the British fashion? That was very bad form.

Deciding to look on the bright side, Fenton ignored Hemingway's "don't publish" mandate and instead sent him a copy of the condensed version of his Kansas City chapter, as edited by *New World Writing's* heavy hand. He was "truly sorry" about the "confusion" as to whether he'd offered or promised to submit it to him previously, Fenton said, but was pleased to have Hemingway read the chapter, for his reaction was sure to be valuable. In fact and unless he heard otherwise, he would send successive chapters to Hemingway for his comments, as they were finished.

By the time the Kansas City chapter reached Cuba, Hemingway had heard from his sister Ursula Jepson, then married and living in Hawaii, about Fenton's Oak Park inquiries. Fenton wrote her, unaware that she was Ernest's sister, asking about Fannie Biggs and Margaret Dixon as teachers and other questions about Oak Park high school. "Seems he must be trying to write a scholarly work on the Great Stein," Ursula mused. Should she answer his letter or not? Hemingway told her not to bother, but to send him Fenton's letter. This document, which reached him on 4 August, conformed in almost all respects to the emphasis on Hemingway's literary apprenticeship that Fenton promised to follow. He inquired, for instance, whether the adolescent Hemingway demonstrated "a precocious sense of dedication about writing," and about his attitudes toward Oak Park high in general, but made no inquiries about his family life. All of this was couched in an engaging manner. Could Ursula, unless she'd already exploded with exasperation, reply to this question? Could she refer him to others whom he might "molest" with his interrogations? Fenton would be glad to submit anything he wrote for her approval. In short, as Ursula remarked, "Fenton the fox" seemed entirely benign. "The insidious thing," she supposed, might be "the trail of people he pick[ed] up," including those who wanted to get a little of their longstanding jealousy of Ernest Hemingway out of their system (JFK).

On 29 July 1952, Hemingway wrote Fenton a long letter spelling out a few of the inaccuracies in the Kansas City chapter. In particular, he protested that Fenton had "fallen hook, line and sinker" for the story that Lionel Moise had exerted a substantial influence on his writing. Moise was a memorable figure, but hardly a close friend, Hemingway said. He'd known Moise only slightly. He was impressed by his facility, his undisciplined talent, and his "enormous vitality which, when he was drinking" (and Hemingway had never seen him when he was not drinking), "overflowed into violence." He'd always felt that "Lionel Moise's morals were his own business," Hemingway added, "and that he was a very picturesque, dynamic, big-hearted, hard-drinking and hard-fighting man and I have always regretted that his talent was not canalized into good writing." But Moise had not taught him how to write and certainly not how to live.

Fenton had made the mistake of trusting unreliable sources, Hemingway believed, and as a result he had to ruin an entire working day trying to straighten him out. In the future, he anticipated an "endless task" trying to keep his inquisitor "out of serious trouble" as he wrote about the Toronto and Paris years. Cooperating with Fenton involved nearly as much effort as writing his own autobiography, and that was something he'd always intended to do. Moreover, he was wasting time and money on Fenton's project. He averaged between fifty cents and a dollar a word for his work, Hemingway pointed out. He sent Fenton letters ranging in length between 500 and 1,500 words that Fenton then incorporated in material he sold for two-and-a-half cents a word. "Mr. Fenton," Hemingway commented, "I hope you will agree that this is economically unsound." Any man's autobiography was his own property, and he should certainly not feed it piecemeal into letters for another man to use. Under the circumstances, he thought Fenton "ought to drop the entire project." Or "organize it in such a way" that both of them might profit adequately from the material.

At this stage, three-fourths of the way through his letter, Hemingway suddenly reversed course. You rarely knew, reading a letter from Hemingway, what was going to come next. Go ahead and publish the Kansas City article as it stood, he surprisingly instructed Fenton. To hell with trying to correct it. Moise would be pleased, and he must be an old man by now. Besides, reading the manuscript had refreshed Hemingway's memory, so he could write a good story about Kansas City now. Fenton also had his permission to use quotations from his letters. Still, there remained two basic misconceptions in his reliance on the testimony of others. Most people did not remember things accurately, and everything had changed in America. You needed local knowledge, needed "to have seen the hill before the bulldozer hit it."

Hemingway was thinking of Oak Park, and how time had changed the place over the years. In one of his caustic unmailed communications to Fenton, he described the deterioration of his boyhood home from a town on the edge of the prairie to one full of subdivisions and apartment buildings. He recalled the high school group called the Inner Circle, "morally certified youths" who served as informers to the principal. He mentioned Edward Wagenknecht, the star student of the class everybody liked and respected but no one really knew. He called up these reminiscences, Hemingway said, to illustrate that anyone coming along 35 years later, like Fenton, would not be able to "get the true gen" [intelligence]. What he'd get instead was "survivor's gen"— badly remembered incidents and slanted anecdotes—and there was nothing scholarly about that (*Selected* 774–78).

Fenton dispatched two separate letters on July 31, thanking Hemingway for his "patience" and his "illumination." He'd been skeptical about Moise himself, Fenton said, but four different sources cited him as a particular companion of Hemingway's on the *Star*. Now, however, he'd revised the script to reduce Moise's role. He'd been hard at work, and the 50,000-word Toronto chapter was nearly complete. That represented "a hell of a thing to unload on you," he told Hemingway, but he'd send it along in a few weeks unless he heard to the contrary.

On 2 August 1952, Hemingway wrote a lengthy, interesting, and again unmailed letter full of anecdotal reminiscences about Kansas City, where he'd been assigned to escort labor reporter Bill Scurry to the Turkish baths to sober him up; about Toronto, where Harry Hindmarsh, son-in-law of the *Toronto Daily Star*'s owner, made his life miserable, and about Paris, where Fitzgerald as timekeeper let the round go on too long while Hemingway tired and Morley Callaghan kept landing jabs.

Then Hemingway shifted to the issue of Fenton's project. If he planned to reprint anything Hemingway had written for the *Toronto Daily Star* and the *Toronto Star Weekly*, they'd have to reach an accommodation. After all, this was work he himself had decided not to republish. He did not like what Fenton was doing. He was convinced of Fenton's scholarly approach and of his "desire to be accurate, truthful and fair" but not at all convinced that his "method of interrogation and cross interrogation" arrived at an approximation "of the true facts. Too many professional survivors."

Hemingway went on to advance in detail the amazing idea that the two of them should collaborate. "[T]his is what I propose . . . You write the apprenticeship book. I will provide letters, as I have done so far giving you the actual true gen as I remember it." The resulting book would be published commercially, with profits to be shared fifty-fifty between them. It should make them both pots of money, and in that way, when Hemingway wrote letters for Fenton to quote he could consider it a legitimate part of his working day. There might even be sequels concerning 1925–1935 or 1935–1945. As a side benefit, Fenton could help him deal with the Ph.D. candidates who were beginning to harass him. One professor, Hemingway figured, ought to "know how to tell another professor to fuck off; that he is working this side of the street." Think it over, he advised Fenton. Was it sound for them to cooperate or should Hemingway start throwing in the road blocks?

Word of this intriguing proposal did not reach Fenton, who fulfilled his promise by dispatching the Toronto chapter to Hemingway in Cuba. At this time, Hemingway was enjoying the tremendous popular and critical success of *The Old Man and the Sea*, printed in its entirety in a single issue of *Life* magazine. The success of the book produced a flood of correspondence, delaying his letter to Fenton about the Toronto chapter until 9 October 1952.

In the first pages of the chapter, Hemingway said, he found so many errors of fact that he could spend the rest of the year giving Fenton the true gen and have no time left to write anything of his own. One such mistake had young Hemingway tutoring the two Connable children. Well, he had served as a companion to Ralph Connable, but Ralph's sister Dorothy had graduated from Wellesley and served in the Red Cross during the war, so that Fenton would look silly saying the 21-year-old Hemingway had tutored her. He was also upset about Fenton "collect[ing]" the articles he'd written for the Toronto newspapers. Morally, and perhaps legally, he had no right to publish such pieces. "I would no more do a thing like that to you than I would cheat a man at cards or rifle his desk or wastebasket or read his personal letters," Hemingway said. Fenton should "make an examination of conscience" before continuing the work he'd "been warned to cease and desist on and which [would] lead him if not to jail at least into plenty of trouble" (*Selected* 786–87). This kind of antagonism may well have been inspired in part by the publication of Philip Young's *Ernest Hemingway*, whose psychological argument infuriated Hemingway. Also that fall, Hemingway was mildly disappointed by Carlos Baker's *Hemingway: The Writer as Artist*, which, he thought, discovered far too much unintended symbolism in his fiction, and by John Atkins's "excessively confused" *The Art of Ernest Hemingway: His Work and Personality* (*Selected* 867, Baker *Life* 599).

Back at Yale, where he was trying to finish his dissertation-book, Fenton was alarmed by the implied threats in Hemingway's 9 October letter. He must have decided, in consultation with Norman Holmes Pearson, that keeping silent would be the safest policy, for the next Fenton-to-Hemingway letter that has surfaced—others have been lost or remain in private hands—was dated more than a year later, in November 1953.

During the long interim, Fenton continued his research and writing. He followed up on Hemingway's comments about the Connable family, for example, by writing directly to Dorothy Connable for information. Before answering, she asked Ernest how she should proceed. On 17 February 1953 Hemingway answered "[g]ood, fine, lovely, beautiful Dorothy." "The man Fenton is one of those who think that literary history, or the secret of creative writing, lies in old laundry lists," he said. He was as bad as Mizener, and he advised Connable not to cooperate with him in any way. It was a miserable thing to have people writing about his private life. "The only way to stop these buzzards is to tell them *absolutely nothing*." Hemingway thought he could prevent Fenton from publishing anything about him after the Kansas City piece in *New World Writing*, he concluded, but it might take a little doing (*Selected* 805–06).

The following day, 18 February 1953, Hemingway sent Fenton a registered letter, with a copy to Wallace Meyer at Scribner's, denying him the right to quote from any of his work, just as he had with Philip Young. He also claimed that he himself had in preparation a book on his apprenticeship as a young writer. It was his property, and he warned Fenton once again to cease and desist on a project which had "degenerated, or enlarged, into a full scale invasion of privacy." In an effort to be helpful when it seemed that Fenton was conducting a bona fide study of a journalistic apprenticeship, he had interrupted his own work and lost irreplaceable working hours. The only way to recover that loss was to write such a book himself, and to do it right (Baker *Life* 599, Bruccoli 298).

Hemingway also maintained that he had copyrighted his bylined articles for the *Toronto Daily Star*. This was evidently not true, for there is no evidence that he went through the legal maneuvers to gain copyright on material the Toronto papers had already copyrighted. Hemingway did, however, write his attorney Alfred Rice on 26–27 April 1953 about a plan to scare Fenton off. He instructed Rice to send Fenton a letter at his Yale address worded as follows: "My client, Mr. Ernest Hemingway has asked me to write you to ascertain why he has not received an answer to his registered letter to you of February 18th 1953. In the future, since Mr. Hemingway is traveling, will you address all communications to him through me?" This letter was to be registered, and if Rice had no reply within a week, he was to send another registered letter to the Department of English, Yale University, enclosing the previous letter to Fenton and asking them to be sure it was delivered.

In explaining his actions to Rice, Hemingway described Fenton as an unsuccessful writer who hated fiction and constantly confounded it with fact, and as an amateur FBI operative who by naming people in his account prevented Hemingway from writing fiction about them and exposed him to possible libel suits. Fenton had also interfered with his privacy "to an unbelievable extent," Hemingway said, and cited one instance of the sort of thing Fenton was writing. In the Toronto chapter, discussing Hemingway's feature article on shoplifting, Fenton commented that there was "no actual proof that Hemingway was ever at any time a shoplifter, but . . . ." Furthermore, Hemingway had backed away from writing a "wonderful story" about "some very bad and interesting trouble" he'd experienced during boyhood up in Michigan—the time that the game authorities were pursuing him for illegally shooting a heron—because Fenton moved in and started identifying the people who were involved.

He didn't want to go to law, Hemingway told his attorney, but he wanted Fenton "off balance," and he wanted Fenton's publisher "too worried to touch the book." The objective was to drop a good road block on Fenton, ahead of him and behind him, and he understood that blocking this sort of publication boiled down to a question of who bluffed who. The thing now was to send the registered letter requesting an answer, for "[j]ust the sight of a legal letterhead spooks most people" (*Selected* 818–20).

Rice's letter (if it was sent) drew no response from Fenton, who continued to plug away at the dissertation that would earn him his Ph.D. in June. Hemingway had done nothing, after all, to forbid him from completing that work. And for the most part Fenton based his later chapters on a close examination of the articles Hemingway turned out for the Toronto papers, on both sides of the ocean. No longer needing information from other sources, as he had done for the Oak Park and Kansas City chapters, he cut back on the "trailing around" of sources that so aroused Hemingway.

In June, Fenton sent Hemingway a copy of his 630-page dissertation. Hemingway scanned it while crossing to Europe on the French line's *Flandre*, as always finding errors. For one thing, he thought Fenton's spelling was just as bad as his own. The Café Rotonde was spelled Rotunde throughout, and "[t]hat's against scholarship, kid." More important was "the whole question of the reliability of witnesses on something that happened 30 years or more ago." Among the unreliable witnesses Fenton used were Frank Mason of I.N.S., to whom Hemingway had sent a marvelous putdown in cablese during a dispute over his expense accounts at Lausanne: "DEAR FRANK: SUGGEST UPSTICK BOOKS ASSWARDS ERNEST." Mason was obviously "a prejudiced source." So was Donald Wright, a "miserable character" who had once shared quarters with Hemingway in Y. K. Smith's house near Chicago. At the same time, however, Hemingway included some ameliorating comments. He felt "pretty damned friendly" toward anyone who had worked as hard as Fenton had on this project, even if he disliked many aspects of it. He also thought Fenton had done "a wonderful job on the journalism" and was grateful to him for uncovering many things that he'd written and forgotten.

This letter apparently was not sent. When Hemingway did get around to acknowledging receipt of the dissertation on 2 August 1953, he contended that the ground Fenton covered amounted to the "note book, oil resource, and basic material" for three novels he had yet to write. It would be "wicked for anyone to publish it," Hemingway said, "when I have saved it all my life to write it in novels." Unless he died in Africa, where he and wife Mary were about to go on safari, he instructed Fenton not to publish his dissertation (Sotheby).

Over the summer and fall Fenton labored to reduce his "rock-like treatise" from 630 to 300 pages, cutting 70,000 words and correcting a multitude of small errors. Nothing new was added, a lot was removed, and the result, he wrote Hemingway on Thanksgiving Day 1953, was "a good, sound, honest book" that invaded no privacy and left "completely undamaged all the material" Hemingway might want to write about himself. Therefore he presented himself "in the bloody unpleasant role of supplicant" asking permission to use fifteen short quotations from Hemingway's letters to him, five from his correspondence with Sherwood Anderson, three from his letters to Gertrude Stein, and one from a letter to Ernest Walsh. He'd stripped down quotations from Hemingway's dispatches to the *Toronto Daily Star*, Fenton added, and used only minimal quotes from his published work.

Near the end of this letter, Fenton introduced a proposal of his own. Hemingway had told him that it made no sense for him to "help set up something"—Fenton's book—that would bring him no profit. Fenton could see his point, and so he'd stopped asking Hemingway questions. Still, would Hemingway now "like to write a Preface-Introduction-Rebuttal-Note to this book," in which he could say whatever he liked "about it, me, scholarship, the Ivy League, etc.?" In that way Hemingway could "get some return on the inconveniences" Fenton had caused him. Probably it was a lousy idea, Fenton said, and for his own part he would rather have the book stand on its own "without the undoubted immense prop of even—or maybe especially—a denunciation by you."

He didn't have the time or any desire "to dispute facts or questions of taste with [Fenton] in a Preface," Hemingway replied from Africa on 5 December 1953. He trusted Fenton to be straight, and if he was not let him "hang and rattle." On the other hand, it was "perfectly ok for Fenton to use the quotes" he'd requested permission for. On safari the Masai had been coaching him how to throw a spear, and if it would mean anything to Fenton to have a spear Hemingway could bring him one "from [his] fucking never-ending apprenticeship." After a comment on not winning the Nobel Prize—he was probably the only candidate, Hemingway noted, who'd been checked out on how to use the dynamite the Nobels made their money from—he signed off "Best always, your friend Ernest Hemingway." In another brief note dated the same day, Hemingway addressed Fenton as "Dear Charlie" for the first time and complimented him on his "superior" letter of 26 November (Sotheby).

The struggle was over at last, with no restrictions on quotations. Back in New Haven, Fenton could finally exhale. He had never been sure, when he opened a letter from Hemingway, whether it would reveal the author in an abusive and threatening or a friendly mood. Soon thereafter Fenton's world-renowned subject increased his fame by surviving two African plane crashes in two days—crashes that left Hemingway suffering the worst of the many physical injuries that periodically befell him. In March, April, and May the *Atlantic Monthly* published outtakes from *The Apprenticeship of Ernest Hemingway*. In letters of 14 April 1954 and 3 May 1954, Hemingway continued to address Fenton as "Dear Charlie." After describing in some detail the debilitating aftereffects of the plane crashes, Hemingway wished him good luck with his book as one professional to another. "Hope you make some dough out of [it] and that all this shit [the publicity deriving from the plane crash] helps. Dough is the least part. Doing it well is first. Money is last" (Sotheby).

In his 6 May 1954 letter, Fenton commiserated with Hemingway about his injuries. He knew that "nobody ever really walks away from a crash," although the phrase "roll[ed] winningly from the lips." His own kidneys had "packed up" back in 1943, "partly from too much cheap liquor, partly from the flying, partly from being scared too often," and he'd been fined for "destroying the King's mattresses," but that hardly equated with the multiple severe internal wounds Hemingway suffered in the second crash. Fenton thanked Hemingway for wishing his book well (he'd sent him a copy at his Paris address), and sank back exhausted from the effort he'd put into it.

Simply getting the facts right, arriving at an accurate account of when and where Hemingway did this or that, and weighing the reliability of various witnesses, from Hemingway himself to those who knew him and had reacted to his outsized personality in one way or another, had been arduous tasks. If he were ever to undertake "another biography," he wrote Mark Schorer, the subject would have to meet "some harsh requirements: he must have been thoroughly anti-social, and absolutely without either friends or enemies; he must have resided his entire life in a single community, preferably in one dwelling place from birth to death; he shall have been a bachelor and childless; and he shall have kept a scrupulous list of all correspondents and all contributions to magazines, books, anthologies, symposiums, and lecture circuits."

Happily, there were compensations. Most reviews of *The Apprenticeship of Ernest Hemingway* were highly favorable, with the exception of John W. Aldridge's in the 11 July *New York Times Book Review*. By applying "the cold, deadly hand of modern classical scholarship," Aldridge said, Fenton had managed the considerable feat of making "Hemingway seem dull and his career commonplace" (4). That was a rough judgment, and not entirely unjust, for Fenton could surely have written a much livelier book. As Norman Holmes

Pearson later commented, "he knew the color better than any one" but had held back in the light of the "cease and desist" warnings and the registered letter from Hemingway. As opposed to Aldridge's waspish review, however, Carlos Baker in the 29 May *Saturday Review* praised Fenton's "thorough and revealing study of Hemingway's seven-year apprenticeship to the art of writing," beginning with the Oak Park high school's *Trapeze* in 1916 and ending with his resignation from the *Toronto Daily Star* on 31 December 1923. Fenton had done the necessary leg work and literary work to correct "the vague and often contradictory" accounts that proliferated in much of the writing about Hemingway, Baker pointed out. Hardly a page went by which did not "contain some new information, straighten out a tangled chronology, explode an old rumor, or settle a moot point." The book was "also continuously informative and interesting, avoiding the sensational, carefully charting out the moves by which the artist was made" (14). Fenton could hardly have asked for a better evaluation of his accomplishment.

Authors are prone to think that a first book will transform their lives, while for ninety five per cent of them, publishing a book proves to be rather like launching a feather at the rim of the Grand Canyon and waiting for the reverberation. Fenton, however, belonged among the fortunate five per cent. Poor as his timing had been when he began his study—arriving in the wake of articles and books that angered Hemingway and made him suspicious of anyone looking into his past—Fenton's book could hardly have been *published* at a better time. The African plane crashes, accompanied by false news accounts of Hemingway's death, caused renewed public interest in the author. Then in October 1954, it was announced that Hemingway had won the Nobel Prize for literature, a final recognition of his accomplishment and genius.

Previously, Fenton had published stories and articles in well-regarded magazines and anthologies, but with the apprenticeship book he established himself as a leading authority on Ernest Hemingway. In advance of publication, the Kansas City chapter appeared in *New World Writing* and the *Atlantic* printed its three-parter. Six months *after* the book came out, a magazine called *Saturday Night* published separate excerpts in five successive issues. Yale promoted him from instructor to assistant professor, and awarded him a grant to pursue his next book, a biography of Stephen Vincent Benét. Actress Faye Emerson interviewed him on network radio. He was the only academic invited to participate in NBC radio's hour-long "Meet Ernest Hemingway" documentary in December. This kind of public attention struck some of his Yale colleagues as excessive and unseemly, but it had to have been an exciting time for a newly-minted doctor of philosophy.

Fenton told Hemingway some of this good news in a letter that has gone missing. On 29 December 1954 Hemingway responded that he was glad to hear about Fenton's promotion and grant, and asked his advice about whether it would be "of any value" for him to write, "truly and censoring nothing," about Joyce, Pound, Anderson, Stein, and other authors he'd known. He'd tried to tune in the NBC documentary, Hemingway said, but missed most of it because he was aboard his boat the Pilar, lying at anchor during an electrical storm. At the end of the letter Hemingway reverted to the plane crashes. He'd had no religious reaction either time, only thinking "shit" during the first crash and "I'll be a sad son of a bitch" during the second.

Carlos Baker was right to characterize *The Apprenticeship of Ernest Hemingway* as a valuable and useful book. In supple prose Fenton traced Hemingway's development from journalist to artist with sensitivity and accuracy. In the penultimate chapter, for example, he showed how Hemingway transformed a five-paragraph 1922 dispatch for the *Toronto Daily Star* into a brief pictorial account for the *Little Review* in April 1923, and then into the even shorter version that appeared as a vignette in the lower-case *in our time* in 1924 and as an inter-chapter in the upper-case *In Our Time* of 1925 (229–36).

In all three passages Hemingway described the evacuation of civilians from Eastern Thrace during the Greco-Turkish war. The copy he cabled to Toronto was first-rate. Lincoln Steffens remembered it years later as "a short but vivid, detailed picture of what [Hemingway] had seen in that miserable stream of hungry, frightened, uprooted people." Steffens's own adjectival account mirrored Hemingway's original dispatch, which contained almost thirty adjectives. In the *in our time* vignette these were cut to ten, gerunds were introduced to carry the story line, and Hemingway submerged himself entirely, refusing to guide the reader's response.

> Minarets stuck up in the rain out of Adrianople across the mud flats. The carts were jammed for thirty miles along the Karagatch road. Water buffalo and cattle were hauling carts through the mud. No end and no beginning. Just carts loaded with everything they owned. The old men and women, soaked through, walked along keeping the cattle moving. The Maritza was running yellow almost up to the bridge. Carts were jammed solid on the bridge with camels bobbing along through them. Greek cavalry herded along the procession. Women and kids were in the carts crouched with mattresses, mirrors, sewing machines, bundles. There was a woman having a kid with a young girl holding a blanket over her and crying. Scared sick looking at it. It rained all through the evacuation.

This remarkable passage breaks almost all of the rules. It is full of simple subject-verb-object sentences and sentence fragments. The passive voice is used repeatedly—"the carts were jammed," Hemingway says twice—to help convey the slow-moving seemingly endless procession on the Karagatch road. Nowhere are the political and military facts of the matter—the Turks, the Greeks, the burning of Smyrna—communicated. Until the last word, we don't even know what is being described. Yet the vignette succeeds in communicating the terrible human cost of war. Part of this emerges from the sogginess of the soaked-through evacuees who can no more escape the weather than the woman, in the single significant action of the passage, can escape childbirth. The eye is powerfully drawn to the scene of the frightened young girl holding a blanket over her and crying.

As Fenton concluded in the final words of his book, Hemingway had lived in many places during his seven-year apprenticeship—Kansas City, Chicago, Toronto, and Paris among them—"and he had been a newspaperman, but he had become a writer" (263).

Fenton faithfully stuck to the apprenticeship theme throughout. Other than necessary background, there was nothing in his book to confirm Hemingway's fears that his privacy would be violated or that personal material he might want to use in his own writing would be pre-empted. Nonetheless Hemingway continued to disparage Fenton to others. In conversation with A. E. Hotchner, he linked Fenton with the two other academics who had written books on his work: "Professor Carlos Back-up and Professor Charles Fender and Professor Philip Youngerdunger, wearing the serious silks of Princeton and Yale and N.Y.U." (Hotchner 179). And in April 1955, Hemingway remarked that Fenton was "a disappointed creative writer and a disappointed FBI investigator," and that his book was "overdone" (Baker *Life* 530). Fenton did follow the FBI practice of interviewing and corresponding with many of Hemingway's friends and acquaintances, it's true, but his goal was entirely different. The FBI was interested primarily in wrongdoing and character flaws, and by contacting multiple sources sought to arrive at a reliable composite portrait of the person under investigation. Fenton aimed to discover how one particular young man made himself into a great writer. Therefore he left out intimate personal details—one Kansas City informant told him that Hemingway was well-known in every whorehouse in town—and papered over the ethical irregularity of his representing three different news organizations when under contract to but one. He'd promised to lay off such material, after all. Besides, he'd committed enough youthful indiscretions himself to feel comfortable finding fault with Hemingway's.

Chapter 5

Carving a Career

George McGough—the Charlie Fenton counterpart in *Fish Flying Through Air*—thought he should easily be able to establish himself as "the greatest living authority on the contemporary American novel" inasmuch as the academic community in general believed that twentieth-century American novelists were hardly literate and not worth studying (262). This was an exaggeration, but not by much. In the 1950s most English departments resisted instituting American literature courses, and modern ones in particular. Emerson and Thoreau, all right; Henry James, perhaps, but not Hemingway—he was still alive!—and certainly not anyone younger.

The only senior professor interested in working on such writers at Yale was Fenton's mentor and friend, Norman Pearson. In supervising Charlie's doctoral dissertation on Hemingway's apprenticeship, Pearson contributed not only his counsel and encouragement, but also his own detailed knowledge about Gertrude Stein and her literary relationship with Hemingway (*Apprenticeship* 277). In addition Pearson called on his extensive connections in the literary community to benefit his protégé. Within Yale's English department, however, the witty and engaging Pearson could be of little help. He did not conform to the pattern of the customary English professor of the period. Although excellent in the classroom, his enthusiasms were suspect, he did not publish enough, and he would not indulge in the backbiting and gossiping that struck men like Peter Matthiessen as endemic in the English department.

Pearson was undoubtedly Fenton's leading advocate at Yale, but there were others as well. The eminent Chester Kerr, who directed the Yale University Press for three decades, recognized Fenton's writing talent and energy when he saw sections of his dissertation, and offered to publish it. Eventually the Hemingway book went to Farrar, Straus & Young, a distinguished commercial press, but Yale later brought out both Fenton's biography of Stephen Vincent Benét and a volume of Benét letters he assembled. Kerr edited both books and became Fenton's friend as well. Another supporter was Thomas C. Mendenhall, the professor of history who was Master of Yale's Berkeley College during 1950–1959. Fenton had his office in Berkeley throughout his time on the Yale faculty, and developed a warm relationship with Mendenhall, a scholar known for his bow ties and informal style who often joined students for meals, unannounced and with no fanfare.

At the time, Yale had a prejudice against promoting from within. The danger was that senior faculty might develop disciples who too closely resembled themselves, thus depriving the institution of new blood and new ideas. Yet given the momentum following release of the Hemingway apprenticeship book, the auspices looked bright for Charlie Fenton. He had established himself as an extremely popular teacher who spoke to students without pretension and in a language they could understand. Perhaps even more importantly, he welcomed the challenge of producing accessible and valuable books and articles. Yale boosted him in that direction by awarding him the Morse fellowship for 1954–1955, a competitive grant for junior faculty in the humanities that gave him a year's leave at full pay.

Still, Fenton was not at all sure that he wanted to invest too heavily in a future at Yale. Mark Schorer at the University of California, an accomplished writer and scholar who had started work on his massive biography of Sinclair Lewis, reviewed Fenton's Hemingway book in highly favorable terms. On the strength of that, Fenton wrote him on 13 December 1954, inquiring about possible future employment. He'd just been promoted from instructor to assistant professor, and given a three-year appointment at $5250 annually. That was pleasant, "of course, but quite frankly the prospects for future mobility at Yale [were] not intoxicating." Then too, Fenton added, two of his three children suffered from asthma, and the cold and damp New England weather made things worse. He was looking for a better-paying job in a more salubrious climate. Did Schorer know of a university with a good library that was looking "for a bright, not so young, rather greedy type" like himself? Schorer did not, but the two men arranged to foregather at the Modern Language Association's annual meeting later that month to solidify their friendship.

In the spring of 1955 Fenton had another proposal for Schorer. Doubtless through the agency of Pearson, Fenton secured summer employment as director of a course in American literature for high school teachers from France. Co-sponsored by Yale and the U.S. Office of Education, the program was designed to supply these French visitors with information they could dispense in their own classrooms. In his capacity as director, Fenton asked Schorer to come to New Haven during July and August to deliver eight lectures to these visitors for a fee of $400. Schorer could not take the assignment; he had not been teaching any courses in American literature, and had nothing prepared. Next Fenton approached Malcolm Cowley, a well-established man of letters, and raised the fee to $700. Cowley hemmed and hawed. He had plenty of things to say, but balked at driving the hundred miles round trip from his home in Sherman, Connecticut to New Haven three times a week. Cowley finally accepted, though, after some encouragement from Pearson and after the honorarium was raised to $1,000.

The connection with Cowley established during that summer had happy consequences for Fenton's career. Cowley served as a scout for Viking Press, and when Fenton approached him in August with a proposal for an anthology of stories about World War II, Cowley encouraged him to go ahead. Two years would elapse before Viking published *The Best Short Stories of World War II*, edited and with an introduction by Fenton. The delay resulted in part from Cowley's insistence that Fenton first survey a number of leading writers and critics, asking which stories they would recommend, in order to give the volume greater authority, and in part from difficulties encountered in obtaining permissions from various authors.

Fenton was far from idle during the interim. He continued to assemble material toward his biography of Benét, and undertook several other projects as well. During the half decade of 1955–1960, in fact, Fenton produced a tremendously impressive record of publication, turning out three books and dozens of articles—several of these in highly regarded mainstream magazines. He also wrote a great deal that remained unpublished at the time of his death in July 1960, including work of considerable merit that would surely have seen the light of day had he lived to guide it through the publishing process.

Beginning in the fall of 1955, Fenton directed much of his attention away from literary studies toward evaluating the unhappy condition of higher education in the United States and suggesting remedies. His best known article on this topic, "The Ivy-Covered Wild Blue Yonder" in the November 1955 *Harper's*, examined the brand-new Air Force Academy in Colorado Springs, and found its educational program "a lot less impressive than its publicity" (40). The crux of the problem, Fenton wrote, lay in the new academy's being too closely modeled after the United States Military Academy at West Point. It could hardly have been otherwise, he pointed out, inasmuch as the leadership positions—superintendent, dean of faculty, commandant of cadets, director of intercollegiate athletics—were all manned by West Point graduates. Good things as well as bad were imported from the USMA, like its exceptionally high ratio of instructors to cadets. West Point was the home of the fourteen-man section, and the Air Force Academy decided to go one step further, cutting the ratio to but twelve students for each instructor.

What was taught in these sections, however, Fenton subjected to considerable criticism. Too much emphasis was placed on training cadets "to speak clearly and with poise," a phrase repeated in the official description of each of the three English courses required of all Air Force Academy students. This represented a basic and essential competence for a literate officer—or civilian—but, Fenton believed, training in elocution and basic composition skills belonged on the secondary school level. Certainly it was not the same as offering "a genuine undergraduate experience in historical or literary study" (43). It seemed unlikely, his downbeat conclusion asserted, "that a slightly hopped-up version of the old service-school education is going to make new kind of men for a new kind of military job" (44).

This article generated a barrage of protesting letters to the editor of *Harper's* and a fair amount of hate mail sent directly to Fenton. Why was he so unpatriotic? If he didn't like it here, why didn't he go somewhere else? Fenton was not particularly surprised, and not at all inclined to alter his ways. When he found fault, as he was constitutionally inclined to do, he would say so, and never mind if that made him unpopular. Sometimes, his rather extreme views paid off. He'd begun serving on the local board of education in Madison, and when it was proposed that art instruction be temporarily suspended at the high school for financial reasons, Fenton vigorously objected. "A student with no aesthetic appreciation is better off dead," he told the board, which then approved hiring a part-time art teacher.

In the same month when he unsettled chauvinistic readers with his article on the Air Force Academy. Charlie Fenton published a defense of "The Writer as Professor" in *New World Writing*. The article began by citing one American professor's pronouncement on the insidious effects of associating the creative process with the scholarly. "Writers must not become academics," the professor declared. "[A] creative writer should never have to be both creator and judge": these were separate functions, and could not be practiced together (163). Having set up his straw man, Fenton proceeded to knock it down.

The single most telling argument in favor of bringing writers into college classrooms, he pointed out, was that otherwise many of them would not be able to survive financially. Writing was an intensely competitive proposition in post–World War II America, Fenton added. For all but a fortunate few, royalties from book sales and payment for articles offered only meager recompense. The majority had to find some other way to support themselves, and teaching university students about their craft—even at less than princely salaries—helped pay the bills. It was true that teaching itself would exhaust much of these writers' energy, but most colleges operated on a nine-month basis, leaving three summer months free for their own work. As a consequence, the writer as professor had become a fixture on American campuses.

There was scarcely an English department in the United States, Fenton asserted, that did not employ a practicing poet or novelist, short story writer or playwright, to teach "a seminar or two in creative writing, perhaps a course in contemporary American literature, and, maybe, if his position [was] insecure and his chairman unfriendly, a section of Freshman English." The field of writer-professors had been pioneered by men like Wallace Stegner and Robert Penn Warren, continued by the likes of Mark Schorer, Richard Wilbur, and Saul Bellow, and was now in its third generation (164).

By and large, Fenton said, this was a good thing. Students and faculty were exposed to a professional worker in the arts, one who often played the role of "the wild man" in residence (165). The writer got a much-needed modest compensation, and might also acquire valuable subject matter for his or her next book, especially if the academic climate at the institution was unpleasant. Several novels with jaundiced depictions of university life appeared just before or shortly after Fenton's article: Mary McCarthy's *The Groves of Academe* (1952), Randall Jarrell's *Pictures from an Institution* (1954), and Bernard Malamud's *A New Life* (1961), for example.

To clinch the argument, Fenton cited the case of Dylan Thomas, the alcoholic Welsh poet who died in New York City in November 1953. "Why are all your poets on university faculties?" Thomas asked an American friend during his last months. After Thomas's death letters of his to a wealthy patroness surfaced in which the poet answered his own question. "It is so difficult for me to live and to keep my family alive," he said. The problem kept him "treadmilling small nightmares all the waking nights." The poet's situation was not significantly different from that of his American counterparts, Fenton observed. Artists had not been supported by an aristocracy for several centuries. There was little federal patronage. The book-buying public paid the way for only a tiny minority of those producing good work. It seemed a "a happy compromise," he concluded, "that a fraction of our writers should be modestly sustained by our universities . . . in return for professional and academic instruction" (170).

In addressing the question of "The Writer as Professor" in the fall of 1955, Charlie Fenton was really reflecting on his own situation. At Yale, he played the role of the writer as professor on campus. His qualifications for the post were modest. He had published only a few short stories in literary magazines, but he had also produced novels and plays that barely escaped publication. When he talked to student writers, they listened to him as they would not have to, say, a Chaucer or Shakespeare scholar assigned to teach a creative writing seminar.

Where his future was concerned, Fenton faced a dilemma. Since prep school days he had dreamed of making his mark as a creator of fiction. During the war, and immediately after, he'd devoted himself to that ambition. But it hadn't panned out: he could not support himself, much less a family, on the minimal rewards of professional authorship. As a consequence he'd qualified himself for academic employment by earning a doctorate. He was determined to make his mark as a professor, either at Yale or at another of the leading American universities. If he could accomplish that goal, Charlie knew, it would please his father immensely, and in some measure make up for the years when—immersed in drink and debauchery—he had disappointed both his parents and himself. At the same time, however, Charlie was not ready to abandon his dream of becoming a writer. Perhaps he did not have to. Perhaps he could succeed both as a professor and a writer. He understood that the two professions usually attracted diametrically opposed personalities. Most college professors led respectable, even stuffy, lives, while most creative artists were bohemians at odds with the status quo. As he continued his career, Fenton uneasily tried to combine these two propensities in his own nature.

Money was much on Charlie's mind during his early years in the academy. He was forever on the lookout for additional sources of revenue to supplement his Yale salary as assistant professor. At lunch one day, the psychologist Leonard W. Doob happened to mention that he was looking for an interviewer to see candidates applying for faculty teaching fellowships under the sponsorship of the Ford Foundation. On leave at the time with his Morse fellowship, Fenton immediately volunteered himself, served for two years in that part-time role, and, Doob recalled, did "a wonderful job" into the bargain.

During the last months of 1955 and into the new year, Fenton frequently drove up from New Haven to Watertown, site of the Taft school, where his father had fallen mortally ill with colon cancer. Daniel Fenton stayed on the job as director of studies at Taft as long as he could, retiring on 1 January 1956 and dying scarcely more than a month later. In his Latin classes at Taft, Daniel Fenton "looked like a statesman or a diplomat," and demanded hard and conscientious work from his students. Witty and erudite, sometimes sarcastic, he struck them as a college professor, not a high school teacher (Shepherd). Charlie spent as much time as he could at his father's bedside during his last days. In the family dynamics, he was the son more closely associated with his father, while his younger brother David bonded with his mother. Daniel was proud of his son for overcoming his youthful misbehavior and actually becoming a professor, especially at Yale. Charlie was glad that he had been able to finish *The Apprenticeship of Ernest Hemingway*, so that his father could see it—and its dedication to him—before his passing.

On February 17, two weeks after Daniel's death, Charlie participated in a debate on "Higher Education" in Watertown. His "opponent" in that debate was the famous Robert Maynard Hutchins, onetime boy wonder president of the University of Chicago. Sharing the platform with Hutchins, according to the newspaper account, would be "37-year-old Charles A. Fenton, who [was] rapidly rising in the academic field much as Mr. Hutchins did 20 years [earlier]." Actually the two men did not diverge widely in their views. One of Hutchins's first steps at Chicago had been to abandon the football team, and as he said, "overnight we became an educational institution." Although Fenton did not go quite so far in his opposition to football, he deplored the overemphasis on the sport and its increasing commercialization on college campuses.

Both of Fenton's prep schools connected with their former student as his visibility in the literary and academic community increased. In the spring of 1956 he was asked to run for the Eaglebrook alumni board—he lost—and to serve as class agent for school's new Alumni Fund—he declined. That same June, however, he returned to Taft to speak to the graduating seniors. Charlie had his reservations about the youths who were matriculating at Yale during this period. For an article on 6 March 1957, the *Nation* asked several prominent young professors who were also writers—Carlos Baker at Princeton, Leo Marx at Minnesota, and Charles Fenton at Yale among them—to comment on the question: "Who are the leading intellectual, artistic and ethical influences on the present generation of students?" In response, Fenton characterized his students as so eager for affirmation of American life that they rejected the critical stances of commentators like H. L. Mencken and Sinclair Lewis. "This is a talented undergraduate generation," he wrote, "industrious and attractive, and a pleasure to teach, but most of them are company men" ("The Careful Young Men" 202–03).

Fenton's characterization of his students echoed that of *The Organization Man*, William H. Whyte's widely read book of 1956. According to Whyte, an entire generation of middle class men had "left home, spiritually as well as physically, to take the vows of organization life," and in so doing had sacrificed their individuality. He warned them to abandon groupthink, and to fight against the comfortable but false assumption that their interests and those of the organization they joined were really, after all, almost wholly compatible (3, 297, 404). Another influential assessment of the time, David Riesman's *The Lonely Crowd* (1950), deplored the change from the inner-directed man of the past to his mid-twentieth century counterpart: the other-directed man who responded "to conformist pressures from contemporary influences, including friends, acquaintances, and the mass media." Inner-directed people channeled their energies into production, other-directed ones devoted theirs to consumption. The procedure signaled an America in decline, and threatened the survival of the individualism Americans prided themselves on, for people lost "their social freedom and their individual autonomy in seeking to become like each other" (Dunar 189–90).

The common stereotype of the 1950s sees the decade as one of mindless conformity, mass consumerism, political conservatism, and coffee klatches in little boxes on suburban hillsides. Norman Mailer called it "one of the worst decades in the history of man" (Castronovo 13). William Manchester castigated its youth as "withdrawn, cautious, unimaginative, indifferent, unadventurous and silent" (Safire). To be sure, some undercurrents of revolt roiled the waters of the decade. It was the time of Jack Kerouac, Allen Ginsberg, and the beatniks, after all, as well as that of *The Man in the Gray Flannel Suit*, Sloan Wilson's signature novel of 1955. But by and large, the image was accurate enough.

"Outside the academy," as Alvin Kernan, like Fenton a young instructor in the Yale English department, described it, "another world was taking shape in the fifties, prosperous, powerful, conformist, America the world power. Powerful but banal. [Its inhabitants lived] in identical Levittown tract houses, manipulated by advertising, dominated increasingly by big business, exploited by cynical politicians, their thinking programmed by the media, more and more in debt to buy washing machines, cars and Frigidaires . . . Sex was Marilyn Monroe, happiness was making money, government was General Eisenhower, fun was watching *I Love Lucy* on TV, and what was good for General Motors was good for the country" (97). Kernan, like Fenton, regarded it as an obligation to shake students out of complacent acceptance of this world. The difference was that Fenton, through his outrageous flouting of authority, presented students with an example—a dangerous one—to follow.

Charlie Fenton's career in the academy almost precisely coincided with the 1950s. The "Fifties male," according to poet Robert Bly, "got to work early, labored responsibly, supported his wife and children, and admired discipline . . . [H]is view of culture and America's part in it was boyish and optimistic. Many of his qualities were strong and positive, but underneath the charm and bluff there was . . . much isolation, deprivation, and passivity. Unless he has an enemy, he isn't sure that he is alive" (1). Fenton refused to be passive, and never lacked for enemies. Most of the enemies belonged to the Establishment and occupied positions of authority. He took them on, out loud and on the page, and it cost him.

During the mid-1950s, Fenton was doing all he could to improve his "not intoxicating" chances of securing promotion and tenure in the Yale English department. Mere articles, and particularly articles in mainstream magazines rather than scholarly journals, wouldn't do him much good. Books mattered far more, and so, in a burst of energy during 1955–1957, he whipped his collection of World War II stories into shape, applied for and received a Guggenheim grant to support the writing of a Benét biography, and produced a lively 250-page history of the National Institute and American Academy of Arts and Letters.

By the end of 1956 Fenton was ready to sign off on the final table of contents for *The Best Short Stories of World War II*. Both he and Cowley wanted to include a J. D. Salinger story as well as Hemingway's brief and moving "Old Man at the Bridge" (despite its origin in the Spanish Civil War), but permissions could not be obtained for either of these. The book, published in August 1957, contained 20 stories in all, with contributions from a few well-established authors (Faulkner, Benét, Stegner) outweighed by stories from several younger writers, among them Schorer, James A. Michener, James Jones, Norman Mailer, Irwin Shaw, John Horne Burns, Ralph Ellison, and William Styron. In his headnote to Styron's "The Long March," the final story in the book, Fenton reprinted Styron's 1953 comment that "there are signs that this generation can and will produce literature equal to that of any in the past" (359). Fenton felt himself part of that generation, and shared Styron's optimism about its future.

On August 15, Cowley complimented Fenton on having put together "a most impressive volume." He regretted the absence of Salinger but felt that Fenton, by using an epigraph from Hemingway's *Green Hills of Africa* pretty well made up for the loss of "Old Man at the Bridge." The epigraph stressed how advantageous it was for a writer to have gone through a war. Those who lacked this experience "were always very jealous and tried to make it seem unimportant, or abnormal, or a disease as a subject, while, really, it was just something quite irreplaceable that they had missed," Hemingway wrote.

Fenton paid further tribute to Hemingway in his introduction. In reading hundreds of stories about the war, he'd detected his influence everywhere. Sometimes the prose was almost eerie in evoking Hemingway's rhythms.

It was cold and the hills behind the city were all autumn and . . . we walked to the house along a hill at night. The summit was dark and the slope below was lamp-lighted at the street crossings. We were together and alone and Jan was ready to cry. I held her hand and she smiled. She controlled herself very well walking on the hill in the cold in the fall.

"It would have been plagiarism," Fenton observed, "had it not been so obviously a helpless captivity" (x-xi).

Although Hemingway's voice was ubiquitous in the war stories by younger writers, Fenton added, they had not adopted the philosophical drift of his early novels toward nihilism. Their attitude was closer to *For Whom the Bell Tolls* (1940) than either *The Sun Also Rises* (1926) or *A Farewell to Arms*

(1929). "Compassion and involvement, not adjustment and separation—Robert Jordan rather than Jake Barnes—[were] the primary characteristics" of his generation's authors, Fenton believed. They absorbed their technique from the early, their values from the later Hemingway (xii). These observations appeared not only in Fenton's introduction, but also, in somewhat briefer form, in an article of his for the *Saturday Review*. He was one among very few university professors whose work was welcomed by the best midcult magazines of the time: *Atlantic Monthly* and *Harper's*, the *Nation* and the *Saturday Review*. They published his material because it was timely, dealing with current or recent events, and because Fenton—unlike most of his academic colleagues—was an accomplished professional writer.

Some professors in the Yale English department were envious of Fenton's ability to reach a wide audience. A few disapproved of his doing so. But all must have been impressed when in the spring of 1957 he won a Guggenheim, the most coveted of all scholarly fellowships, to finance the writing of the Benét biography. In his application, Fenton emphasized a basic theme of the book: that in relating the story of Benét's productive years from 1920 to 1943, he was presenting "a portrait of the role of a serious, popular writer in a democracy." His ultimate goal as a scholar, he said, was to "narrate and interpret literary history as accurately and imaginatively as [he could], and for as wide an audience as is decently possible." Moreover, he was ready to write his book, with the research almost entirely completed. Within a year, Fenton said, he should be able to produce the biography.

With time off from the Guggenheim, and a supplement from Yale to make up the difference between the grant and his salary, Fenton met that deadline. *Stephen Vincent Benét: The Life and Times of an American Man of Letters, 1898–1943* came out in October 1958. Fenton initially harbored hopes that Viking might publish the book. But Cowley, who had supported Fenton's Guggenheim application, read the first three chapters and responded with only minimal enthusiasm. He did not share Fenton's conviction that Benét ranked among the really important writers of his time. Benét started out with an enormous talent, publishing his first book of poetry while still in high school. Yet out of that early promise, Cowley asked, how much had emerged? "*John Brown's Body*, yes," but not much else except for a few brilliant short stories with soft spots where Benét "used glittering words to conceal limp thoughts." With an editor so inclined, Fenton tactfully withdrew from seeking an acceptance from Viking and went instead to the Yale University Press, where Chester Kerr was eager to publish the biography. There were strong connections to Yale, after all. Benét graduated from Yale, and maintained his ties to the institution. Almost all of his papers were housed there. Fenton himself had three Yale degrees and a position on the faculty.

The new Ph.D. in his doctoral robes, 1953. Fenton Family Photo

Spurred by his own Guggenheim 30 years earlier, Benét emigrated to Paris in the spring of 1926 and after two years of hard research and writing produced his masterpiece, *John Brown's Body*. American readers responded to his epic poem about the Civil War with a warmth they had not shown since the publication of Longfellow's "Hiawatha" and "Evangeline" in the 1850s, and no long poem since has commanded so extensive a readership. *John Brown's Body* came out in 1928, when Benét was thirty years old, and for the rest of his fifteen years he received letters from every corner of the country celebrating his accomplishment. Especially after 1941, when his publishers issued an annotated edition with footnotes and an essay on the causes of the Civil War, students read his poem in their junior or senior years in high school, learning about the nation's terrible war while absorbing an exposure to the art of poetry. In an outtake from his biography for the *Atlantic Monthly*, Fenton finished with Benét's comments in verse about that edition. He had not written *John Brown's Body* to educate the masses or the elite, Benét pointed out.

> I wrote it poor, in love, and young,
> In indigestion and despair
> And exaltation of the mind,
> Not for the blind to lead the blind;
> I have no quarrel with the wise,
> No quarrel with the pedagogue,
> And yet I wrote for none of those.
>
> And yet there are the words, in print,
> And should an obdurate old man
> Remember half a dozen lines
> Stuck in his mind like thistle seed,
> Or if, perhaps, some idle boy
> Should sometimes read a page or so
> In the deep summer, to his girl,
> And drop the book half finished there,
> Since kissing was a better joy,
> Well, I shall have been paid enough.
> I'll have been paid enough indeed ("Writing of *John Brown's Body*" 51).

A romantic himself, Fenton found the sentiment in these lines irresistible. He admired Benét, too, for the manner of his death. Benét died in March 1943, "his health broken by the immense amount of radio material he had been writing for various war agencies." He had no patience with writers who worried that their reputations might suffer from writing such propaganda. The government had as much right to call on him for his abilities as a writer as it did to call on a chemist for his, Benét believed. He couldn't just "sit on [his] integrity, like a hen on a china egg, for the duration" (Benét headnote, *Best Stories*).

In mid-1957, before he took the Benét biography under consideration for Viking, Cowley passed judgment on Fenton's history of the National Institute and American Academy of Arts and Letters. This manuscript developed out of Fenton's research on Benét, who had been instrumental in restoring the Institute and Academy to respectability in the 1930s. As Fenton saw it in *The American Man of Letters in the Twentieth Century: A History of the National Institute of Arts and Letters and the American Academy of Arts and Letters. 1898–1968*, the Institute—the more inclusive organization—and the Academy, which selected its limited roster from members of the Institute, were handicapped from the beginning by the dominance of the genteel tradition. Many early members were so fixated on protecting the American language against slang and grammatical violations, and on protecting readers against exposure to the dark underside of industrial progress, that they refused to grant recognition to the major proponents of realism and naturalism in their midst. So, for example, they did not elect Theodore Dreiser, who was not a gentleman and whose novels proved it.

Instead, and even worse, Fenton believed, the Institute began choosing its members from the ranks of college presidents—worthy men, no doubt, and capable administrators, but hardly qualified as writers or artists. Nicholas Murray Butler, president of Columbia, more or less ran the organization for a number of years. Then the patrons took over, especially Archer Huntington, heir to a railroad fortune, who gave copious funds to the two organizations and financed the building of their palatial headquarters on New York's W. 155th Street: generosity that was rewarded with election to membership. By the 1920s the Institute and Academy were in sorry shape, as Sinclair Lewis made clear in a diatribe against them. Then Benét, and the composer Walter Damrosch, and the lawyer-novelist Arthur Train, rode to the rescue. In telling the story of the Institute and Academy, Fenton arrived at a happy ending, but his best and most vigorous writing concentrated on the organization's unfortunate early years. He was at his best when puncturing the balloons of the pretentious.

Cowley, who happened to be president of the Institute, liked Fenton's manuscript enough to suggest some changes and to advise him on the best way to see it into publication. He could envision no market for it as a commercial trade book—a university press would be better—and yet, Cowley said, it might come out as a trade book if the Institute-Academy could be moved to give it a subsidy. With that in mind, he proposed showing Fenton's script to Felicia Geffen, the secretary of the Institute, and discussing with her the possibility of a subsidy. "I wouldn't be optimistic about it," he warned Fenton in his letter of 25 August 1957, "but there's enough chance to make the experiment worth trying." This effort did not succeed, but Fenton made the suggested revisions and—as of the end of 1959—wrote Cowley that it looked as if the Duke University Press was going to publish "that monograph of mine on the Institute and Academy."

In his memoir *In Plato's Cave,* Renaissance scholar Alvin Kernan pre-sented a vivid picture of Yale in the postwar period. He was a graduate student in English from 1951 to 1954, and an instructor from 1954 to 1957, almost exactly mirroring Fenton's years there. Most of his fellow graduate students in arts and sciences were drawn from liberal arts colleges and the middle class, for "the financial rewards were too small to attract the more affluent and socially savvy people to what Bernard Shaw described as a life of "being half mad from reading undergraduate papers." They all were smart, with a few notably smarter than others: Harold Bloom, for example, who came to Yale from Cornell heralded by Meyer Abrams as "a prodigy, beyond anything I've ever seen" and proceeded to astound students and colleagues alike by his prodigious energy, vast acquaintance with literature of all peri-ods, and photographic memory. "Every work he picked up," Kernan recalled, "came to life in his hands" (68–69).

Most of the graduate student-instructors, benefiting from the G.I. bill, came from less privileged backgrounds than those of the students they taught and the faculty they sought to join. The Yale students thought of them "as prep school masters . . . servants hired by their fathers at low wages to give them culture, to teach them how to write, and to expose them to the small amount of literary polish required by their station in life." Seeking redress from those who looked down on them socially, Kernan and others resorted to "dazzling displays of learning" in the classroom and tried to jog their mostly unrecep-tive students into actual thinking.

At times, it worked. As a way of getting into a discussion of Milton's *Para-dise Lost,* Kernan directed a question to Smithers, his generic representative student. "Smithers, what do you think of original sin?" Long pause before a reply. "Well, sir, it's all right, I guess." Rather than giving up at so inane an answer, Kernan managed a quick, somewhat bemused riposte: "You don't sound entirely convinced, Smithers; what exactly are your reservations?" This led to a merry forty minutes in which the students "gradually picked up and played with the idea, novel to Americans, that there is something ineradi-cably corrupt about human beings" (88).

As of 1950, the majority of ensconced professors at Yale came from backgrounds similar to those of the students. A life in the academy—filling the role of a scholar and a gentleman—was one of the options for patrician youths. Whereas the first or more ambitious son might go into the family business, second sons were advised to consider the law, or the clergy, or the military, or even the university: all respectable occupations. Most senior fac-ulty members, particularly in the Ivy League, lived comfortable genteel lives, protected by their inheritance—or that of their wives—from descending into the middle class. That tradition was about to change. The war itself "really ended the old faculty gentility," Kernan noted, for the G.I. bill brought fresh candidates to the campus from less privileged families. Yet it would take time for them to secure tenured positions and replace those who were retiring. In the meantime, the respectable elders made the decisions, and they were in no hurry for the Yale English department to "get its instructors off the New York subway," as Benjamin Nangle, the permanent associate professor who served as the department's director of undergraduate studies, remarked (86–87).

The competition among aspirants for promotion and tenure at Yale was "almost unbearably intense," Kernan observed. "To survive you not only had to teach well, you had to establish yourself as a scholar and . . . a writer on your subject with an international . . . reputation" (90). Moreover, politicking was frowned upon. Any overt campaigning with the established professors could destroy a candidate's chances. Fenton did no such campaigning: quite the contrary.

In the spring of 1958, Yale's English department decided to make a permanent appointment in American literature. Yale did not ordinarily promote its own, preferring to let them prove themselves elsewhere before returning, but in this case the two principal candidates for the post were already on campus. Both had studied at Yale as undergraduates and graduate students, and both, oddly enough, shared the same initials. The contest was joined between Charles Fenton and Charles Feidelson. One of them would be promoted from assistant to associate professor and granted tenure. The other would not. The choice rested with the department's senior professors. Fenton brought to the table his considerable success in the classroom, and by way of publication his book on Hemingway, the volume of World War II stories, and—then in press—his biography of Stephen Vincent Benét. Feidelson, on the surface, seemed to have less to offer. Gaddis Smith, who took a course on Henry James with Feidelson—a "shy southerner," as Kernan described him (87)—thought that he and Fenton were 180 degrees apart as teachers: Feidelson rather pedantic, Fenton breezy and witty.

Part of Fenton's success in the classroom was dependent on a presentation of himself as significantly different from the run of serious scholarly professors at Yale. In class and out, he regularly expressed his disdain for excessive academic bookishness and reserved his enthusiasm for creative writing and its practitioners in the present or the recent past—unexplored territory for almost all of the Yale professoriate. As his friend the psychologist Leonard Doob put it, Fenton "played the scholarly game in his fashion, not quite approving of himself but at least picking people and themes"—Hemingway, Benét, the making of the artist—"with which he had deep sympathy."

Lawrence J. Schneiderman, who took Daily Themes in the fall of 1952, has never forgotten the day that Fenton read aloud a comic piece of his to the class. Schneiderman was a work-scholarship student, assigned to assist Professor Frederick A. Pottle, the renowned scholar who spent most of his life editing the voluminous journals of James Boswell, the disciple and biographer of Samuel Johnson. Pottle's edition of Boswell's *London Journal*, in which the young mid-eighteenth century Scotsman recounted his sexual and literary adventures upon first coming to London, became a best-seller. Most of Boswell's writings aroused considerably less commercial interest. For Pottle and his meticulous assistant, who shared his devotion to the cause, no detail was too fine, no individual too obscure to escape their notice. Schneiderman was assigned to transcribe into typewritten form substantial amounts of what seemed to him to be entirely trivial material. It was tedious work, dealing with the minutiae of dry-as-dust scholarship. For Daily Themes, he wrote a satirical sketch about the time Pottle triumphantly located the source of an elusive note, resulting in a chorus of exclamations from his devoted lieutenant: "Oh," "Oh," and yet again "Oh." Fenton read this sketch to the class, reciting all the "Oh's" with great mockery and eliciting howls of laughter from the students. In so making sport of a distinguished senior colleague, Fenton undoubtedly compromised his own future at Yale. Remembered tales of Fenton's drinking days dimmed his prospects still further.

Then too, his rival Charles Feidelson, who was to become one of the first Jews among the department's professors, had produced an important book— *Symbolism and American Literature*, published by the University of Chicago Press in 1953. This ranked as a major work in the field, wide-ranging in its focus on writers of the American Renaissance: Poe, Hawthorne, Melville, Whitman, and Emerson. The closely contested decision came down in favor of Feidelson. Fenton, at the crossroads of his career, had to decide what to do.

Pearson and other adherents on the faculty urged him to stay at Yale. He might have to wait a few years, but there was every chance that he would still earn promotion and tenure. At just this time, an alternative came to light. Duke University, in Durham, North Carolina, was looking for young blood to invigorate its program in American literature. Duke had been the home of *American Literature*, the leading journal in the field, since its inception. Arlin Turner, who would one day become editor of that periodical, was going to take over as chairman of the English department. Born of deep southern roots, Duke was eager to transform itself from a regional to a national institution. A man like Fenton, an excellent teacher whose books and articles were receiving wide and favorable attention, would surely aid in that transformation. So Duke made Fenton a remarkable offer. They offered him a full professorship with tenure, in effect eliminating the several years in the associate professor rank that ordinary mortals in the academy were obliged to experience. And a healthy raise in salary. And his choice of courses to teach.

These were powerful inducements, but Fenton's ties to Yale were not easily severed. A delegation from the English department, with Pearson at its head, implored Yale university president A. Whitney Griswold to intervene. Griswold arranged a meeting with Fenton, and that decided the matter. The two men knew each other fairly well, for Griswold taught Fenton both as an undergraduate and in graduate school. During their interview, Griswold told Fenton that the issue boiled down to whether he wanted to sign himself "Fenton of Yale or Fenton of Duke." *Why,* Fenton thought, *the pure arrogance of the bastard.* "They didn't think I would leave," he later remarked. "They thought my blood was Yale blue." He drove out to Madison, and when Gwendy returned from shopping, Charlie came running out of the house swinging a couple of empty suitcases. "I've made a decision!" he hollered. "I've made a decision!"

On April 25, he wrote Cowley that he'd accepted a full professorship at Duke. "You know the academic jungle well enough to appreciate this bonanza, since I am presently an asst. prof. here. All my teaching will be American literature, my wife and kids should profit immensely from the move, it's a good library, almost double the salary . . . All in all it's very giddy." To lighten the euphoria, he added, "Tenure. Sweet Jesus. I will grow a beard and become a shit." He was to start teaching in September, the same month the Benét biography came out, and did not idle away the summer. Instead he took another crack at converting his experiences in World War II into fictional form. In August he sent Cowley the resulting short novel, first called *The Trotters* and later *The Long Summer*, for consideration by Viking.

An excellent judge of fiction, Cowley responded with one of the most heartening letters of rejection ever written. He'd read *The Trotters*—"trotters" was British slang for men who'd deserted or gone AWOL—and so had Tom Guinzburg, Viking's president, and editor Catherine Carver. As it stood, Cowley said, it was not a book Viking would publish. But it was the most honest and persuasive writing about the bombing squadrons Cowley had ever seen. The characterizations were good, the dialogue was good, the picture of the differences between the airmen of different countries was convincing. "With this manuscript," Cowley told Fenton, "you have struck into a new level of writing." There was but one trouble: the book didn't have a plot. Or rather, it started out to have a plot and then didn't deliver. One of the characters died, but killing him off didn't end the book, it merely stopped it.

Cowley thought he understood what was wrong and how to fix it. Fenton had to come out from the shadows, and tell the truth about his own months "on the trot." He suspected that "Professor Fenton, late of Yale and presently of Duke, couldn't quite bring himself to write a first person narrative in which the first person hero did truly disgraceful things." Cowley went on to suggest specific changes. Fenton's hero might go AWOL and then return to sweat out his thirty missions. There ought to be a girl in the story too—some fictional embodiment of Betty Lyon who had taken Fenton in and hid him from the Special Police. A novel reconfigured along these lines might even generate Hollywood interest, and he hoped that Fenton would make the revisions. "Now that you have nothing in the world to do except move to O. Henry's home town [Durham] and prepare a few courses to regale the students, why don't you give some serious thought to constructing a plot for *The Trotters*? Everybody here thinks it would be a marvelous novel if it were a novel."

In a review for the *Nation* that doubled as a farewell to Eli, Fenton reported on the world premiere of Archibald MacLeish's *J. B.*, presented by the Yale School of Drama. MacLeish chose to launch his Pulitzer prize winning drama in New Haven, where he had taken his undergraduate degree. In reviewing the production, Fenton managed to praise *J. B.* (a modern version of the Biblical Job) while delivering sarcastic comments about those he was leaving behind. "Someone inquired if A. Whitney Griswold was going to play Job. The Department of English sent its masters of biblical exegesis to inspect this native talent. One sensed that they did not plan to enjoy it. After all, to have seen [T. S. Eliot's] *The Cocktail Party* was sufficient bounty for one critical lifetime." The audience, resenting MacLeish's career as a public figure, arrived "with an air of expectant cannibalism." But the moving play overcame their expectations. The intellectual snobs—the same ones who had voted against his promotion—spilled out on York Street afterwards, grumbling that *J. B.* was too simple, too readily understood, that it should not have moved them, dammit. Fenton particularly admired two things about the play: its theme of regeneration, and the implicit notion that the individual was superior to the institution (426). He took those ideas with him when he drove down to North Carolina in August.

Chapter 6

A Different Planet

"Mr. Fenton's leaving is a great loss to all students in American Studies," Norman Holmes Pearson told the *Yale Daily News*, "He will make a distinguished addition to an already distinguished faculty in American literature at Duke" ("Fenton Leaving"). It was an adventurous appointment for Duke, whose English department was run at the time by a stodgy and hidebound group of full professors, many with genteel southern roots. But Fenton brought with him an expertise in modern American literature that was needed, along with an excellent record in teaching and publication. "Wanting to transform Duke University from provincial to international status," a colleague characterized the university's decision, "the administration was apparently so dazzled by CAF's Ivy league background, publishing successes, good looks, teaching skills, and war record that they overlooked his iconoclastic tendencies and limited diplomatic skills"—and, in addition, his being a Yankee.

Neither Charlie nor Gwendy Fenton had spent any time in Dixie, and they were shocked by their first exposure to wholesale segregation. Duke's campus buildings, for example, were equipped with six toilets: two for faculty, two for students, two for staff (African Americans). In the movie theater, there were two balconies, the lower one for whites, the higher for blacks. A devoted liberal, Gwendy recoiled from such inhumane behavior and played Billie Holiday's "Strange Fruit" (about the lynching of blacks) on the phonograph. She went to the supermarket and came home shaking her head. What was the trouble? Well, she said, "I liked the colored people very much." The whites, though, were really incredible, Charlie wrote Chester Kerr at the Yale University Press, before signing off with "All the best from outer space." Daughter Wendy, about to enter Duke as a freshman, was the last member of the family to arrive in Durham, after finishing high school and a summer job in Madison. "You're going to have to get used to it," Charlie said when he met her at the train. "It's like living on a different planet."

Charlie himself felt like something of an alien in the South, but Duke after all had valued him more highly than Yale and he was determined to make the best of his new situation. "We have a perfectly swell house [at 2535 Perkins Road]," he wrote Kerr, "the kids are making friends easily, and the library is first-rate in American Lit." Subsequent letters to Kerr—his Benét biography was nearing publication—struck similarly cheerful notes while reporting on the mores and customs of Duke. Freshmen were required to wear beanies. His arrival coincided with the inauguration of an honor system for undergraduates, reminding him of his schoolboy reaction to such naïveté. "They've got the honor," the lads chanted, "and we've got the system." Everybody called him "Dr.," and when so introduced he bristled, looking around for "some son of a bitch in white." He signed himself "Fenton, I guess, of Duke."

Among his perks as a full professor was a minimal teaching load of seven ("yes, 7") hours a week, information that he encouraged Kerr to circulate on the Yale grapevine so as to foment mutiny among the troops. Because of his Guggenheim grant, Fenton had not met a class since May 1957, and he was pleased by his initial exposure to Duke students 16 months later. Yale might have a few more "really first-class" students, but the Duke undergraduates seemed "much more impressed by the magic of being in college, and a hell of a lot more attentive in class." Before long the word got around campus about Charlie Fenton, the charismatic newcomer from Yale. Daughter Wendy began hearing about how marvelous her father was. By the end of his first year, according to one colleague, Fenton had become "by far the most popular professor at Duke—much to the resentment of the stodgy old liners in the department."

As a tenured full professor, he was for the first time in the position of voting for or against the retention and promotion of young instructors. It was surprisingly difficult to vote no, he found, but he managed to, "since [his] colleagues among the bearded sages always vote for everybody, on the highly professional grounds that 'he's such a nice fellow.'" Fenton was not at all reserved in disparaging these elders, expressing himself vigorously within and without the English department. Louis J. Budd, an assistant professor with a distinguished future ahead of him, kept expecting Fenton to get into a fight with the dogmatic and dictatorial Clarence Gohdes, editor of *American Literature*, who said outrageous things and ordered people around in department meetings. One day, Budd felt sure, Fenton would say "Oh, bullshit" to Gohdes, but the explosion never came. Each of them, Budd retrospectively concluded, must have recognized in the other someone who had no fear and played for keeps, and so avoided conflict.

Where the Duke administration was concerned, there was conflict aplenty brewing. On one of his first days, Fenton paid a visit to the nearest notary, who turned out to be the secretary of President A. Hollis Edens. While Fenton was in her office, the president swept by, pausing to shake his hand en route: "his hand was damp, he needed a shave, and his eyes were furtive—but otherwise an impressive figure of a man." On his heels came Vice President Paul Gross, who also shook Fenton's hand. The two administrators, he soon discovered, were bitter foes in a "palace revolt," with Gross "preparing to jap" Edens. This controversy—any controversy—struck him as "a fine thing all around," Fenton told Kerr in a letter of 29 October 1958. He added that he had "been approached by a secret society more loathsome than B-n-s [Skull and Bones] in its pomposity," that he had "issued an inflammatory statement about integration," and that he was generally enjoying himself. In mid-November, Fenton heard that Tom Mendenhall had been named president of Smith College. As a fellow deserter from Yale, he took a "certain small and ill-becoming satisfaction" in Mendenhall's departure. But also, as he told Chester Kerr, he felt real satisfaction for their friend, and "the profession at large will benefit from it. Goddam. I'm delighted."

At just about this time, six weeks after Fenton met his first class at Duke, his *Stephen Vincent Benét* biography appeared, earning the widespread national attention that most professors only dreamed about. The book was reviewed everywhere, and for the most part favorably. Perhaps the strongest review came from Paul Engle in the *Chicago Sunday Tribune*, who declared that "no reader of American literature, no library with an address on this continent [could] afford to be without this book . . . one of the best biographies of a literary figure to appear in a long time." His admiration was "immense," Mark Schorer wrote from California. He'd learned things that would be of real benefit to his own Sinclair Lewis biography. The subtitle of the Benét biography, *The Life and Times of an American Man of Letters, 1898–1943*, spoke to Fenton's own purposes and ambitions. In Benét's trials and his devotion to his craft, his family and friends, and his country, he found a model to live by. He was also attracted to the resolute liberalism of Benét's politics, as he had been to Hemingway's. He set about putting together a volume of Benét's letters, and on a more ambitious scale started collecting notes toward a major study of the Spanish Civil War and its impact on the United States.

At Duke, "numbers of creatures" climbed the five flights to Fenton's library office with copies of the Benét book for him to autograph. "[N]oticeable among them" were "instructors up for promotion," he joshed to Chester Kerr. Actually younger members of the faculty gravitated toward Fenton, who despite his full professorship was not yet 40 years old. Some of these had arrived as he did in the fall of 1958. Gaddis Smith, his former student at Yale, came to Duke to teach beginning history classes while finishing his dissertation. The English department brought in several men on temporary appointments who like Smith had not yet completed their doctorates. Among these was the writer Reynolds Price, who graduated from Duke, went to Oxford as a Rhodes scholar, started writing his first novel *A Long and Happy Life* (1962), and returned to his Alma Mater to teach. Price was the only one among the "class of 1958" additions to be retained in the English department after a three-year appointment. He stayed for a long while. In the spring of 2008, Duke honored him with a celebration of his 50 years of teaching and of producing novels, poems, plays, essays, and memoirs.

Charlie Fenton heard about Price's fiction and made it a point to look up the issue of *Encounter* containing "One Sunday in Late July"—a substantial chunk of Price's novel-in-progress. One day Fenton accosted Price on campus: "that's a whopper of a story," he said in his side-of-the-mouth bantering way. Price, 14 years Fenton's junior and a beginning instructor to the older man's full professor, was naturally pleased. Like many others on campus, he was impressed by Fenton's "manufactured (or maybe not) Hemingwayesque persona" and his general air of informality. Fenton was the first full professor Price had ever seen who met his classes without wearing a tie. He would arrive in freshly ironed khakis and immaculate tennis shoes, roll up the sleeves of his buttoned-down Oxford cloth shirt, and start the 50-minute hour. This approach immediately distinguished him from the senior professors in the department who were sometimes amiably referred to as "the old farts." Fenton openly ridiculed them, much to the amusement of the younger faculty and the cadre of graduate students.

The most important thing about teaching, Fenton believed, was not to "put off students" with an air of superiority. He was "trying to shake up things," said Bill Combs, another instructor who started at Duke in 1958, trying to change the pedagogical style of addressing students *de haut en bas*. The word about Fenton's classes rapidly spread around campus. In spring of her senior year history major Mary Church and several of her friends enrolled in his undergraduate American literature class, and were swept away by the experience. They'd never encountered a professor like this tall, slender, and engaging fellow, with the furrowed brow of a craggy New Englander. Fenton was witty, vital, exciting. The class was like "going to the movies." Above all he communicated with his students, was interested in them, managed to make them feel co-equals in the fascinating business of learning. "He brightened our lives," she recalled. "He was our hero."

At least four students in that class, including Mary Church and her fiancé Henry (Hank) Rouse, switched fields in order to study for a master's degree in English with Fenton. When they embarked on their graduate studies,

Fenton called them up to his "wonderful" office in the tower of the library—pictures of World War II bombers on the walls—and immediately steered them toward fresh and unexplored thesis topics in twentieth-century American literature. For Mary it was the early writings of Willa Cather; for Hank, the baseball writings of Ring Lardner. "He was the best teacher we'd ever had," she said. "He took the extra step for us."

Among other graduate students who became close friends of Fenton were Calvin Skaggs, Merrill Maguire, Michael True, and Frank Gado. "We were all very excited about Charlie Fenton," recalled Skaggs. The other full professors were "august and austere," and students were expected to approach them with reverence. Fenton, in contrast, seemed to be "one of us." You could talk to him, have a conversation as with anyone else, and this was true in class as well as out. Skaggs, who taught for fourteen years before embarking on a major career as a producer and director of films, learned a great deal from Fenton about teaching as well as literature. In his classes, he recalled, Charlie spoke with passion and conviction about the prose writers he most admired—Hemingway, Faulkner, Fitzgerald. He paced in front of the classroom, relating layer after layer of the text to the students' own imagination and experience. And he relaxed the atmosphere with humor, drawing people out and inviting questions, even personal questions. Perhaps a third of his students were bewildered by this approach, so much less rigorous—on the surface—than what they were used to. The other two thirds were "bowled over," and half of those—say, 10 in a class of 30—actually became Fenton's friends. A few took away from his courses "the greatest gift of all: the sense he radiated that teaching and writing about American literature" was a calling worth pursuing.

Merrill Maguire began her studies at Duke simultaneously with the arrival of Fenton in 1958. This was not a coincidence, for she had won a three-year graduate fellowship that required her to spend at least the first year at a university in the South. Her brother John, studying at Yale, consulted Norman Holmes Pearson about where she might go. Pearson advised her to choose Duke, where his protégé Charlie Fenton was about to begin his classes in American literature. Merrill came, discovered that Fenton was "like a breath of fresh air in that environment," and stayed at Duke to finish her doctorate. She married Cal Skaggs in August 1960, and in due course became professor and dean at Drew University, and a leading authority on the work of Willa Cather.

Both Mike True and Frank Gado enrolled in Duke's graduate program in the fall of 1959, took Fenton's courses in late nineteenth-century and twentieth-century American literature, and chose him to direct their graduate writing—in True's case a dissertation on Randolph Bourne; in Gado's, a thesis on Hemingway and Camus. He was "an amazingly good teacher" and "extraordinarily generous to me" as a youthful aspirant in the field, True said. Gado too admired Fenton for his teaching, and especially his meticulous preparation. The lectures were written, but in accessible prose, not at all "embalmed on the page." Gado was not a note taker, relying on memory, and Fenton would catch his eye in a classroom full of students with bowed heads, busy making notes. There was a certain kinship between Charlie and both of these young men as rebels against privileged establishments. True was a devoted adherent of nonviolent and peace movements, Gado a more generally and less religiously inclined defier of authority.

Not everyone at Duke regarded Fenton so favorably. He was an iconoclast, after all, someone interested in knocking down statues and violating accepted standards. He was "certainly not my ideal of a university professor," the wife of one of his colleagues observed. She was particularly offended by Charlie's derogatory comments about his seniors in the department. According to Bill Combs, who came to Duke in 1958 on a three-year appointment, "the faculty had some good old-fashioned professors and some not so good, who'd got lazy." Fenton joked about the gentleman scholars of the old guard and excoriated the lazy among them. These men—very few women had yet entered the profession—were not amused when word of their new colleague's disparaging remarks filtered back to them, but they could not help being impressed by his accomplishments as a scholar and author. Impressed, and resentful. Charlie Fenton rode down out of the north and published twice as much as anyone else. He became a spokesman for the young instructors in the department. Graduate students broke off dissertations with others to begin again under his tutelage. In the faculty dining room, he usually sat alone, or with his juniors.

He may have been generating envy, but over the months Charlie Fenton settled in at Duke, happy in his work and his status. Gwendy Fenton did not. Her mother died in 1955, and her brother and only sibling in 1957. Her father then remarried, and Gwendy and the stepmother did not particularly like each other. So it must have seemed as if the foundations were collapsing around her as she dutifully accompanied her husband to Durham. She felt whisked away from her Madison, Connecticut home, the friends she loved, what remained of her family, and never felt comfortable in the South. Nor did she readily adjust to the role of the submissive faculty wife. Faculty wives of the time were supposed to take care of the house and the children, fit in socially, and keep themselves informed on arcane matters in their husbands' fields. Sometimes they were asked what department they belonged to (Kernan 93–94, Pritchard 113). Gwendy valued her independence too much to play that game.

Soon after the Fentons arrived in Durham, another couple in the English department invited them to dinner. They accepted, but a few days in advance of the engagement, Gwendy called their hostess-to-be. "Charlie says to tell you we can't find a babysitter," she said. The hostess recommended a couple of sitters, one living near the Fentons' house on Perkins road. Gwendy then said, "Do you want us to come, or would you like to ask someone else?" Of course she wanted them to come, the hostess insisted. On the night in question, the Fentons did not turn up for the dinner party, cutting off any further social connection between the two young academic families.

At the cocktail parties they did attend Charlie and Gwendy frequently descended to squabbling. They quarreled about money, Gwendy complaining about their poverty and Charlie berating her about the phone bills she was running up to keep in touch with her sister-in-law Alice and others in Madison. These "loud disagreements" at parties, Reynolds Price thought, predicted the "George and Martha shouting matches" in Edward Albee's *Who's Afraid of Virginia Woolf?*

For the Christmas season in 1958, Gwendy and the children decamped for Madison while Charlie remained at Duke to do research in the library. She also went north during the summer of 1959, renting a beach house while her husband taught summer school and worked on manuscripts. Charlie's letters during those absences let her know how much she was missed. "[M]e and the animals are still alive, though all of us very lonely and gloomy," he reported on 20 December 1958. Mister, the German Shepherd and very much Charlie's dog, was the principal animal, the others being Poopsie and Wandy, more or less Gwendy's cats. Some of the loneliness was relieved when Richie, then enrolled at Southern high school in Durham, came back from Connecticut. On Christmas eve, he and Charlie drove around the area looking for someplace to have dinner, and ended up eating their steak "surrounded by darkies" in a festive "colored restaurant" in Chapel Hill. On Christmas Day they were the guests of outgoing English department chairman Charles Ward and his wife. Also in attendance were Lionel Stevenson, an authority on the nineteenth-century English novel, his "motormouth" wife, and "the very dear Will Irving," the former department chairman. "Richie had not believed my description of Mrs. Stevenson," Charlie wrote Gwendy at 6 P.M. Christmas day, "and was dumbstruck by her chatter." The fruit cake Gwendy left for the occasion "was a colossal hit, and there were many regrets" at her absence. The turkey was good, the stuffing terrible and not enough of it. Richie and he gorged themselves anyway, "not knowing God knows when our next meal [would] occur, having been deserted by she who should be looking after us." He urged Gwendy to get back soon, perhaps in time for the New Year's Eve party at Professor John Fisher's house. She could catch the 10 A.M. train in New York and he'd meet her in Raleigh that same evening. He'd been watering the plants fairly regularly and feeding the cats, but, he warned in conclusion, he could not be counted upon to do either chore much longer. She'd better come home.

In the relationship between the Fentons, Gwendy played the nurturing wife to her rather pampered husband. When in residence, she took care of all practical matters—not an unusual pattern in mid-twentieth century American marriages.What was different was this particular husband's attractiveness. Fenton was "a good-looking guy," Lou Budd recalls. Budd's wife was annoyed at the way that women, young and old, flocked around him at parties. And he cut a rather dashing figure driving around in his Hillman Minx convertible, even if—in "car nut" Tom Greening's view—that sporty British import was "a lousy, underpowered car." Fenton was driving, as it turned out, without a valid license, for somehow he'd managed to flunk the North Carolina driving test and never bothered to retake it.

Joanne Marshall, a neighbor girl then in her early teens, developed a schoolgirl crush on Charlie. Later to become the well-known writer Joanne Mauldin, she spent a good deal of time at the Fentons. "He secreted hormones," she said, and he was nice enough to talk to her "thoughtfully and patiently" about the books she was reading and her literary aspirations. One day when Charlie was walking his German Shepherd, Joanne rode up on her bicycle and Mister, startled, bit her on the leg. When she got home with the news, her mother called Gwendy to say that she would have to take Joanne to the hospital. Which Gwendy did. Gwendy struck Joanne as less well-groomed than other faculty wives; it was rumored that she cut her own hair with nail scissors, and she kept an untidy house. But she was always kind to the teenage girl who hung around the place, obviously smitten with her husband.

In April 1959 Wendy Fenton and Paul Nielsen, another Duke undergraduate and like her a "faculty brat," the son of a physics professor, met and fell in love. Early in June, when Wendy went back to Madison with her mother and siblings, Paul wrote her in distress. They had to be together. Couldn't she find a way? She could, pleading the need for a summer school course in Geology, and so came back to live with Charlie—and see Paul—by midsummer.

From the first Nielsen was as bedazzled by Charlie and Gwendy Fenton as by their daughter. Durham itself was still a provincial community at the time, he later realized, "a 1950s kind of place," very reserved, and that was true of his own family as well. It was quite different at the Fentons. Both of Wendy's parents treated him as an adult, and that surprised and pleased Paul, then a rather naïve college freshman. He thoroughly enjoyed the repartee, the kidding, the lack of reserve in the Fenton household. Paul thought of them as cosmopolitan, urbane, witty, and not the least bit shy about their sexuality. Paul vividly remembers the time Gwendy grabbed Charlie by the crotch, saying "Your pants too tight? Your pants too tight?" There was not a snowball's chance in hell that Nielsen's mother could have done or said that.

Nielsen especially admired Charlie, who erected no barrier of dignity. "He was always more alive than anyone I'd known," Paul remarked. He regarded Fenton as a model of male possibility: worldly and charming, warm, welcoming, handsome, and occasionally "wicked," as during his drinking days. Both Charlie and Gwendy meant a lot to him, and never more so than in the fall of 1959, when he and Wendy decided to tell them their secret. Gwendy was the first to get the news, and when Charlie came home around five, and went to his study to read, she relayed the word that "Wendy's pregnant" as the two young lovers stood in the doorway. Charlie put down his valise, smiled, shook hands with Paul, kissed Wendy, and said "Congratulations." Gwendy immediately began planning the wedding. There wasn't the faintest hint of parental disapproval.

The Fentons managed to spend a pleasant week at Longboat Key, in Florida, with Charlie's brother Dave and his wife over spring break in March 1959. It was the only vacation the four of them ever took together. Early in June Gwendy drove up to Madison in the family Ford while Charlie remained in Durham to teach both summer school sessions at Duke, turn out articles, and add to his research notes on the Spanish Civil War. His letters to her depict a devoted husband, strongly bonded to his wife sexually and genuinely lonely in the absence of his family. Son Richie characterized their relationship as "terrific and strained." The strain emerged when they quarreled in public. The letters show the terrific side. "My darling Gwendy," he wrote the day after she left, "I miss you all terribly." As soon as he could wangle some travel money from Duke, he'd come to see her.

Much of the news from the home front involved the pets, and especially Mister, his German Shepherd, who misbehaved badly when left alone in the house. On separate occasions Mister managed to knock out the screen for the breakfast nook over the driveway, to destroy another screen beside the front door, and when more securely locked inside to leave a foul-smelling mess in the hallway. Mister also scared the trash man so badly that he threw the can at him and it went bouncing down the driveway. Strictly a "one-man dog," Mister belonged to Charlie, who forgave him, cleaned up after him, and walked him through the woods in the afternoon. Fenton's schedule took him to campus in the morning, with a visit home around two for the walk with Mister. Several times a week, he followed this routine with nine or eighteen holes on the Duke golf course. His favorite partner was Al Tischendorf, a professor of Latin American history at Duke and a close competitor. Charlie told Gwendy about these outings—one day, he reported proudly, he shot a 78—while acknowledging that he'd much rather be playing with her. Charlie's work did not greatly interest her. Golf and bridge and the children they had very much in common.

And sex. Repeatedly Charlie wrote of his yearning for her. Gwendy did not write as often, preferring to pick up the telephone instead. "It certainly was wonderful to talk to you today," he wrote on June 26. As a consequence of their talk, he made arrangements to fly to New York on Monday, June 29, and booked them a double-bedded room at the Biltmore. He had the rendezvous all planned. Aunt Alice could look after Andy for the night. Gwendy could catch a train from New Haven to arrive at Grand Central around 5:30 or 6:00. He'd meet her at Grand Central. "We will have a chance to get acquainted at the Biltmore before dinner," Charlie promised, "and we can get well acquainted before taking a train back to New Haven Tuesday morning."

Still, the specter of jealousy hovered in the background. When it had been determined that Wendy would come down to attend the second summer session starting in mid-July, Gwendy made a crack about Wendy's presence "cramping Charlie's style." He had no style to cramp, he insisted. Wendy's "not going to take my typewriter away from me, is she, or forbid me to go to the Library in the evening?" In fact, Wendy's arrival improved matters considerably at the house on Perkins Road. She often cooked for the two of them—or for three, when Paul Nielsen came to dinner and cleaned up the dishes afterwards, a chore that Charlie was inclined to put off. During that time, Wendy also agitated "furiously that she simply must have her name changed" to Fenton—Charlie had been her father, after all, for 15 years—and he consulted a lawyer about that possibility.

Summer school would be over in three weeks, Charlie wrote Gwendy early in August, so he proposed another reunion in New York, this time at the Hotel Delmonico. She'd sent him a picture of herself in a skimpy bathing suit, displaying her shapely legs. He'd put the photo in his workroom, over the desk. "It certainly will be exciting to attack you, baby," he told her. "[T]ake care of yourself, and be assured of my undying love and lust." Gwendy was not so assured. It seemed to her that he sounded entirely too cheerful in his letters. "Only a gallant pretense," Charlie responded, but finally her jealousy boiled over and she called him with her accusations. "I forgive you for being so horrid [on the phone] but only because I love you so much," Charlie wrote her the next day. It made him miserable to think of Gwendy upsetting herself with such fantasies. "I am glad that you are jealous of me, as I am certainly jealous of you, but don't make yourself wretched for nothing—you have all my heart and no girl ever had a more devoted and single-minded mate than you have." As the summer school grind wore down, he reiterated this reassurance.

*The Fentons at home, ca. 1958: clockwise, Richie, Gwendy, Wendy, Charlie, and Andy.
Fenton Family Photo*

"You are all of life to me, baby, and my lust is overpowering. God forbid that I should ever be separated from you again." Before long, this feeling would change. It may well have begun to change already. For Gwendy was right: there was a girl, and her husband was falling in love with her.

Charlie Fenton's career reached its ascendancy during the months ahead. Despite his emotional turmoil, he had never been more productive. There were several books and articles in the works. He did some reworking of his war novel, transforming it from *The Trotters* to *The Long Summer*, and sent it to Malcolm Cowley at Viking. Fenton began with a sort of hero in bomber pilot Johnny Frome and ended with his accidental death in an accident, but as the novel proceeded Frome became peripheral to the experience of the first-person narrator. "In this rewriting," Cowley wrote, "it becomes more and more apparent that you don't especially want to tell Johnny's story. This is your story. It is the story of how you sweated out 30 missions with the percentage all against you. Johnny's death is only one crisis in that story, which doesn't end with the summer but with the 30 missions somehow flown, or you excused from the last of them for some reason, or you going on the trot. I don't know, you may have some resistance against telling this part of the story, but if the book is going to be a true one and a complete one somehow you have to give. That's the trouble now—at some point the reader feels that you have stopped giving, that you have started something and not carried it through to the end." And it was wrong, too, to omit love and sex on the grounds that "all that business has been so overdone." The "honest thing to do," he felt, "would be to give." At the same time, though, Cowley made it clear that the door was still open at Viking Press for "this marvelous material." He suggested that Charlie put it aside for a while, perhaps until the next summer, and then "reshaping and making the story a whole story." In reply Fenton thanked Cowley for once again reading his "saga of the dear days with the English. Believe me, I appreciate your labors with it. Send the son of a bitch back and I'll have another go at it."

At Duke, Fenton applied for a subsidy to support publication of his history of the National Institute and American Academy of Arts and Letters. The Duke Research Council, with historian John Tate Lanning as secretary, received two strikingly divergent readers' reports on Fenton's manuscript. The first somewhat negative report came from the eminent Harvard professor Howard Mumford Jones, himself a member of the Institute. Jones disliked the early section of the book, where Fenton made fun of the founders of the organization. What Fenton derided as the last gasp of tired gentility Jones regarded as "an idealistic tradition" that continued to offer "a far better basis for cultural democracy than Mencken's plea for an enlightened few or the picture of the American presented by Faulkner, Hemingway, Eliot and others." Upon reading this and by detective work discovering Jones as its source, Fenton commented that "[n]o wonder the sage was so vexed by my tone. Those were his buddies that were being knocked."

A second and extremely favorable report was contributed by Mark Schorer, as ever Fenton's advocate. The Research Council agreed on a subsidy, publication seemed assured, and Fenton wrote Cowley on 30 December 1959 asking if it was all right to dedicate the book to him. Cowley accepted with gratitude, adding the caveat that it be made clear Fenton was articulating his own and not necessarily Cowley's opinions in his occasionally inflammatory prose. In closing his letter to Cowley, Charlie contemplated the sunniest of futures. "Life is increasingly delightful down here," he wrote. "My work is thriving and now that my dependents have become heartily adjusted to life away from New England I am feeling more and more my good fortune in clearing out of New Haven when I did."

A week later, Fenton got word that he had won a $6,000 ACLS grant to complete his ambitious "history of the Spanish Civil War (1936–1939) as an American experience," defining its impact on such national institutions as "the arts, the press, the universities, the federal government, the church." Looking ahead, he planned to use the grant to support a leave from January to September 1961 and a trip to Spain. Duke agreed to supplement the ACLS money with a non-taxable $600 grant of its own.

Back at Yale, Chester Kerr was guiding Fenton's edition of Stephen Vincent Benét's letters through the publishing process. And President Whitney Griswold invited Fenton to deliver a talk on Alumni Day (20 February 1960) as part of special ceremonies honoring three centuries of publications by novelists and poets and playwrights who had attended Yale. On that occasion Fenton, who shared the platform with Robert Penn Warren (Yale M.A., 1952), concentrated on Benét's devout anti-Fascism, stimulated in good part by the war in Spain, on the liberal stance he adopted in his late stories, and on his refusal to kowtow to editors and publishers.

Benét got into a dispute with the *Saturday Evening Post* over a story called "Schooner Fairchild's Class." Wesley Stout, the *Post*'s editor, felt that Benét had placed unduly partisan and inauthentic sentiments into the speech of Yale undergraduates in the story, and asked for revisions. Benét's livelihood depended in good part on the $2,000 a crack the magazine was paying for his stories. But, as he told his agent, he simply couldn't make any revisions. "[If] you have to class-angle a story for the *Post* as you'd have to for the *New Masses*, only in reverse — well, there's no point in my trying to write for them. . . . Where the hell does Stout think he gets his three million circulation? From the Union League Club?" Fenton admired Benét for taking such a stand. It was part of a devotion to "the American republic" and "the cause of human freedom and anti-totalitarianism" that he shared with Benét ("Yale Writer" 22–23). He was broadening his compass, turning away from strictly literary studies to more comprehensive subjects.

After his talk to the alumni, Fenton joined a number of Yale friends at Berkeley, his old college. The psychologist Leonard Doob was there, and got the distinct impression that Fenton resented Yale for letting him go, yet at the same time wanted to be asked to return. Fenton's "pleasantest impression" of the visit came from A. Whitney Griswold's offhand comment upon bidding him farewell. "Hope to see you back here soon," Griswold said. That, along with the invitation to address the alumni, must have struck Fenton as a latter-day recognition that Yale had made a mistake in delaying his promotion.

At Duke as well, he was in demand as a speaker, as to the several hundred graduates of Duke University Woman's College who assembled for Alumnae Day on 9 April 1960. The ACLS grants, officially announced to the press on April 18, gave evidence of Fenton's increasing prominence among the nation's scholars. George Winchester Stone, executive secretary of the massive Modern Language Association, sought out his assistance on a delicate matter. The MLA wanted to elect a few leading contemporary creative writers as "Honorary Fellows," Stone explained, but did not want to embarrass itself or these writers by refusals. Ernest Hemingway had been unanimously chosen by "a distinguished committee." Would Fenton sound Hemingway out as to whether he would accept the designation? Fenton would not, thinking the proposal nonsensical.

During his two years at Duke, Fenton learned a great deal about how universities should conduct themselves, and expressed his views in a series of articles. In these pieces, he was no longer content to knock down the existing edifice of higher education. Instead he began to propose ways of rebuilding. Seeking out constructive solutions represented a considerable alteration in Fenton's outlook, who had once told a student of his at Yale that "academic life is like a cesspool: the biggest turds rise to the top." As a full professor at Duke, however, Fenton was increasingly called upon to influence academic decisions. He hoped to make a real difference in the profession.

In the fall of 1959, for example, Fenton became involved in two important matters on campus. The English department decided to hire "a good young critic" to expose their graduate students to some "decent instruction in critical theory." Fenton, who was "practically stone cold deaf" on the subject, nonetheless took a leading role in the search. In correspondence with Schorer, then chairman of the department at the University of California, he mentioned various candidates while amusingly denigrating his Duke colleagues. They were liable to make remarks like, "Well, yes, he seems to have done good work, but is he the sort of person who'll fit in?" In a last note on the subject in

January 1960, Fenton wrote that the great "Search for a Critic" was continuing. "I'm now pressing for Leonard Unger [at the University of Minnesota]. One of my colleagues murmured, 'Jewish name, isn't it?' Charming."

The second issue had to do with Duke's athletic program weakening academic standards. Fenton served as chair of a Graduate School committee investigating "the practice here and elsewhere of permitting graduate students to participate in intercollegiate athletics." In other words, the committee was charged with looking into "redshirting": the then-unusual and later commonplace custom of holding student-athletes out of competition for a year to let them recover from an injury, or—less justifiably—to better suit the needs of the team involved. Such a student might either delay graduation, or graduate and still be eligible for another season of competition. In that way, for example, a football coach with two or more gifted quarterbacks on his team might shunt one to the sidelines for a year and call on his services when the other talented player had used up his eligibility. It was primarily football—a sport over-emphasized at Duke as on most college campuses—that resorted to redshirting.

Seeking advice "elsewhere" as recommended, Fenton wrote to athletic director Delaney Kiphuth at Yale. The Ivy Group, Kiphuth replied, had adopted an eight semester rule as a safeguard against redshirting. All students were required "to use up their athletic eligibility . . . during their first eight terms of attendance at college." The Big Ten was also observing this rule, Kiphuth added, and he recommended that the Atlantic Coast Conference, to which Duke belonged, follow suit. The ACC did not do so, the Big Ten reversed its position, and redshirting continued at Duke as at most other universities: an example of the over-emphasis on athletics at the expense of the academic program that Charlie Fenton—like many professors—deplored. Unlike most of them, he was bold enough to say so, and in print.

Intercollegiate football was one of three Duke institutions he attacked in an editorial forum on "The Purpose of the University" in the *Duke Chronicle*— the undergraduate daily—for 10 February 1960. The university's function was to extend human knowledge through teaching and research, Fenton began. Athletic training and competition constituted "a valid division of university life, since they contribute to our understanding of both the body and the spirit." Yet then, with characteristic brio, he castigated the "surrender" of football to "bands of athletic directors, public relations experts, alumni, and trustees . . . No amount of pious gabble about financial profit, the support of minor sports, the opportunities for education for deserving athletes, or the acquisition through football of national luster, can disguise the various degradations of the university ideal which are inevitable by-products of big-time football."

Fenton was surely tilting at windmills, for fifty years later it remains true that faculty idealists are basically powerless to change the athletic programs of their institutions. In addition, by expressing his convictions so vehemently, he alienated many readers of the *Duke Chronicle*. The adversarial position he took on fraternities was also sure to produce indignation among alumni. Briefly a member of an undergraduate fraternity at Yale himself, Fenton of Duke declared that they corrupted the very values of the university. As with football, he disparaged fraternities by dismissing the usual arguments in their favor. They could "be defended," he wrote, "only by a fatuous double-talk about social adjustment, good fellowship and the mystic opportunities for personal growth."

Having offended football fans and fraternity members and supporters, Fenton proceeded to address the even more sensitive subject of segregation. Duke did not, in 1960, admit African-American students. This was wrong, Fenton declared. "Any university—and most explicitly a private university—should be open to all candidates for admission who are qualified to profit from an association with the university. The cause of human knowledge is not served by segregation, whether it is the segregation which says that the Negro is an outlaw, or that the Jew is an alien or that residents of one region have a prior claim beyond the claims of residents of a more remote region. You can't segregate knowledge. You can't ration the truths of a university among an elect and a non-elect."

These were ringing, even statesmanlike words, and heartened more than a few students and colleagues. But they outraged others who felt strongly about maintaining the status quo. Duke and Durham were, at that precise time, in the throes of racial unrest. On 2 February 1960, eight days before Fenton's remarks against discrimination, four black students at North Carolina A&T College had marched into Woolworth's at Greensboro, NC, sat down at the lunch counter, and refused to leave unless they were served. Their intrepid action attracted nationwide publicity and inspired other college students in the South to follow their example. Shortly after Fenton's impassioned appeal was printed, a number of Duke students participated in sit-ins at the downtown lunch counters of Woolworth's, Kress, and Walgreen's in downtown Durham. They surrounded and welcomed the African-Americans who came in to order lunch in these segregated areas. Some blacks and demonstrators were arrested, Woolworth's closed its lunch counter, and six days later Martin Luther King, Jr. came to Durham and told a crowd of 1,200 at White Rock Baptist Church not to fear going to jail for standing up for their rights. "Maybe it will take this willingness to stay in jail to arouse the dozing conscience of our nation."

In speaking out on this issue, Fenton well understood that he would make enemies. That was precisely what Duke University itself should be doing, he declared in the final paragraph of his comments. According to cultural anthropologists, he said, Americans "often place too high a value on being loved." Not Fenton, and if he had his way not Duke. The best way to evaluate a university's achievement, he felt, was to judge it by its enemies. It was not a coincidence that Harvard, the leading university in the United States, had been detested at one time or another in its history "by the least attractive elements in our society," and not a coincidence that the major individual figures in American university life were regularly "abused by the Klan, the Legion, the DAR, and the most ignorant public officials. If you were curious about a university's fulfillment of its mission, he concluded, "ask yourself who its enemies are" ("Purpose").

Fenton's controversial statements in the *Duke Chronicle* ran alongside high-minded generalizations drawn from the speeches of President A. Hollis Edens. To wit: "We have a heritage on which we are building and to which we owe much: the spirit of free inquiry, the perennial concern with good teaching, the spiritual and moral tone that pervades the institution." Nothing to get aroused about there. A Southern gentleman and "good old boy," Edens was loathe to displease anyone. Besides, he was in the last days of his power struggle with Vice President Paul Gross. The board finally resolved matters by disposing of both men. "All is panic and alarms here," Fenton wrote Malcolm Cowley at the end of March. "Five weeks ago the Trustees forced the resignation of the President, an oaf, and last week they fired the Vice President, a sensible and energetic man. So the faculty is whirling dizzily in its confusion, sharply divided into two camps, each with an equally insane position. I spoke my piece loud and clear and then retired to my office, spitting on both camps."

Fenton was still playing the rebel for Cowley. Actually, he had begun to think that he might induce some reform in higher education through the vigor of his writing. Fraternities and football were sacred cows, he knew, yet someone needed to speak out against them. As for integrating the student body, Duke was only two years away from admitting a few token African-American students. He had other causes in mind, too, pertaining directly to his experience on university faculties. He wanted to redefine the role of the writer-intellectual as a standard bearer in American society. In his final year at Duke, as his young colleague Gale Carrithers put it, Charlie Fenton "forged a series of articles—compelling, witty, always impassioned, always controlled—on responsibilities in undergraduate and graduate education. His concern was no less than how our democracy may know itself and train its leaders" (Carrithers).

As Fenton finished these pieces, he sent them to Ashbel Brice, editor of the Duke University Press, as part of a book tentatively titled *The Writer as Professor, and Other Essays.* Often he added a self-deprecatory note: "[h]ere's another statesmanlike pronouncement to add" to the work-in-progress. As he envisioned it, the book would be divided approximately in half between literary essays deriving from the war and his studies of Hemingway and Benét, and between articles addressing the current status of American universities in general and English departments in particular. The articles in part one had all appeared in journals or as introductions to books during the 1950s. On 1 January 1960, he drafted a preface about the origin of these pieces. Several had been written, he noted, at the suggestion of "a fine and generous teacher, Norman Pearson. Some were written at home, some in a gothic office [at Yale], and one of them—and not, embarrassingly, the worst—was written while proctoring a three-hour final exam. One of them paid some very old bills, and one bought a sailboat [that was for Richie], but most of them bought nothing but the package of fifty reprints and the two free copies of the magazine" ("Preface" vii-viii).

Part two, by contrast, was to consist of the essays he composed during 1959–1960, about the current state of the university. The titles tell the story: "In Defense of Literary History," "The Care and Feeding of English Departments," "Publish or Perish Revisited," "The Sweet, Sad Song of the Devoted College Teacher," "Graduate Schools and the Humanities," "Duke's Mixture: A Harvard for the South—Maybe," and—most audaciously–"Down with the Trustees." In these essays Fenton had important and invigorating things to say about the profession he had joined.

In his book on Hemingway, Fenton described how one talented youth converted himself into a professional writer. In his biography of Benét, he wrote about how such a writer might best fulfill his function in a democracy. Hemingway and Benét, both ardent supporters of the leftwing Loyalists in Spain, led Fenton toward his projected book on the Spanish Civil War. Working early and late hours in the library, he assembled enough notes toward *The Last Great Cause* to fill twelve boxes. In the process he was stretching himself into international politics, as filtered through the context of American observers and participants. In his articles about higher education, he was also spreading his wings.

As a preliminary piece to his investigations into the state of higher education, Fenton included Sinclair Lewis's evisceration of the American Academy of Arts and Letters in his Nobel Prize acceptance speech of 10 December 1930. At the time, Fenton said, the members of the Academy and Institute were firmly committed to electing young writers "as little unlike themselves as possible," or at least likely—by virtue of their "Eastern birth, Ivy League education, and Anglo-Saxon parentage"—to shrink into facsimiles of themselves. For a decade the academicians had been slandering Lewis and his work. Upon hearing of Lewis's winning the Nobel Prize, for example, Academy member

Henry Van Dyke—popular writer, Presbyterian minister, Princeton professor, and according to Justice Oliver Wendell Holmes "the kind of man who could strut sitting down"—took umbrage. The award was an insult to the United States, Van Dyke declared. "It shows the Swedish Academy knows nothing of the American language. They handed Lewis a bouquet, but they have given America a very back-handed compliment." *Main Street* and *Elmer Gantry*, in his view, were far from the best in American writing. Why, there wasn't a single girl in *Main Street* "with whom you could fall in love."

Lewis heard about these remarks on the boat that took him across the Atlantic, and in Stockholm he lashed back. The American writer "has no institution, no group, to which he can turn for inspiration, whose criticism he can accept and whose praise will be precious to him," he declared. He listed those writers that the Academy had excluded in addition to himself, "all the rejects of official American literature: Dreiser, Mencken, Nathan, O'Neill, Millay, Sandburg, Jeffers, Lindsay, Masters, Cather, Hergesheimer, Anderson, Lardner, Hemingway," et al. The Academy did not "represent literary America of today. It represent[ed] only Henry Wadsworth Longfellow." This tale, drawn from Fenton's monograph on the Academy and Institute, ran in the Autumn 1959 *South Atlantic Quarterly*. ("The American Academy . . . vs. All Comers" 582–85).

Thereafter he turned his attention to issues that more immediately concerned higher education. In his article on "The Care and Feeding of English Departments," for instance, Fenton uncovered problems that continue to beset those departments to this day. The young instructor or assistant professor of English faced a difficult future, he wrote. He was part of a vocational paradox. "The chemist is a trained technician. He is what he teaches: he is a chemist. The sociologist is fully capable of professional work in the field. Only the English teacher, with rare exceptions, has not practiced regularly what he teaches. He has traditionally been a great reader of books, but not a writer of them." Hence he earned little respect from his students, who logically considered him a stereotype of someone "who teaches because he cannot do" (204). Usually, also, the beginning English professor was paid less—sometimes far less—than his counterparts in other fields. This unhappy situation was made still worse by a departmental hierarchy in which senior professors hoarded their privileges, year after year demanding to teach their favored courses and assigning the ill-paid junior ranks to elementary courses alone. As a corrective Fenton advocated at least a modest redistribution of advanced undergraduate and graduate courses to energetic younger teachers.

Another conspicuous division within English departments pitted specialists in American and British literature against each other. For generations, the British teacher-scholars ruled, but by 1960—and increasingly thereafter—American literature was making inroads against that dominance. Students gravitated toward courses on American authors, and away from the traditional core curriculum in English literature. Inevitably battle lines were drawn between teacher-scholars in the two fields, with some disciples of the new specialization going so far as to propose a separate fiefdom of their own. Fenton, although an Americanist, was dead set against such a breach. "It would be a professional catastrophe," he wrote, "if graduate students in American literature were allowed to complete their training without a coherent base of instruction in British literature." English literature laid the essential groundwork for its transatlantic counterpart. Not for nothing, Fenton pointed out, was Bryant called the American Wordsworth and Cooper the American Scott (205).

These schisms between old and young, English and American, worsened the notoriously bitter relationships that characterized English departments, then and now. As Fenton put it, one "would be hard put to locate any other Department which contains more small wounds and more aggrieved members who must never under any circumstances be invited to parties attended by certain other departmental colleagues." The pattern of ongoing animosity within English departments, undoubtedly facilitated by the members' capacity to express their views in vivid and forceful language, derived from Charlie Fenton's experience at Yale and Duke in the 1950s. Yet it remains accurate when applied to other institutions fifty years later.

While he was at it, Fenton inveighed against "the shocking practice of employing first- and second-year graduate students as part-time instructors" of freshman classes, especially classes in composition. These instructors usually chose to enter the profession for the excellent reason that they would be paid to talk about literary works they valued and admired. Then, with little or no instruction, they were put to work evaluating relentless outpourings of dreadful prose. These teachers, their students, the department, and the reputation of the university all suffered from such a system, Fenton commented. The only winners were the bottom-line budget-makers who through use of "sweated, untrained personnel" were enabled to pay wages far below those of the competitive market (205–06).

As to course work, Fenton had a few specific changes in mind. He advocated a course on the practice of literature as a profession, for example, and instituted such a course himself at Duke that looked into such customarily ignored matters as writing fiction for a particular market, the role of publishing houses and editors and agents, and the nature of popular taste in a democracy. Students of American literature in particular, he also felt, "*must* be reprieved" from the "meaningless and antique" requirement of a course in Anglo-Saxon literature. Adequate courses in the neglected field of colonial American literature "*must* be added" to the curriculum. Dissertations on living or recently dead authors "*must* be allowed without reservation to qualified doctoral candidates" (207). Not *should*, but *must*: Fenton did not pussyfoot.

In two other essays, he tackled "the sanctified principle of publish or perish" ("Publish or Perish Revisited 5), endorsed by nearly every English department in the United States. As a prolific professional writer himself, Fenton stood to profit from the emphasis on publication. But he nonetheless predicted, correctly, that for departments to rely heavily on publication as the single most important factor in hiring, promotion, and tenure was "going to become increasingly contradictory, increasingly difficult, and increasingly absurd" (4) in the years ahead. At 1960, American universities were rapidly growing, with the wartime baby boom about to generate an influx of students and a corresponding demand for teachers. Only a small percentage of those new instructors, Fenton believed, would have acquired the basic training in research to enable them to compete in the academic publishing market. His own case was unusual: at Yale he had benefited from the mentorship of Norman Pearson, Richard (Ditsie) Sewall and Benjamin Nangle (fellow instructors in Daily Themes), and Chester Kerr. But few other beginning instructors, he knew, would be so fortunate. And besides—though he did not say so—only a fraction of the well-trained would also possess the talent and the drive to become consistent publishers. Perhaps twenty per cent would be qualified to become regular contributors of books and articles, and eighty per cent would not. This would result in unendurable tensions within departments, with the disadvantaged majority in revolt against the stars—a few of whom would inevitably descend into sluggards when awarded premature promotion.

Manifestly, then, departments needed to widen their standards. Exceptional teachers should be retained and promoted as well as exceptional scholars. The problem was how to determine who these teachers were. Too often, then as now, judgments were arrived at on the basis of "second-hand faculty innuendoes or casual student reaction." Fenton proposed two different methods for evaluating good teaching: widespread use of student questionnaires and classroom visits by at least two senior professors. The systematic use of questionnaires, common enough in the twenty-first century, was strongly resisted in 1960. A popular and successful teacher himself, Fenton cited some of "the pious objections" of the time to questionnaires: undergraduates were too immature, colleagues too vulnerable, findings too inexact. Yet at the very least, he maintained, a judicious and unbiased use of questionnaires would "indicate the extremes among the instructional staff," pointing almost infallibly to the outstanding instructor and the least effective one in a group, say, of half a dozen.

Classroom visits, unlike student questionnaires, have not yet become commonplace in the profession. Many teachers still resist them. The presence of an authority figure in their classroom—where the instructor customarily rules as king or queen—might throw them or their students off stride, they argue. In addition, the need to visit classes would significantly add to the workload of a department chairman or director of undergraduate studies. There was also the objection born of snobbery: visitations might be all right for a teachers college, but improper and out-of-place in a liberal arts college or university. This kind of "genteel distaste" Fenton condemned as intolerable, especially in the light of the alternatives. "A system of visitations which permits cross-checking of professorial response is a great deal more desirable than a system which encourages professorial whim, momentary spleen, or downright malice" to dictate career-shaping decisions. Unless English departments instituted such measures, he asserted, they would be in the position of the farmer who told the government agent that "he didn't want to read any goddamn pamphlets on better farming methods: he wasn't even farming *now* . . . as well as he knew how" (6–9).

Feeling as he did about the importance of both teaching and research, Fenton abhorred the periodic attacks—they have not stopped—against "publish or perish" from college teachers who complained that their contributions were ignored while all academic rewards went to dry-as-dust scholars who couldn't or wouldn't teach. It simply wasn't true, he wrote in "The Sweet, Sad Song of the Devoted College Teacher," that "the conscientious teacher is somehow, magically, conspiratorially, victimized by the alleged emphasis on research and publication." Teaching 9 or 12 hours a week was hardly a full-time occupation, he declared, much to the consternation of most of his colleagues. Research, the obligation to contribute to human knowledge, was also part of the job. "[T]he teacher who honors and undertakes research is in reality an infinitely more devoted teacher than his colleague who bleats that research interferes with his devoted teaching" He has more to teach, more with which to inspire his students who might otherwise succumb to the national emphasis on "vocationalism and careerism and conformity and adjustment." Teaching and research were so entangled, he said, that they must not be separated. "No teacher can undertake a scholarly book or an extensive laboratory project without enlarging in some way his classroom effectiveness and his utility to his students."

Yes, Fenton admitted, every campus had its pedants who yearned for post-doctoral programs in which classroom teaching might be nonexistent. He had no patience with these pedants, but thought they did less harm to the profession than teachers who sought to make a virtue out of doing no research. The pedant only bored his students. "The stagnant college teacher . . . corrupt[ed] them by his own fluent superficiality" (361–64).

Fenton was here responding explicitly to "the dirge entitled 'Too Many College Teachers Don't Teach,'" which appeared in the *New York Times Magazine* of 21 February 21 1960, "under the coy pseudonym, John Q. Academis." His reply ran in the *AAUP Bulletin*, after editor William P. Fidler persuaded him to tone down the bitter sarcasm—note "dirge" and "coy" above—on the grounds that "a slight relaxing of indignation" would result in a more effective argument. Fidler hit upon a problematic strain in Fenton's writing. He liked confrontation and cultivated controversy, a habit of mind that disqualified him from positions of leadership (not that he aspired to them) in any university administration. His intemperate prose made enemies. It also got people's attention, which was what he was after.

In other essays written during his last months, Charlie Fenton spelled out in specific terms how Duke might grow into one of the nation's great universities. Founded and funded by tobacco tycoon James B. Duke, the institution had in thirty years transformed itself "from an obscure Methodist college with an enrollment of four hundred—Trinity College—into a stable university with an excellent Medical School, a fine Forestry School, a modest Law School, a Graduate School which annually award[ed] about a hundred advanced degrees, a student body of five thousand, and a faculty of eight hundred" (2). But, Fenton pointed out in "Duke's Mixture: A Harvard for the South—Maybe," the young university had been "prematurely decorous and conservative" (3) from the beginning, and that would have to change before Duke could achieve a distinct identity of its own. "Cells" of Harvard graduates occupied major positions in the administration and on the faculty. The college hierarchy would make no move, plan no new departure, until it was satisfied that there were precedents at Harvard or Yale or Columbia. These were excellent models to imitate, but such professional caution inhibited local inventiveness and prevented initiation of "fresh or radical proposals" (8).

Still, Fenton observed, Duke was attracting quite good students. A primary reason—and one of the institution's great advantages—was coeducation. Duke Women's College was located on one end of campus, the male students of Duke itself at the other, but the twain met for classes and of course for social occasions as well. Here, as Fenton put it, was a neo-Ivy League college "which furnishe[d] desirable companionship," very much a rarity in 1960. He quoted a Duke sophomore on the subject: "When I finished four years at Exeter, I said to my mother, 'Mom, I gotta go where there's girls." But that lad, and others like him, would discover that a "covey of attentive big brothers, vice presidents, YMCA directors, and student counselors" hovered over the social scene at Duke, lending to campus gatherings the air of church socials (10–11).

This "bureaucratic paternalism" that harassed Duke undergraduates with a "web of restrictions" was paralleled by the administration's "benevolent emasculation" (12) of the faculty. There had been one shining moment, he felt, when the faculty denied the president's request to bestow an honorary degree on Richard M. Nixon, a graduate of the Duke Law School. Usually, though, the faculty stayed submissive, and for good economic reasons. Few universities in the United States could rival Duke in its support of faculty needs, Fenton acknowledged. Salaries and fringe benefits were generous. Money was available for travel and clerical aid. The university subsidized publication of scholarly books and monographs. The excellent library was well-financed. Under the influence of such benevolence, most faculty members were disinclined to object to what Fenton considered the worst aspects of the university (12–13).

Leading his list of these was the understood but not-to-be-spoken-of policy of excluding African-American students. It was "shameful," Fenton wrote, "that the single major private university in the South should permit a group of parochial trustees to block even token admission of Negroes" (9). He also found it objectionable that the institution encouraged and supported fraternities by providing them with buildings on campus, yet another instance of its "fond" and misguided paternalism. Another reform he advocated would do away with what seemed on the surface a desirable practice. Unlike the Ivy League universities it aspired to emulate, Duke bestowed tenure at the end of three years instead of six. In theory, this promised a young instructor, "humanely, that he [would] not be retained until the threshold of middle age and then released into a cold marketplace." In practice, however, this meant that only a handful of instructors were ever retained, for three years was "far too brief a time, particularly in the humanities, in which to assess a [candidate]'s potential for mature scholarly achievement." It also opened the door to errors in judgment, so that the few who did get "premature tenure" were liable to prove unworthy. Better to follow the six-year policy of the Ivies, he believed, even in the face of the accusation that "Harvard and Yale take the best years of a man's life and then throw him out" (14–15).

The real and admittedly harsh truth, Fenton wrote in conclusion, was that a great university could not be built "on charity and decency and good will alone." In an earlier article, he concluded that universities might best be assessed by the enemies they made. Now he added that they could only become great by building upon their losers: the teachers who did not get promoted, the applicants who were not admitted, the seniors whose degrees were withheld at Commencement, the alumni who were not placated. Duke had come far in its short history, but not yet far enough. "A good university is no common thing," he acknowledged, "and it [was] awesome that one should have been created in the South within thirty years, but a great university require[d] cruel rigor as well as warm benevolence" (15).

In "Down with the Trustees" Fenton argued that greater participation in governance by the faculty would be needed in order to grow Duke from a good to a great university. As the resolution of the Edens-Gross dispute made abundantly clear, the institution was under the control of its Board of Trustees, as was the case at virtually all American universities. Ultimate authority rested with the trustees, who at Duke were strongly connected to the Methodist church. They governed, Fenton wrote, from behind the smokescreen of "a managerial agent, the president or chancellor" (5) whom they could hire or fire at will. In a business society, the Boards of Trustees had for fifty years "been composed of industrialists, corporation lawyers, managerial executives, bankers, large stockholders, brokers, and the heirs of long-established family firms"—men of wealth, men of business. But "[e]ducation [was] not a business." A university was concerned in large part with present intangibles and future unknowns, and had "no fundamental kinship" with the money-making objectives of corporations. Business success had little or nothing to do with university excellence (11).

Besides, Fenton observed, Boards of Trustees exemplified the worst sort of absentee governance (15). Ten or twelve times a year they assembled on campus for a day or two, with their time tightly scheduled by public relations functionaries to prevent exposure to voices of dissent. To improve upon this model, Fenton advocated "establish[ing] a beachhead of faculty representatives" on Boards of Trustees. Specifically, he proposed that one-third of the trustees be "practicing teachers and scholars—not deans or vice-presidents." That would "benefit all the parties to the university compact" without destroying the voting majority of the residual trustees (14). "Down with the trustees," he proclaimed, "up with the faculty" (17).

Chapter 7

Sailing through Air

At the beginning of the 1960s, the future looked bright for Charlie Fenton. Nationally his reputation was growing. Yale welcomed him back to talk to the alumni. He won an ACLS grant to write his book on the Spanish war. His book of Stephen Vincent Benét's letters was in press, and three other books of his were on their way to publication. At Duke he was extraordinarily popular as a teacher. In addition he was developing at 40 into that rare creature: a faculty member with important and controversial things to say about the profession. He was off to a brilliant start on what promised to be an extremely productive career. He had less than seven months left to live.

In trying to reconstruct what led to Fenton's suicide, I learned a great deal from several sources. The Fenton family has been wonderfully supportive throughout my attempt to do justice to Charlie's life and untimely death, readily contributing remembrances as well as letters. Fenton's students and colleagues at Yale and at Duke remembered him with a vividness and affection undiminished by the passage of half a century. I consulted archives at various universities and prep schools and the RCAF. It was clear from the beginning that a romantic relationship operated as a contributing factor to his untimely death. But I was still stumbling toward understanding, after finishing a preliminary draft of this account, when it finally occurred to me to look at the papers of Norman Holmes Pearson in Yale's Beinecke library. Months earlier, I had read through the very useful Charles A. Fenton archive there. But the Pearson papers really opened my eyes, for after the death of his student and protégé, Pearson embarked on a campaign of his own to discover the reasons why, and his wise reflections proved invaluable. Even more enlightening were the letters Pearson exchanged with the graduate student at Duke Fenton fell in love with in the spring of 1960.

No hint of that emotional complication was in evidence on the occasion of daughter Wendy's marriage to Paul Nielsen. They spoke their vows early in January in an alcove of the Duke chapel. Andy Fenton, 8, remained riveted throughout the ceremony by the sarcophagi along the walls. At any moment, he expected a ghost to emerge from one of them.

Less than a week later, his head still spinning, bridegroom Nielsen walked into his examination in Introductory Ethics, looked at the questions, froze, and handed in a nearly empty bluebook. Nielsen's philosophy professor failed him, but Fenton came to the rescue. He called the professor and "raised holy hell," demanding that under the circumstances Paul be given a re-exam—which he managed to pass. In the spring semester, Charlie once more intervened on behalf of Nielsen, seeing that he was transferred from his assigned section of Sophomore English to the one taught by Gale Carrithers, a rising star among the younger faculty. Nielsen was grateful for these acts of kindness, and acutely aware of the prominence and popularity on campus of his new father-in-law.

Duke students had their own secret societies at the time, the White Duchy for female and the Red Friars for male campus leaders, tapped for membership much as Yale students were for Skull and Bones. Yet another organization, the Order of the Chair, sprang up to ridicule the solemnity and self-importance of the exclusive groups. Fenton was the sole professor invited to attend and be inducted during the Order of the Chair's mock ceremony in the spring of 1960. Paul Nielsen, who with Charlie heartily approved of making fun of the privileged few, was on hand, but Fenton decided not to go. Had he been on hand when "Yale's Charlie Fenton" was hollered—no discreet shoulder taps—Fenton would like the other mavericks chosen have been led, blindfolded, to sit on a commode, consume a spoonful of grits, and shout, "I love my grits." This kind of folderol cooled the hothouse atmosphere at Duke, Nielsen thought.

In his classroom and around campus, Charlie saw Virginia (Ginger) Price, one of the university's brightest graduate students, almost every day. Ginger was born and brought up in the South, traveling around Georgia and Florida as her father's business career demanded before settling in Virginia. She was valedictorian of her high school class, graduated from Randolph Macon magna cum laude and Phi Beta Kappa with honors in English, and came to Duke on a Graduate Assistant working-scholarship in the fall of 1957. The following year she was appointed one of the first Tutors at Duke, and in 1959–1960 she was awarded a University Fellowship as she finished her master's thesis on William Dean Howells. The curmudgeonly Clarence Gohdes directed the thesis. One of the two secondary readers was Charlie Fenton, and she expected to write her dissertation, on William Carlos Williams, under his direction. Ginger received her M.A. in English and American Literature on 6 June 1960, by which time she had won a scholarship for a year's study abroad in Strasbourg, France, beginning in September.

Ginger Price took two classes with Charlie Fenton, and impressed him as very pretty, very bright, very interested. She made intelligent comments and asked penetrating questions, and after a time they continued their conversation after class. She shared his passion for literature, and eventually—and not for the first or last time—a mature professor and young graduate student fell in love. Before long Charlie resolved to end his marriage to Gwendy, a union that several observers at Duke felt had been "waiting to crumble" since the Fentons arrived in Durham. In February they agreed to a divorce, but decided to keep the decision private until June, when both Richie and Andy would have finished the school year. Meanwhile, Charlie and Ginger made plans for the future, and tried to keep a low profile.

In a 2007 article entitled "Love on Campus," William Deresiewicz suggested how such student-teacher liaisons originate and develop. His article began by noting "a remarkably consistent pattern" in movies of the 2000s: an English professor and failed writer who is vain, selfish, resentful, and immature "sleeps with his students, neglects his wife, and bullies his children" (36). After exploring various sociological reasons for this special animus against professors—and especially English professors—Deresiewicz acknowledged that "the relationship between professors and students can indeed become intensely intimate," but that this intimacy was customarily "an intimacy of the mind," or "an intimacy of the soul." One might occasionally uncover a predatory professor who took physical and sexual advantage of this intimacy, but Deresiewicz believed—I think correctly—that these offenders were rare. For evidence he described a conversation with a young graduate student. Did she ever have a crush on an instructor in college? Yes, she had. Did she want to have sex with him? No, she said, she wanted "to have *brain* sex with him" (43).

Professors, for their part, were attracted to students because they still believed, as almost no one else did, that ideas matter. Professors and students thus sought each other out in what Deresiewicz called an "eros of souls" (44)—a love that dare not speak its name to a "sex-stupefied, anti-intellectual" culture. "Teaching, finally, is about relationships," he wrote. "It is mentorship, not instruction. Socrates says . . . that the bond between teacher and student lasts a lifetime, even when the two are no longer together . . . the feelings we have for the teachers or students who have meant the most to us, like those we have for long-lost friends, never go away" (46). So the relationship between Charlie Fenton and Ginger Price began. In their case, the "eros of souls" was accompanied by a powerful physical attraction: she was uncommonly attractive, and he (in the words of another female graduate student at Duke) "the sexiest man alive." And yet, both of them maintained, this intensity did not lead to sexual congress. She was a well-brought-up young woman of 24, taught that sex should be reserved for married people only. He was a widely experienced man of 40, but still a romantic who wanted their relationship to be different. At his insistence, they imposed a chastity rule on themselves. With her sometimes coquettish Southern ways, Ginger was unlike any woman he had ever known. She gave him the love and admiration he coveted, and that was enough.

In retrospect Paul Nielsen recalled a winter afternoon in 1960 when he and Wendy were walking up to Perkins library as Charlie and Ginger came tumbling out. At first Charlie seemed delighted to see them, then looked somewhat abashed. It would be only a matter of time before Gwendy found out, Charlie knew, but he wanted to delay the break until June at the end of the regular academic year. Gwendy had her suspicions—later she told her children that Charlie had uttered Ginger's name while asleep—but did not demand a confrontation until the drumbeat of local gossip reached her ears. In early April she had a call from Hessie Baum, the somewhat deranged widow of Professor Paull F. Baum (she had been his student before they married). She did not mean to make trouble, Hessie said, but she had seen Charlie and Ginger going into the Duke Forest almost every afternoon and thought Gwendy ought to know. This was not true. "For once in my life, I'm innocent," Charlie told Reynolds Price. "Jesus Christ, there are enough motels between here and Greensboro: I don't have to take to the woods opposite Hessie Baum's." But Gwendy could not ignore it, and demanded to know Charlie's feelings. According to neighbor Joanne Mauldin, Gwendy was washing his socks when Charlie admitted that he was "deeply in love" with Ginger.

At this point, their son Andy recalls, his mother "went ballistic." Furiously, she burnt photos and letters as Charlie and Andy watched in silence. As the word spread about Charlie's betrayal, other faculty wives rallied to Gwendy's support. Joyce Tischendorf steered her to local lawyer E. K. Powe to draft a separation agreement; Joyce's husband Al, Charlie's erstwhile golf partner, took his wife's side and broke off their friendship. According to the terms of the agreement, Charlie was to send Gwendy $350 a month, to sign over all benefits from his life insurance policies (Fenton's only real financial assets), and to pay all expenses related to their house until it could be sold and the proceeds split between them. To make sure that news of the affair reached everyone at Duke, Gwendy telephoned the garrulous wife of Lionel Stevenson, naming Ginger as Charlie's partner presumably in sin. Then, without telling Charlie, one day in mid-April she packed up the household goods, and with Richie and Andy drove up to Madison to stay. Two weeks later, Charlie ran across Reynolds Price at the entrance to the library, and unburdened himself of the story. Gwendy took everything, he said. "She didn't even leave me a washcloth." All she left were photos of Andy, to remind him of what he was losing.

Gwendy took the position that if Charlie did not want her, he was not to have any part of the family. Andy did not want to leave Durham, he remembers, but as a third grader could hardly object. Richie came back to Durham to finish his last six weeks of high school, but moved out of the house on Perkins Road to escape the man who had been his father for 16 years and live with the parents of a classmate. Already admitted to Duke, he was mandated to withdraw and enrolled instead at the University of North Carolina nine miles away. Only Wendy, who was living with Paul in their apartment, stayed at Duke and saw Charlie regularly. At 2535 Perkins Road, Fenton was alone but for Mister, who continued to express his doggy displeasure about being left during his master's long days on campus. After a few weeks, Charlie started taking Mister along to his office.

At first he was optimistic about the future, even though it immediately became clear that there would be money difficulties. On April 24 he sent Gwendy a check for $250, $100 short of the agreed-upon monthly sum but all he could manage after making the mortgage payment on the house and other bills. He'd send the balance, Charlie promised, the minute the house sold or he had a check from *Harper's* for the "Down with Trustees" article they were considering. To encourage a quick sale of their house, Charlie spread the word that he'd "be perfectly willing to sell to either a Negro or a Jewish businessman," an announcement that did not endear him to the more militantly racist elements of the community. If in fact the Fentons had sold to an African American, it would have been in violation of a covenant they signed upon originally purchasing the house—a covenant mandated of all buyers by Duke University, the original owners of the land.

Charlie expected, perhaps naively, that the scandal about his affair with a graduate student would soon blow over. "The great moral crisis has settled down a good deal," he told Gwendy. In fact he thought it was being "kept alive solely by the diseased tongues of your dear friend Mrs. Tischendorf and that loonie Mrs. Baum." He was wrong about the house, which did not sell for nearly three months, and even wronger about the "moral crisis," which was building momentum and would turn a wide swath of the university community against him and Ginger Price.

With Gwendy gone, the two lovers walked around campus in the spring, talking with curious intensity but without touching. Usually it was Charlie who talked and Ginger who did the ardent listening. They also appeared together at weekend parties of graduate students and young instructors. Often they formed a foursome with Merrill Maguire and Calvin Skaggs, who were engaged to be married. Merrill and Cal thought it thrilling to have a friendship with "this electric and fascinating, funny and occasionally rebellious professor." Cal hesitated, then made the bold suggestion that Charlie be an usher at their wedding in August. "Of course," he said. "I'd love it."

On a Wednesday night that spring, Cal borrowed a car—Charlie's Hillman would not comfortably seat four—and equipped with a couple of six-packs of beer and something to eat the four of them drove out to a trysting place and parked. Two carloads of Durham teenagers then arrived, shouting threats against them as over-privileged Dukies and rocking the car. Cal was afraid that the townies would bash in the car, beat up him and Charlie, even assault the women. To escape they drove through a creek, up a bank, and into a clearing with a chain preventing any exit. So they had to stop, the boys thundering behind them. "You guys stay quiet and let me do this," Merrill heard herself saying. *One Yankee syllable out of Charlie and we're cooked*, she was thinking. They all got out and Merrill started talking "hick" to the youths, in an accent and language they understood. "Why aren't you boys at prayer meeting?" she drawled. "Do your parents know you're out here?" Ginger chimed in, too, in her southern accent, and the boys backed off. Charlie would have been most at risk, they all realized, if the incident got into the papers: Eminent Professor in Rumble/ With Student Girl Friend.

On a perfect day early in May, the four of them spent an afternoon at the beach. They lay in the sun for a couple of hours, the women tanning and the fair-skinned men turning red. When it was time to leave, there was the clear outline of a white hand on Charlie's scarlet chest, where Ginger had rested her hand while they were sunning. It was the only time he ever saw Charlie totally relaxed, Cal recalled. Usually he was "more or less manic, with incredible energy."

In mid-May Charlie had a call from his mother in Watertown, who was worried about him in his exile. He had not kept in close touch with her since his father's death, and now, living alone in Durham, he tried to make amends by reassuring her—and himself—about his situation. Dorothy Fenton was particularly concerned about her son's separation from Andy, the apple of his eye. Charlie acknowledged that it caused him "real pain to have given up Andy, even temporarily," but he simply "could not have endured the prospect of another twenty-five years of the appalling boredom which marriage represented": an uncharacteristically cruel comment, shifting the blame for the breakup to Gwendy. Were he of a different temperament, less reckless and more expedient, Charlie added, he would never have permitted the separation to take place. But being the way he was, the break was inevitable, "and it would have come sooner had [he] been able to afford it." He was not drinking. He was not running around madly. He was doing his work "and gradually putting together the pieces of the kind of life" he wanted for the rest of his days. And besides, his "young woman" (in correspondence he circumspectly withheld her name) was "enchanting, and someone [his mother] would like and respect a great deal."

It was the letter of a happy man, as he and Ginger were discovering more to like about each other. To her Charlie represented everything "that was noble and fine and extraordinary," and he could not possibly have felt more deeply about her qualities. She opened his eyes and ears, drawing him into her enthusiasm for music and art. He started listening to classical music because she enjoyed it, but soon began listening for himself and talking about it. He discovered a great truth about the difference between Sinatra and Vivaldi, Charlie told her: you could grade papers to Sinatra, but not to Vivaldi, for the music kept intruding on your consciousness. On another occasion he burst into a half-hour eulogy and analysis of baroque music. Ginger, who thought him a genius where literature was concerned, was stunned by Charlie's musical insights. It became a new source of excitement for him, and so did art. Ginger took Charlie to a museum on a day when he was feeling weary, and suddenly he came alive and began discoursing on the painting in front of them. Charlie started with the artist himself, trying to understand him as a person and what he was saying with his lines and colors, and what he felt about the people in the painting. They stayed in the museum for three hours, talking and talking. Charlie used to say in jest, "I have the strength of ten." That afternoon he did, and made Ginger feel she did too.

Ginger was intellectually gifted in her own right. The two of them learned and profited from one another. She was bold enough to tell him that an article he was writing seemed "hasty" and that she thought his novel *The Long Summer* lacked unity. They read Chaucer back and forth to help prepare him for his summer school class, Charlie apprehending one thing after another that she'd absorbed from her graduate studies. He valued her intelligence, felt her sympathy, and spoke to her—about himself as well as their shared professional interests—as he had never spoken to anyone. Seeing Charlie and Ginger together, Gale Carrithers could not help thinking about the wonderful life that lay ahead for them.

But there were complications. Probably no one understood Charlie Fenton better than Norman Pearson at Yale, who early recognized his promise and guided his career. He characterized his protégé in a letter to the psychologist Leonard Doob, another Yale colleague who knew Fenton well.

Charlie always had two very strong pulls in his life: one was toward the solid citizen's status, respected in his community, a member of the school board and the golf club, consulted on matters of importance and responsibility, being a good father, eventually a trustee, and if an academic the holder of honorary degrees. This was an image he tried to break away from and yet coveted. It was related to his father's image and the image of the Yale man. On the other side was the desire to be free, to be the writer who was respected by writers, to be the champion of the weak, to be (safely) the Bohemian at least in speech and sometimes in drink. His marriage was rocky from the beginning, yet he clung to it out of a sense of responsibility for first his stepchildren and then his own son; he used to talk against the irresponsibility of a Hemingway who left wives and issue at the side.

Despite his airy pronouncements about escaping 25 years of boredom, the "solid citizen" in Charlie undoubtedly took on a burden of guilt for breaking off the marriage with Gwendy Then, too, he was financially strapped. As his remark to his mother about being able "to afford" a separation indicated, he had long relied on Gwendy's support. He pursued his professional career, successful but hardly remunerative. She took care of the domestic side of things and contributed to the family finances through the trust fund her first husband set up on behalf of Wendy and Richie. In her bitterness after the breakup, Gwendy told others that Charlie stayed with her until the trust fund was about to run out—that is, when Wendy and Richie reached legal age—and "when the money was running low, he dumped me." On his own, Charlie soon found how difficult it was to get along without the trust fund money *and* without the sizable share of his salary he'd agreed to send Gwendy each month. Nor did he know how to take care of the house, which probably made it harder to sell. Richie came by in mid-May for a brief visit, and found the place in total disorder.

At Duke the gossiping grew worse. "Everybody knew about Charlie's affair with a graduate student," Gaddis Smith recalled. "My trouble is I have a Ponce de Leon complex," Fenton joked to Reynolds Price, but it was not a laughing matter to those who saw in Charlie the prototype of a philandering professor who seduced his student, abandoned his wife and family, and— worst of all—offended the proprieties by appearing in public with her. For her part, Ginger was subjected to censure from faculty wives who rallied to Gwendy's side. At least two of these wives, who did not themselves know Ginger, circulated tales that she had made advances toward other professors. In her extremity Gwendy was more than willing to accept this libel, which was almost certainly false. Ginger was not at all that kind of person, those who knew her best maintain. As then-instructor Bill Combs put it, "[t]here were both women undergrads and grad students at Duke who could be interpreted to be putting themselves in the way of faculty men," but Ginger was not one of them. He remembers her as "a lovely, vivacious, intelligent young woman," a conventional southern girl who seemed less worldly than most graduate students. Ginger was manifestly in love with Charlie, but if he had to bet, Combs said, he would bet that she was waiting until after they were married to consummate their love.

That was exactly the way it was between them, according to both Ginger and Charlie. Ginger told Jim Boatwright (later editor of *Shenandoah*) and Mary Ann Wimsatt (later professor of English at South Carolina), two of her closest friends in Duke's graduate program, that she remained chaste throughout their relationship. Charlie said as much to Chester Kerr and Mark Schorer and others. And it was his decision, not Ginger's, to keep things that way. To many observers at Duke, of course, such an interpretation was hard to accept. They knew what they knew. Fenton had after all given up wife and child, and where there was that much smoke, there had to be fire. He was a bounder and a cad, his "young woman" a marriage-wrecker and sexual opportunist. Ginger and Charlie could not help overhearing the clacking tongues of those who construed their relationship in the worst possible light. Not all of the judgmental were faculty wives, and not all of them were at Duke. Ginger's mother quickly came to like Charlie, for example, but her father threatened to disown her and refused even to meet the man—16 years Ginger's senior, and married!—that she'd gotten herself involved with. And despite her concern for her son, Charlie's mother told him that "of course [she was] sticking by Gwendy."

For Ginger it was a stressful spring: negotiating the maze of her master's thesis, the many hours of separation, the persistent doubts, and the terrible awareness that Charlie had given up for her more than any human should have to bear—wife, family, and house, to begin with. Charlie, full of confidence and courage and plans, got her through that period. Ignoring the disturbing buzz around them, they looked ahead to a happy future. She would take her M.A. in June and embark for France in September. He would teach first semester summer school, go to Mexico for a fast divorce, come back for the fall term at Duke, and use his ACLS grant to travel to Spain early in 1961, where they would be married. It might even have worked out that way.

It seems doubtful that any single event in a man's life can determine his fate. But certain happenings, especially in one's formative years, can play a crucial role in that determination. In the masterful short stories of Frank O'Connor, he sought to recreate such moments of change, events of such significance that "the iron was bent, and anything that happens to that person afterwards, they never feel the same about again" (quoted by Wilkinson, 44). For Charlie Fenton, that event may have been the beating he suffered at the hands of two fellow students during his year at Eaglebrook school. He told Ginger Price about it one day in April 1960. He'd never told anyone else about it, neither his parents or Gwendy or the children. He'd always been afraid to let anyone know about it, he said, but he wasn't afraid now. Remembering the story as Charlie told it, she passed it along in a letter to Norman Pearson.

"I was twelve or thirteen [actually, fourteen] and unhappy with school," Charlie said. "At Eaglebrook everything was organized alphabetically, and so I was thrown in with Darlington and Dayton. We became friends of sorts, and then one day I did something, committed some kind of heinous crime—heinous in boy's code, anyway. I can't remember what it was," he said, "I've tried everything, and even considered writing one of them and asking, but I can't remember. I think that if I could, this mess would evaporate. At any rate this dastardly act somehow concerned Darlington and Dayton, and they came in my room that night and gave me the worst beating of my life."

"When I woke up the next day, I thought the depression came from bruises and because they wouldn't talk to me. But it got worse. I can't explain it. It became a kind of living thing for me—it even affected me physically and I used to look into the mirror to see if my face had changed and to watch my hands shake. I thought maybe I could sweat it out, so I got up early and ran before classes. I'd come back exhausted, shaking and wet, then run some more in the afternoon. But it didn't work. My grades went down. I was afraid to see anyone, afraid to try to talk to them, afraid to do anything except eat and sleep and run. But then I had trouble sleeping too. I'd go to bed aching with fatigue, fall asleep and then jerk awake, wet with cold sweat and terror."

"After six weeks it went away and I've never felt so good. I could read and write and do damn well at both. I had more energy than I could use in a day. After a while I forgot about the depression but it came back again. Soon a pattern became established—a long period of energy and being able to do things and then three months of being a bloody zombie. But I haven't had it in a long time, over two years now," Charlie said. "I think it's gone and it surely can't come back now. Jesus, it's unthinkable."

Ginger was frightened by the story, which Charlie had told with a nervous self-consciousness uncharacteristic of him. When they talked about it later, he would mock himself for letting something so stupid concern him. Yet the more he joked about it, the more significant it became. That he could not recall the nature of his "heinous crime" inevitably invokes the dark realm of repressed memory. What could he have done so awful that he could not let it come to mind?

The school, the place, the other students were real enough. Cully Darlington and Bob Dayton were new boys along with Charlie Fenton during the 1933–34 school year at Eaglebrook. Both Darlington and Dayton were seventh graders, while Fenton, only six months their senior in age, was in the ninth grade. All three boys lived on the same floor in Gibbs house, Fenton in a single room. Although Eaglebrook maintains thorough records, there is nothing in them about the beating Charlie suffered or anything leading up to it. Had the authorities known of the incident, Marshall Coleman of Eaglebrook said, they would surely have taken disciplinary action. Bullying was not to be tolerated.

As aftercomers, looking back two thirds of a century, we are left with a mystery. None of the boys themselves are alive, nor are any classmates who might be able to contribute clues to its solution. The three lads became friends of a sort, then Charlie did something "heinous," was severely beaten, and thereafter scorned by the other two. Several readers, confronted by these bare facts, have jumped to the conclusion that a sexual violation must have precipitated the beating. Such things happened in boarding schools, after all. But that explanation conflicts with what we know of Fenton himself. He would simply have brushed any such incident aside, Ginger feels sure. The man she loved and admired "never had any fears of being homosexual or of having a gay man make a pass at him." What seems more likely is that Charlie did something that betrayed not only a "boy's code" of honor but also his own integrity. He may have made cruel fun of the other boys, or acted superior to them, and in revenge they administered the beating. Apparently, he did *not* go to the headmaster or his house master to turn in Dayton and Darlington, an action that would have violated his lifelong distrust of those in authority. Yet whatever he did so compromised his sense of himself that he repressed the memory.

Gradually Ginger learned more about Charlie's other bouts of depression. During World War II in England, Betty Lyon took him to a doctor who diagnosed a thyroid ailment as the cause of his depression, and gave him medication for that. For a while he felt sure that the thyroid pills were relieving his gloom. "I was capable of getting stinking drunk in those days," he told Ginger, "but even if they had to carry me home, I'd scream for that bloody pill before I passed out." After the war in New York he consulted a psychiatrist, but when he tried to talk about his despondency, it didn't sound real even to him. He dismissed the episodes with false light-heartedness, and the psychiatrist responded accordingly. "Everyone has periods of depression, Mr. Fenton," he was advised. "Don't concern yourself overmuch about them. Plunge into your work when you feel one coming on."

He'd tried to follow that advice when depression overtook him at Yale. There were times when his lectures, his writing, everything seemed worthless. Each day he had to force himself to drive from Madison to New Haven and confront his students and colleagues. He used to shut himself in his office and quake at the thought that somebody might come in. Occasionally he invented excuses to avoid the trauma. On one day he called in sick, and on another, half-way to campus, he called to say his car had broken down. He felt a sense of shame about these episodes, and concealed them as best he could, even from family and friends. Gwendy and the children knew that Charlie suffered occasional "black Irish moods" when he turned mean and hurtful, not his usual witty personable self. Gwendy did her best to talk him through these periods, but no one in the family, least of all Fenton himself, wanted to make much of these episodes. "I lived with him 16 years," son Richie recalled, "and never thought of him as seriously afflicted psychologically." Norman Pearson, as ever perceptive, learned that sometimes Charlie held back from him, not wanting to seem weak, and that he would conceal the facts "with a shroud of untruth. Only one could never be angry with him any more than one could be angry with a son."

During the first eighteen months at Duke, there had been no sign of depression. On the contrary, Fenton's freewheeling ways and imprudent writings managed to offend most of the senior professors in his department and leading members of the administration, making him vulnerable in his marital crisis. Even before Gwendy's departure, the university's new president—Dr. Julian Deryl Hart—came by with the Fentons' next-door neighbor Sally Verner, the wife of Dr. John Verner of the Duke medical faculty, to commiserate with Gwendy, offer his regrets, and express his outrage at her husband's misbehavior. The judgmental posture stiffened as Charlie and Ginger appeared together at campus gatherings, their affection for each other interpreted as a parading of their illicit love. In the late 1950s, early 1960s, divorce was not done on university campuses, especially if a professor-coed affair was involved. Such a messy parting of the ways could undo a career. Ugly rumors flourished and made their way back to him. "I was electrified to learn recently," he wrote his mother, "that it is regarded as a fact among these dirty-mouthed Methodists that my appearance at Yale [in February] was just an excuse to take my young woman to New York for the weekend. *How vile are the righteous.*"

The permanent consequences of the Fentons' separation became increasingly apparent as the spring semester wound down. Gwendy decided to return to Durham for a few days to ship furniture from their unsold house to the one she'd just purchased in Madison. Charlie was instructed to absent himself from the premises during her visit. On May 30 he wrote requesting her to leave certain items behind: the love seat, for example, because otherwise he had "absolutely no living room furniture," the dining room table and chairs, the corner cabinet in the dining room and the Yale china, the record cabinet, either the "North Carolina" or the "Florida" painting, the two mirrors in the front hall. He was "short of everything except books."

He was also short of funds, and once again sent her a check for $250 instead of $350. The separation agreement he'd signed as the offending party rendered it extremely difficult to make ends meet. The sale of the house promised financial relief, but finally Charlie gave up on selling it himself, hence saving a commission, and turned it over to Durham Realty. He had to borrow $750 to pay off the worst of the bills, he told Gwendy, and though there were rumors of "another big across-the-board raise" at Duke (the previous year he'd had a 12 per cent hike to $11,500) he was beginning to have an uneasy feeling that he might receive no raise at all for the coming year. "There's a remarkable amount of venom still encircling me," he explained, and he asked Gwendy please not to "stir up any more trouble" while she was in Durham, for her bread and butter, and Andy's, were at stake, after all.

During her brief stay in Durham Gwendy had a conference with lawyer E. K. Powe, finalizing the trust agreement he'd worked out on her behalf. She also had lunch with Arlin Turner, the rising chairman of the English department, who tendered his regrets and echoed the president's assessment of her husband's moral turpitude. The hard-headed Clarence Gohdes, who had come to admire and respect Fenton, called him into his office one day. His career at Duke was over, Gohdes told him. The first inkling would come when the new salary schedule revealed that he was the only professor not receiving a raise. Charlie would not be discharged, Gohdes said—the administration at Duke, strongly prejudiced against him for his intemperate remarks about blacks and football and fraternities and even the trustees, did not want to stir up a public revolt—but it would be foolish for him to stay there. Gohdes promised to help him get a job at Michigan or Minnesota, and on his own, Charlie began searching for a post elsewhere.

Writing academic friends at the end of May, Charlie confessed that he'd "dropped rather dramatically into the shit" at Duke where his private life was concerned. "For once in my life I'm a vessel of innocence, neither adulterous nor criminal," he insisted, but although the few people he respected at Duke had been "fine," many had found him guilty. So he was looking for a post elsewhere, at "a decent metropolitan university with a good library," and asked the men who'd been his closest mentors and friends—Norman Pearson, Mark Schorer, Tom Mendenhall, Chester Kerr—to keep a weather eye out for him. Despite the uproar at Duke, he told them, there would be no trouble about first-rate recommendations. He just didn't have the appetite to fight the faculty wives.

While acknowledging the uproar at Duke in his 28 May letter to Schorer, Fenton sounded happily optimistic about the future with Ginger. "This is a remarkable girl," he said. "I feel, quite frankly and lyrically, like a man who's been reborn, and rapidly putting together the pieces of the kind of life I've been hoping for for a long time." Schorer, who had just completed his Pulitzer prize winning biography of Sinclair Lewis, assured Fenton that he would land on his feet, and said he would see what could be done at his home institution, the University of California. Kerr, editor of the Yale University Press that was about to bring out Fenton's edition of Benét's letters, replied in the jocular style that marked their correspondence. "The news of your personal life is distressing, sport. You have my keen sympathy—and I mean that. Old Tom [Mendenhall] will be here tonight . . . and we'll plot on your behalf." If he were younger, Kerr added, San Francisco and Berkeley would draw him like a two-ton magnet. "The cosmopolitan west, boy." There was at least an overture from one other source, as well, probably through Gohdes's recommendation. When Richie stopped by 2535 Perkins Road one day, Charlie said he might not be around much longer: the University of Michigan had shown some interest in recruiting him. His teaching and publishing record placed Fenton among the nation's leading scholars. He would have found a place, sooner or later, but nothing was settled.

Early in June, after classes were over and before summer school began, Charlie and Ginger took the trip to Memphis both of them had been looking forward to for months. Ginger had close friends there, with no connection to Duke, and was eager to introduce them to the man she wanted to marry. The long train trip was all pleasure for Ginger, although Charlie was unusually quiet and looked, somehow, different—especially his eyes. The unthinkable had happened. The night before the trip, the old terror spawned at Eaglebrook came back and he wakened in a pool of perspiration. He fought it on the train, but when she mentioned the odd look about his eyes and hands—the "frozen pupils" and "blue fingernails" that announced the advent of his disease—he confessed the truth. In Memphis, sitting on the lawn, Charlie tried to describe what was inside him: the panic, the despair, the raging self-doubt.

Thereafter it became Ginger's role to be forever cheerful and reassuring, to do or say anything to take Charlie's mind off himself. Admiring him tremendously as a teacher and writer and scholar, she now had to praise everything he had done. "Do you really think I did the right thing? Do you honestly find that article well-written?" he repeatedly asked. As the depression took hold, he could rarely think well of himself, yet almost always Ginger was able to brighten the day, lighten the darkness. But only temporarily; it would not go away. "Bleed for me, for I'm in pain," he wrote her—there were many letters, even when they were both in Durham—and bleed she did.

In mid-June Ginger left for Washington, D.C. to live with her parents and take a summer job with the Interior Department. Charlie stayed behind to teach the first semester of summer school. Originally he planned to teach but one course in American literature, but at the last minute he also took on a sophomore survey in English literature—on Chaucer, Shakespeare, Donne, and Milton. That meant a more difficult preparation, and the two classes met one after the other six days a week. It was a draining schedule, but he needed the money. And with Ginger gone he felt increasingly lonely. He had come to rely on seeing her every day, either on campus or at her small off-campus apartment. Daughter Wendy, who hoped that her parents would reconcile, accompanied Charlie to Ginger's place on one of those occasions. She could not help liking Ginger and felt rather guilty about it. Gwendy, hearing the news in Madison, was furious with her daughter.

Charlie Fenton lacked the caution that might have protected him from the verdict of the "righteous." He loved Ginger, she loved him, and he was disinclined to conceal his feelings. Sometimes, Charlie told his young colleagues, it seemed that his life had become an open book. In his admittedly misspent youth, he had broken all the rules in such a cavalier and headstrong way that Roddy Ham constructed a novel about it. At Duke, he had once again become an object of widespread scrutiny, affording people with conventional lives a measure of entertainment and an opportunity for criticism. The difference was that the wildly misbehaving lad of 20 had grown into an idealistic if still temperamentally reckless man of 40, and that he had much more to lose.

The two sides of his personality were obviously in conflict. In a sense it was the rogue in him, the wild artistic streak that spurned convention, that led to the separation from wife and family. The solid citizen in Charlie, on the other hand, insisted on a chaste love affair with Ginger. It was not always easy to observe that chastity. In a preliminary version of this account, I wrote that the two lovers walked around campus in the spring of 1960, holding hands (a Duke colleague remembered it that way). Ginger corrected that comment, emphatically. Had they allowed themselves that kind of touching, they could hardly have stopped there. Charlie demanded of himself—and of her—an ethical standard above and beyond the dictates of the bourgeois world he at once scorned and sought approval from. Despite these self-imposed rules, many of his colleagues and most of the academic community at Duke in the spring and early summer of 1960 regarded him with chilly disapproval. They remembered his scornful comments about themselves and were not inclined to grant him tolerance. The rebellious side of Charlie cavalierly dismissed their judgment. The solid citizen wondered if they might not be right.

Meanwhile he was nearing the end of his rope financially. "Here at last is the bloody income tax form," he wrote Gwendy on June 30. The form needed her signature, and the tax bill also required her contribution of $2500 as well. He'd paid half of that sum, "plus all the Durham taxes, plus the termites, plus the bills," Charlie said. He could do no more, for he was broke and figured to remain broke even after the house sold, what with his commitment to pay the lawyer (Powe was in effect representing Gwendy, but Charlie had agreed to compensate him) and the mover who'd carted off furniture to Madison. Under the circumstances, some bills went unpaid. He was months in arrears on the coal bill, for example, and he was served with a subpoena for a $300 bill Gwendy had run up at a local department store.

His mood was growing ever darker. "[L]ife for me at the moment . . . is hellish," he told Gwendy in an appeal for sympathy she was disinclined to grant. "I'm a local pariah. I'm teaching from 7:30 A.M. to 11 each morning, six days a week, in order to get enough money to pay off that $750 I borrowed . . . I've got an apartment which is hot as hell, and the thought occurs to me with increasing regularity that I'm probably one of the great horse's asses of all time." He was delighted to hear that she was settled comfortably in her new Madison home—and he meant it, Charlie assured her—"and I daresay in time I'll adjust to my situation." Meanwhile, for companionship he was reduced to taking meals at the Holiday Inn with Mildred Anderson and Ben Boyce, two of the more superannuated figures in the stuffy Duke establishment he'd long made sport of. The tone of this letter was far different from that of the businesslike ones he'd sent Gwendy after their separation. For the first time Charlie betrayed a measure of doubt about his decision to opt for a new life.

Most painfully of all—and a piece of news he did not bring himself to tell Gwendy—dogs were not allowed in his apartment and he was forced to have his German Shepherd Mister, a great nuisance but also "a great comfort," put to rest. It was not easy for him to do that. Years earlier, back in Connecticut, he and Gwendy had another German Shepherd who became old and sick and had to be put down. Charlie was supposed to take care of it, and on the assigned day he took the dog in his car—and came back with him. Gwendy had to see to it. Alone in Durham, Charlie had to do the job himself. Losing a creature so loyal to him and dependent upon him had to hurt. He bought Mister a steak dinner before taking him to the veterinarian for the injection, he told Frank Gado. A few days later, having dinner with Merrill Maguire, he spoke about the dog's death with an exaggerated nonchalance that left her aghast. Behind the stiff upper lip she could feel his intense loneliness.

Retrospectively, Gado realized that Fenton was cutting off ties. Mentor and student had similarly bantering styles, but in a late June conversation Charlie spoke to Frank with atypical hesitancy. Both he and Gado were to be ushers at the Skaggs' wedding, with Frank driving them to Jacksonville for the occasion. In the last weeks, though, Charlie told Frank that he couldn't make it for the wedding: he had to go to Mexico instead. But he didn't explain that he was planning to get a quickie Mexican divorce, leaving it to Gado to infer the reason, and he delivered the news with chuckles of embarrassment. "Each of us knew exactly what he was telling me," Frank realized in retrospect, "yet he seemed psychologically incapable of being straight out with it—as though that would nail down in reality what he didn't yet fully believe." A few days later, Fenton called Gado into his office. "Do you think you'll have any problem finishing your thesis?" he asked. "No," Frank said. The thesis was well along, and he could complete it without difficulty. "Good," Charlie said. "I just wanted to be sure you won't have any problems, in case I can't go through the entire process with you." Again, it was left to Gado to assume the unsaid: that Fenton would be leaving Duke, or to intuit the unthinkable: that he was considering suicide.

With his own family gone, Charlie reached out for support to the mother he'd been ignoring for years. She sent him some Berkeley cups (from his college at Yale), and offered to supply flat silver as well for his new domicile. Thanking her for these gifts and for "writing so often—it means a great deal to me right now," he inquired about her holiday plans. Ginger would be in France, and he was reluctant to face the season alone. If Dorothy Fenton was going to be in Watertown, Charlie said, he would love to spend Christmas with her there. Then he was scheduled to read a paper at the MLA convention in Philadelphia on December 27 or 28. At that annual gathering of the professoriate, he could also have spread the word about his availability for a new position or have met and been interviewed by prospective employers.

These plans did not materialize. In the heat of the North Carolina summer, Charlie Fenton withdrew from ordinary social contact. He refused invitations, and failed to show up after accepting one to a cookout at Bill and Marie Combs' house. Around campus he became virtually unapproachable, keeping his head down to avoid conversation. To fight off the melancholy, he went to see Ginger in Washington on a couple of weekends and wrote her often. They were in it together—"I've tied you to a loonie," he wrote her, "I cannot bear it"—and she urged him to see a psychiatrist. Finally he consented, but implored her to come along to talk for him. She did not go, doubting that her talking to the doctor would have done any good or even been tolerated. Neither she nor Charlie—nor almost anyone else, in 1960—knew much about manic depression or bipolar illness. But she did know how sick he was, and in retrospect wishes she had gone down to Durham to help him.

Dr. John Verner, Fenton's neighbor, arranged a consultation for him with Bernard Bressler, a professor of psychiatry on the Duke medical faculty. In preparation for that meeting, Fenton typed out a chronology of past episodes of depression. The part of that document that survives traced only the period from 1934 through his service in World War II. The first entry begins "1934—appears to have been some time between Xmas & Easter that it commenced, after D & D episode [Darlington and Dayton at Eaglebrook]. At this time periods of depression recalled as brief, but equally brief periods of recovery." In the conference itself Fenton told Dr. Bressler that nearly every year since he suffered through "a terribly down period" when life seemed too much for him. In his notes, Charlie also listed "additional physical characteristics" that were troubling him. His flesh marked easily and unnaturally after the slightest pressure. After a shower, he looked for a long time as if he'd been soaking in water. He cut himself often when shaving ("could be nerves not skin"). He was having trouble sleeping. Fenton clearly believed, or wanted to believe, that his recurrent depression derived as much from physical as from mental causes. His illness came along too soon for its symptoms to be ameliorated, if not cured, by drugs. Not until the mid-1960s did the psychiatric establishment begin to shift from the talking therapy alone to a joint treatment with pharmaceuticals (Stossel 17).

To Dr. Bressler, Fenton played down his state of despondency. As far as he could tell, Charlie said, things were going much as they had during his previous battles with depression. He'd survived all of those, and thought he would "come out" of this one too. Concluding that Fenton "was not too deeply depressed," Bressler nonetheless recommended therapy as a way of staving off the recurrence of depressive episodes. Charlie resisted that recommendation: he'd have to think it over, he said. Bressler judged that Fenton "had very strong feelings of shame about entering therapy." And indeed, he'd been brought up according to a code of conduct that held there was something "defeatist" about calling attention to one's problems. Men were supposed to keep their troubles to themselves.

There were other reasons, too, why Charlie decided against treatment. Dr. Bressler made it clear that doing so would involve a considerable investment in time and money, and he had little of either to spare. As a practical matter, he told Bressler, it would be impossible for him to undergo psychiatric therapy in the near future. He was planning to go to Mexico for a divorce, and then had a fellowship that would take him away from the area. What he did not say was that he did not much like the psychiatrist. Bressler told Charlie, for example, that it was guilt that triggered his episodes of depression. He had broken up his family, after all, and in such cases "the superego can come down on conscience like a hammer" (Gass 375). But Charlie resisted that conclusion, and he also formed the impression, as he told Ginger, that the doctor was "positively drooling to hear the details of our sordid affair." At the end of their consultation, Bressler suggested that Fenton contact him soon for another appointment (he did not) and thought little more of it. The doctor did not believe that the man he had been speaking to was liable to harm himself. "Something very traumatic," he commented after the fact, must have occurred to bring him to suicide.

Fenton struggled through the six-week summer school grind, maintaining a high standard in the classroom despite his unshakable despair. "I don't want to sound like the schoolgirl with a crush on her teacher," a bright sophomore in his English lit class told Gale Carrithers, "but he was the finest teacher I've had at Duke." The afternoon after the final exam, she saw Fenton on the deserted campus. As he walked past without seeing her, eyes fixed on the ground, she heard him mutter "God!"

When the summer school session ended in mid-July, Charlie went up to Washington to see Ginger. They selected their china and silver, and visited with her mother, but he was obviously in desperate straits. Usually Ginger could haul him out of his depression—no one else had ever been able to, he told her—but this time she could not. Nothing worked, and she gave up out of exhaustion. She knew that Charlie "had somehow separated himself" from her and that she "didn't have the strength to force him to bring his trouble into the open." Something in her felt relieved when he left on Tuesday morning, July 18. Despondent as he was, Charlie tried to be upbeat. "Don't worry, darling," he told her. "We'll find a fiddle for death." Such "a Charlie thing to say," Ginger thought, and deriving from English slang he'd picked up during the war:

Fiddle Verb: to cheat. Noun: a fraud or cheat.

In 1943 he had managed to cheat death by surviving an unspecified number of bomber missions and then going AWOL, being busted in rank, and doing time in the stockade. It had been hard enough for a tail gunner to beat the percentages. It would be still harder for a deeply depressed man of early middle age to find another fiddle.

Before he left Washington on Tuesday morning, July 19, Charlie shook Ginger by the shoulders. "You are *not* to worry," he told her. "Soon I'll be back. I'll be fully back." He was worried about many things—money, his career, the need to go to Mexico, the havoc he was wreaking on those he most cared about—and when he got to Durham that afternoon, there was only bad news. A last-minute glitch had come up, and the sale of the house had not yet gone through. He heard a rumor that Gwendy had started drinking. His world was collapsing around him. The much-anticipated future was beginning to look like a myth. A new job? But because he had to! And having to go through another uncertain initiation at another university. A new wife? But her father would not receive him. His son Andy? A thousand miles away. He'd dragged Ginger into despondency, and made Gwendy desperately unhappy. Whatever he did was certain to hurt someone, and it was no one's fault but his own. His troubles would be over, and everyone better off if he were gone. He started making plans.

At 9 A.M. on Wednesday, July 20, Charlie Fenton left his stifling third-floor apartment and drove his Hillman Minx to the Lancaster Street apartment of Wendy and Paul Nielsen. Nervous and chatty, he paced back and forth. "I've made a terrible mistake," he told Wendy. "I've got to get your mother back." Then he called Gwendy in Connecticut—he'd not yet had a telephone installed at his own apartment. He pleaded for forgiveness. Ginger was just a silly girl, he said, and he'd never laid a hand on her. He loved Gwendy and wanted to reconcile their marriage. It was as if he were trying to obliterate the past few months. "We'll get the house back," he told Gwendy. But it was about to sell, at long last, so how could they do that? And besides, that prospect was hardly an inducement to Gwendy, who had left Duke and Durham behind. It was a long telephone call, with Charlie more or less groveling. Finally, though, Gwendy agreed to meet him the following day in New York. *That was done.*

Charlie swung into action. He bought a plane ticket to LaGuardia, and arranged with Wendy to drive him to the Raleigh-Durham airport. *That was done.* He tidied up the remaining tasks of his summer school courses, returning papers to students, converting Incompletes to letter grades. *Done.* At the library (where his office was located) he spoke briefly with Reynolds Price at the entrance to the stacks, "looking a bit frayed and harried." When he turned in his grades at Central Records, the secretary mentioned that he didn't seem his usual cheerful self. "Well," he said, "maybe it's because I had my dog put to sleep." Dr. Bressler had given him a prescription for tranquilizers, but Charlie had not had it filled and eventually misplaced it. Urged to do so by Ginger, Charlie called Dr. Bressler's office to get it renewed. He could not get through to the doctor, the nurse-receptionist could not arrange for the prescription, and he gave up. *Not done.*

He wrote a letter to Ginger, postmarked Wednesday afternoon. He told her that the house had not sold, and with the closing date still uncertain, he might not get back to Washington as soon as he had planned. He felt harassed by all the complications he faced, and matter-of-factly mentioned "the low point" of their last day in Washington. He said nothing to her about calling Gwendy. The letter ended, "God bless you, my darling, and take care of yourself. All my love—all all all." *That was done.*

Ginger did not receive that letter until it was too late, but she'd grown frantic about the depth of Charlie's depression after he said goodbye to her in Washington. Unable to reach him by telephone, she called fellow graduate student Paul Hurley in Durham on Wednesday and asked him to find Charlie and have him call her. Hurley contacted everyone he could think of, but could not locate Fenton.

That same afternoon, Gwendy and daughter Wendy spoke woman to woman on the phone. Gwendy said she planned "to tell the son of a bitch where to stick it" when they met in New York, and made it clear that there were "no guarantees" of a reconciliation. Still, Wendy was hopeful, especially when she heard that her mother was having her hair done and buying a new dress for the occasion. "Sure, she would have given him some grief," Wendy acknowledged, but she believed they probably would have reconciled. Charlie needed Gwendy, she felt. She was "his rock": always there, a source of stability.

Fenton came back to the Nielsens' for supper. They listened to the radio news and talked about the election. Richard Nixon was coasting toward the Republican nomination for president, and Charlie, seeming "hyper and excited," hoped the Democrats would choose young Jack Kennedy to run against him. There was talk about the possible reconciliation with Gwendy. At one point during the evening, Wendy cautioned Charlie that "she may not take you back this time." But did he really want to put his family back together, to recover Andy, to restore himself to a position of public acceptability? Was he willing to debase himself to Gwendy if that was required? He had not broken off with Ginger, after all. It was as if he wanted to leave each of them feeling that he cared for her, most of all. Before he left, Charlie said he would swing by in the morning for the drive to the airport. Wendy could have the use of the car while he was away. *That was done.*

Charlie left the apartment about 7:40 P.M. and stopped by Frank Gado's apartment to drop off the copy of Anthony Trollope's autobiography he'd borrowed. Gado invited him in for a visit, but no, Charlie said, he had errands to run. *Done.*

In his autobiography, interestingly, the British novelist Trollope described an unhappy childhood that in important ways paralleled Fenton's. His father, a failed London lawyer and unsuccessful farmer, sent Anthony to Harrow School as a day student when he was only seven. There the headmaster repeatedly flogged him. At 12, he went to Winchester college, where his older brother thrashed him daily as a means of exacting obedience. Perhaps even worse, Anthony felt himself unworthy alongside his fellow students. "What right had a wretched farmer's boy, reeking of a dunghill, to sit next to the sons of peers—or much worse still, next to the sons of big tradesmen who had made their ten thousand a year?" (Trollope 10). Reading about these trials, manifestly worse than his own, Fenton would have been reminded of his boyhood at Eaglebrook and Taft—both the sense of social insecurity and the trauma of being beaten up.

After leaving Gado's, Charlie drove downtown to check in at the Washington Duke hotel, which was in the process of changing its name to the Jack

Tar. He signed the register under his own name, gave his address as Madison Avenue, Madison, Connecticut (Gwendy's new address) and went up in the elevator to his room on the eighth floor of the twelve-story building, the second tallest in town. *Done.*

Fenton barely disturbed the bed linen in his room and may not have slept at all. According to the desk clerk, he left the hotel and returned a couple of times during the night. Once he went back to his quarters at University Apartments, where the occupant of the apartment directly beneath his heard him walking about after midnight. While there he wrote a kind of informal will and testament and then, thinking better of it, tore it up. *Not done.* He also typed a brief description of himself, and left it behind.

Fenton checked out of his hotel room at 4:30 A.M. He may have been having second thoughts. Fifteen minutes later, though, he came back and asked to re-occupy his room. He'd been unable to get his car started, he told the desk clerk, and wanted a place to rest until a mechanic could be summoned. The elevator operator took him back upstairs. Charlie then mounted to the twelfth floor—the only door to the roof was supposed to have been kept locked—and, apparently with the aid of a tool from his car or apartment, managed to remove the tightly secured screen from a hall window on the Market Street side of the building. Had he jumped from there, he would have landed on the parapet of the hotel's lower-level commercial structure. Instead he crept around the narrow outside ledge to the Chapel Hill Street side (or possibly managed to mount to the roof, from where a running start would account for the remarkable trajectory of his fall) and plunged to his death shortly after 5 A.M. *Done and done.*

Two early-morning construction workers on a nearby job—"L.R. Fisher and Amos Cook, Negro"—chanced to look up and saw Fenton "sailing through the air." He cleared the sidewalk and landed on his stomach in Chapel Hill Street. The body was found at 5:18 A.M. Death was instantaneous from hemorrhage and shock, county coroner D.R. Perry reported. "Entire body mangled and crushed. Fell from 12th floor window, Washington Duke hotel. Fractured skull and most of bones of body." The impact ripped all the seams on his clothes, and they contained no identifying documents. After talking with the hotel staff, the police concluded that the body must have been that of Charles A. Fenton, and learned that he had been a Professor of English at Duke. Professor Arlin Turner was summoned to identify the body. By breakfast time the local radio was carrying the news. The *Durham Sun*, the afternoon daily, ran the story under the sort of banner headline usually reserved for the beginning and end of wars.

DUKE PROF LEAPS TO DEATH HERE
Dr. Fenton Seen 'Sailing Through Air' Near Hotel

The story, by Dick Barkley, revealed that Fenton's valise, wallet, and watch were found in his eighth floor hotel room. The wallet contained $102 in cash and a card certifying that in the previous fall Charles and Gwendolyn Fenton had joined the PTA at Lakewood School, where Andy was enrolled. No car keys were located, and there was no driver's license, for Fenton continued to drive without one during the 18 months after he flunked the North Carolina driver's test. The story mentioned the "recent separation," and quoted Sheriff Jennis M. Magnum as saying "he understood that Dr. Fenton's wife and children [were] living" in Madison, Connecticut.

The full impact of the suicide struck hard among friends and colleagues in Durham. Fifty years later, Fenton's plunge to oblivion remained "the ultimate horror story" at Duke, Reynolds Price said. "There's never been anything else as bad as that." Those who knew Charlie Fenton remember where they were and what they were doing when they heard about it.

Gaddis Smith was living in his air-conditioned office to avoid the heat while working to finish his dissertation. Smith's mother did not know that he'd abandoned his apartment, though, and repeatedly tried to telephone him there. Desperate with worry, she finally called the Duke campus police. The police reached Smith on his office phone in the early morning of July 21 and before transferring the call from his mother, asked whether he knew Professor Fenton. Indeed he did, having been his student at Yale and his occasional golf companion at Duke. So, after quieting his mother's anxieties, Smith called the campus police back to find out *why* they asked him if he knew Charlie, and heard the terrible news. The body had just been identified, they said, but a few minutes earlier they were still looking for someone to help with the ID.

Shortly after 6 A.M. Paul Nielsen was about to leave for his summer job when *his* mother called from across town. "Don't go to work," she told him. "Don't turn on the radio. Meet me at the corner outside." There she told him about Charlie's death, and Nielsen broke down, crying as he never would again, not even when his own parents died. Then he had to tell Wendy, still in bed: a young husband, weeping at the bedside of a young wife, neither of them yet 21. Beset by obligations—*who was going to tell her mother?*—Wendy fought off her distress to make the necessary phone calls. She got in touch with her grandfather, who was at a meeting in New York, and he instructed her to call Aunt Alice, Gwendy's sister-in-law, in Madison. Aunt Alice, in turn, relayed the terrible message to Gwendy Fenton.

Around 9 o'clock Bill Combs was sitting in the barber's chair. "Oh, you work over at Duke, don't you?" the barber said, and turned on the radio. Combs was so shaken he thought he might throw up—and still not entirely surprised. Charlie was "kind of an erratic guy," he knew.

Joanne Marshall biked downtown to the scene of Fenton's suicide. She marveled at his navigating the hotel ledge before leaping, and watched, numb, as the police hosed down the street. A charismatic man was gone, and she would cherish his memory. "Be kind to Charlie," she told me when she heard I was writing about him.

Mary Church was badly shaken when she heard the news, and Hank Rouse took her for a long walk in the Duke Forest to recover. She could not forget the last time she'd talked with Charlie, early in the summer. She had a part-time job in Duke hospital's psychiatric ward, where she'd had met a troubled and talented young patient who wanted to be a writer. "Bring him to class," Fenton said when she told him about the youth. "Anything we can do for him, we should." Then there was an awful aftermath. Three years later, when she and Hank were married and living in New York, her husband—suffering from fierce headaches and the side effects of drugs he was taking to control them—took his own life with an overdose of sleeping pills. The following Christmas, her brother, who was a great friend and admirer of Hank's, shot himself. It was as if the three men were granting one another serial permission to commit suicide.

In Ravenswood, West Virginia, on a business trip to the Kaiser Aluminum plant, David Fenton got the call from Wendy. Dave understood that as Charlie's brother and the only adult member of the family able to do so he must take over. He rented a car for the five-hour trip to Durham, arriving at mid-afternoon. He telephoned his wife Boyd in Toledo, who got on a plane to deliver the news to Dorothy Fenton. When Boyd walked into her room unannounced, Dorothy with a mother's intuition grasped the situation at once. "Who is it?" she asked. "Charles or David?"

At 11 A.M., Sheriff Mangum conducted a search of Charlie's N3B apartment with Wendy and Paul Nielsen and the manager of the University Apartments. Wendy found the penciled note on Washington Duke stationery in the wastebasket, torn into six pieces. Taped together, it read:

July 20, 1960

Please notify my daughter of my death—Mrs. Paul Nielsen, Lancaster Street, Durham. Telephone, 89979. My automobile, a 1956 Hillman, is parked in the municipal parking lot. I would like to bequeath it to my daughter, and urge her to redeem quickly the Eastern Air Lines ticket which is in the lefthand glove compartment. All my other worldly possessions, such as they are and such as she wishes, I leave to my beloved wife, Mrs. Charles A. Fenton, Madison Avenue, Madison, Conn.

This note, torn and unwitnessed, was eventually ruled invalid as a will. Fenton left yet another note along these lines, crumpled and unsigned, in his hotel room wastebasket. It read "this is my last will and testament" and stated that he was leaving "all of my property to her," with the "her" unspecified.

A third note was found later in Charlie's apartment. In the center of the page he'd typed CHARLES FENTON, and under that a list of attributes—"Intelligent," "Trustworthy," "Masculine"—as though he were assessing the image of himself he was striving for. At Fenton's funeral Norman Pearson could not stop thinking about that sad epitaph. "The poor bastard," he kept muttering to himself, "the poor bastard."

Police located the Hillman Minx in the municipal parking lot with two parking tickets under the windshield wipers. It was unlocked with the keys inside, and started without difficulty. The airline ticket was in the glove compartment. The cramped back seat area contained Charlie's golf clubs and his Hermes portable typewriter—the first thing he'd bought after returning from the war. Ginger sped down from Washington as soon as word reached her about Charlie's suicide. Thursday afternoon she came over to commiserate with the family. The visit did not go well. Charlie had not written his brother David about Ginger, and David, almost inevitably, could not help regarding her as an intruder. In a gentle way, meaning it as a kindness, he apologized to Ginger that Wendy and Paul had told her about Charlie's apparent reconciliation with Gwendy. *As if that mattered*, Ginger thought. Charlie was dead, and she was devastated. Besides, she could not believe that he ever planned to go back to Gwendy.

Dave Fenton made the arrangements with Hall-Wynne mortuary in Durham for transportation of the body to Swan funeral home in Madison. Thirty eight people signed the register at Hall-Wynne during the brief visitation hours, including Arlin Turner, Grover Smith, Louis J. Budd, Gale H. Carrithers, Jr., John H. Fisher, Ashbel Brice, James Wimsatt, and Paschal Reeves from Duke. In Madison, there was a large turnout for the funeral at the Congregational Church and the burial in West cemetery.

Chapter 8

What Might Have Been

Those left behind wondered if they might somehow—by reaching out to alleviate Charlie's melancholy, by doing or saying the right thing—have been able to prevent the catastrophe. Friends felt that way, and family members, and Ginger most of all, for she knew better than anyone else how deeply Charlie was depressed in his last days. Half a century later the memory of his suicide touches her to the quick. She cannot shake the thought that she might have saved him: if only she had accompanied Charlie to see the psychiatrist, if only she had insisted that he take the tranquilizers, if only she had gone down to Durham in his last days and shepherded him into the hospital. Or, it may be, nothing would have worked.

In *The Suicidal Mind* (1998), Dr. Edwin S. Shneidman reported on his findings during half a century's research into suicide and its causes, based on hundreds of "psychological autopsies" or case studies. Working in collaboration with Drs. Norman Farberow and Robert E. Litman at the Los Angeles Suicide Prevention Center, Shneidman found that "about 90 per cent of unequivocal suicides" issued verbal or behavioral clues within the week or so before they committed suicide. Perhaps Charlie Fenton provided such a clue when he told Frank Gado that he would not be around to be of assistance as Gado completed his dissertation. Perhaps he sent a message by having Mister put down, for giving up "prized possessions" often signaled an impending suicide. The pattern was like that of someone going away on a long trip (51–55). But these clues were hardly overt. By and large, Fenton operated in secrecy. Charlie did what he could in telephone calls and letters to make both Gwendy and Ginger feel as blameless as possible, *after the fact*.

Every year, more than 30,000 Americans kill themselves. The rate goes up during economic hard times, and moderates during periods of prosperity

145

("Suicide Rate"). Three times as many men as women commit suicide. Why should that be true? Edward Hoagland asked a female friend. "I'm not going to go into the self-indulgence of men," she angrily responded: men wouldn't bend to failure, and wanted to make themselves memorable. Hoagland, who was writing during a time of crisis in his own life, agreed that many men were romantics, "likely to plunge, go for broke," declare themselves as mavericks. Most people sidled toward death, outwitting it as long as possible. A few dramatized "the chance to make one last, unambiguous, irrevocable decision . . . leaping toward oblivion through a curtain of pain" (508–16). Fenton did not leave his death to chance by taking pills or turning on the gas. He jumped from the highest possible place to make sure that he would not survive.

Why did he do so? For years, talking about it, I would tell others that Charlie Fenton fell in love with a graduate student and his family left him and so he jumped, as if that were the whole story. But of course there was more to it than that. Did Charlie Fenton kill himself because he thought he was dragging Ginger into a hopeless situation? Because he had destroyed his marriage to Gwendy? Because he had lost his son? Because so many thought him a moral reprobate? Because he'd had Mister put down? Because he felt desperately alone? Because he had to seek a new job, with the scent of scandal following him wherever he went? Because he was in financial trouble? Because of the childhood beating at Eaglebrook? Because of recurrent chronic post traumatic stress disorder stemming from World War II, a disease that constitutes a risk factor for suicide? (Bullman and Kang 175–77). Because he was overcome by the overwhelming despair of depression? Because of guilt and shame he could not shake off? Because of all these reasons, and quite possibly others?

Suicide is often over-determined. In *Night Falls Fast* (1999), Kay Redfield Jamison pointed out that "some type of depression is almost ubiquitous in those who kill themselves" (103). She also commented that "[s]udden heartbreak or catastrophe" frequently occurs before a suicide, exerting an "incendiary effect on the underlying mental condition" (89). But the real motives usually belong "in the internal world, devious, contradictory, labyrinthine, and mostly out of sight" (Alvarez 123)—a realm all but inaccessible to survivors.

Yet a certain pattern of thinking is extremely common among those who decide to kill themselves. Almost always, according to Shneidman, the suicidal mind constricts and narrows (59). Once that tunnel vision takes hold—*there is no way out*—the victim enters the "closed world" of suicide, as A. Alvarez called it in *The Savage God* (1972): a world "with its own irresistible logic . . . a man [who] decides to take his own life enters a shut-off, impregnable but wholly convincing world where every detail fits and each incidence reinforces his decision." The consciousness is trapped in a bell jar, the image that Sylvia Plath—the poet and friend of Alvarez who killed herself in 1963—used to title her novel. No one "ever lacks a good reason" to kill himself, as the Italian writer (and suicide) Cesare Pavese commented (quoted by Alvarez, 99).

One piece of evidence suggests that Fenton may have had a precedent lurking in the back of his mental universe. J. Gerald Kennedy, professor of English at Louisiana State University and a leader in the field of American literature, took his doctorate at Duke. One day in 1970, he was browsing in a Durham bookstore and bought Charlie Fenton's copy of F. O Matthiessen's magisterial *American Renaissance*. Tucked inside it was the *New York Times* account of Matthiessen's suicide on 1 April 1950.

Fenton may well have been reading *American Renaissance* at precisely that time. That volume, with its invaluable studies of Emerson, Thoreau, Hawthorne, Melville, and Whitman, would have been a required text in Norman Holmes Pearson's American Studies seminars at Yale. Pearson knew and admired Matthiessen, with whom he shared a bias toward political liberalism. Both of them were Yale graduates who became masterful teachers: Pearson at Yale, and Matthiessen at Harvard, where the post–World War II "Matty's Boys" included such brilliant scholar-teachers as Leo Marx and J.C. Levenson.

Several coincidences link the suicides, ten years apart, of Matthiessen and Fenton. The "world-famed man of letters" at Harvard leaped to his death from the twelfth floor of the Hotel Manger early in the morning. The previous day he organized his papers, paid the bills, wrote farewell letters to friends, and put out food and milk for his cat before packing an overnight case and checking in to the hotel. He was "depressed over world affairs" and terribly lonely. He was living alone, his longtime companion, the artist Russell Cheney, having died six years earlier. "I can't seem to find my way out of this desperate depression," a letter on his desk said. "I have fought it until I'm worn out. I can no longer bear the loneliness with which I am faced" (Hyde 3–4). He asked to be buried by the side of his mother in Springfield, Massachusetts— the city where Charles Fenton was born and grew up.

One might think that success would be sufficient to ward off suicide, and despite his problems at Duke, Charles Fenton had achieved a good deal in his career and had an extremely promising future ahead of him. Worldly success itself, however, does not provide protection against suicide. Fenton would have known of two writers of his generation who took their own lives in the wake of tremendous public acclaim. On March 1948 Ross Lockridge, author of *Raintree County*, locked the door of his garage, started his car, and died of carbon monoxide poisoning. At the time *Raintree County* led the best seller lists, had won the lucrative MGM award, had been excerpted in *Life* magazine, and had been chosen as the main selection of the Book-of-the-Month Club. On 19 May 1949 Tom Heggen, author of the popular *Mister Roberts*, took an overdose of sedatives and drowned in his bathwater, just as his novel was being adapted into a Tony-award winning play on Broadway and was optioned for what would become a Oscar-winning motion picture. In *Ross and Tom: Two American Tragedies* (1974), John Leggett concluded that both Lockridge and Heggen—men of very nearly opposite personalities—were "equally single-minded about writing, each compelled to it with a force that dwarfed the other elements of his life." And neither of them had been able to put anything down on paper for months. They had lost their energy, Leggett speculated, "knew they had lost it and knew that without it they were useless men." He also suggested that sudden and unexpected success might have stimulated apprehensions about the future: what were Lockridge and Heggen supposed to do for an encore? In that connection, Leggett cited the case of Willa Cather, a writer for whom success "created . . . a deep despair and even a wish for death" (11–15).

One newspaper account of Fenton's death noted that he had established himself as an author with *The Apprenticeship of Ernest Hemingway*, and that his own career as a tail gunner in the war "had some Hemingway in it." So did the manner of his passing. Fenton's suicide preceded Hemingway's by only a year. Hemingway wrote Carlos Baker a wry letter about it on 16 January 1961 from the Mayo Clinic in Rochester, Minnesota, where he was undergoing a series of shock treatments for depression and paranoia.

> Had heard about Fenton jumping out of the hotel window in Durham, North Carolina, last summer. Hope that won't set an example to my other biographers. Wonder what he thought about on the way down. Understand he decided to go down once and then decided to climb up and started all over again. He was supposed to have had some trouble when he was in the R.A.F. and that may have had something to do with it. Never met him but feel very sorry for him although his school of biography and criticism was that type of F.B.I. treatment which I did not care for. I bought his book on Steven St. Vincent Benet and it seemed a fair enough book to cause anyone inclined that way to window jump. Hope this levity is not out of order.

Six days later Hemingway was discharged from the hospital. Six months later, at his home in Ketchum, Idaho, he stole downstairs in the early morning, propped his shotgun against his head, and tripped both barrels.

Once every minute, Karl A. Menninger commented in 1957, "someone in the United States either kills himself or tries to kill himself . . . Sixty or seventy times every day these attempts succeed" (Shneidman and Farberow vii). Many more fail: for every completed suicide, clinical records show, "there are at least eight suicide attempts" (Tabachnik 1). The way that people regard the taking of one's life has changed over time. William H. Gass summarized the issue in a 1972 essay, moving from seventeenth- to twentieth-century reactions. "It was dangerous for Donne to suggest that suicide was sometimes not a sin. It was still daring for Hume to reason that it was sometimes not a crime. Later one had to point out that it was sometimes not simply a sickness of the soul. Now it seems necessary to argue that it is sometimes not a virtue" (375). A. Alvarez, a year earlier, did not go that far. "What was once a mortal sin has now become a private vice," he wrote, "another 'dirty little secret,' something shameful to be avoided and tidied away, unmentionable and faintly salacious" (99).

Whatever we may think of the act, suicide has touched nearly all our lives. We may not have a suicide in our family, but we all know someone whose relatives or friends have done away with themselves. Besides, "who is not mindful of the potential self-defeating impulses within our own personality?" So it is painful and uncomfortable to discuss the topic with others. Suicide, as Shneidman put it, "haunts our literature and our culture. It is the taboo subject to our successes and our happiness" (3). As a corrective, he set out in *The Suicidal Mind* to locate the causes behind most suicides and to propose possible solutions.

In almost every case, he asserted, suicide is caused by *psychological pain.* "Each suicidal drama," that is, "occurs in the mind of a unique individual." Within the closed suicidal mind, the feeling often develops that one's pain is greater than the pain and suffering of others, making it unendurable—a feeling "bordering . . . on grandiosity" (160). This happened when suicidal people cut off ties to others, confining themselves in the prison of their own minds.

The severe psychological pain leading to suicide derived from "frustrated psychological needs," Shneidman believed. Beyond our basic biological needs, human action was motivated by some combination of such intangible needs as "to achieve, to affiliate, to dominate, to avoid harm, to be autonomous, to be loved and succored, to understand what is going on." In his research, he discovered that most suicides fell within one of five clusters of psychological needs: thwarted *love*, fractured *control*, a self-image assaulted by *shame* and defeat, ruptured relationships leading to *grief*, and excessive *anger* and hostility (18, 25). The cluster that dominated in Charlie Fenton's case was that of a self-image under assault by shame and guilt. His particular personality—what was different about him—might be best understood as an example of the constellation of psychological needs called *counteraction*, as defined by Henry Murray in his landmark *Explorations in Personality* (1935):

To master or make up for a failure by restriving. To obliterate a humiliation or rejection by resumed (or increased) action. To overpower weakness; to repress fear; to efface an insult by action; to maintain self-respect and pride on a high level. Counteraction is related to the need for Achievement and the need for Inviolacy (to have one's own psychological space uninvaded). There is determination to overcome; pride; autonomy; zest for striving. Such a person is resolute, determined, indomitable, dauntless, dogged, adventurous; [driven] to make efforts, however disguised, to deal successfully with a formerly traumatic situation; to avenge a rejection; to do forbidden things just to prove that they can be done; to engage in activities so as not to be scorned as inexperienced. (quoted in Shneidman 69)

Such people would be especially vulnerable to attacks on their self-image, their concept of themselves, their personal ideal (159). Fenton's self-image came under assault as he lost his family, lost any chance of advancement at Duke, became a social pariah and—in his own description—one of the world's greatest horse's asses. "The most important question to a potentially suicidal person," according to Shneidman, "is not an inquiry about family history or laboratory tests of blood or spinal fluid, but 'Where do you hurt?' and 'How can I help?'" (6). Yet given Fenton's counteractive personality, he was unable to confront the fragmenting sense of self, to admit that there were some crises he could not handle alone. "People commit suicide," Shneidman's colleague Robert Litman observed, "because they cannot accept their pain, because the pain does not fit in with their concept of themselves, with their personal ideal" (159).

Norman Holmes Pearson's papers—the most essential ones informing this story—document his quest for understanding what happened to Charlie Fenton, the younger man who had been his student, protégé, colleague, friend, and surrogate son. He was launched upon "a prolonged and devastating journey," an "*agonizing questioning*" (Jamison 295) to discover the reason(s) why, not unlike the one I was to undertake half a century later. A few days after the suicide Pearson started putting techniques he had learned during his counterespionage work in World War II to work on the project. Encountering Leonard Doob in Sterling library in midsummer, Pearson told him he was assembling as much information as he could. Early in October Doob (one of many haunted by Fenton's death) wrote him from his sabbatical post in Merano, Italy, wondering what Pearson had found out. In his 13 November 1960 reply Pearson expounded on the "two strong pulls" he had noted in Fenton's life between the solid citizen and the rebellious risk-taker, and passed on details of Charlie's last days gleaned from Gale Carrithers, the Yale Ph.D. who had become Charlie's friend, colleague, and admirer at Duke. Pearson also got in touch with Malcolm Cowley, with members of Charlie's family, including his mother and brother Dave, and—his most valuable source—with Ginger Price.

Ginger suffered through an extended period of trauma following Charlie's suicide. The marriage of Cal and Merrill Skaggs in August reminded her of what might have been, and she could not feel wholly happy for them. As Merrill put it, "I fear our presence just before she left for France" (and her fellowship) "was more painful than helpful." Once overseas in Strasbourg, Ginger wrote Pearson the first of the several letters they exchanged in an enlightening and—for her—therapeutic correspondence.

"I did try not to intrude myself upon you," she said by way of apology, "but I am not getting along well." At Duke she felt constrained from expressing her sorrow openly and helpless before the injustice of a college community only too willing to paint her as a predatory young female. Students there were planning a memorial seminar in Fenton's honor, she told Pearson, but she feared that if she participated it might "discolor" the occasion. Furthermore, Charlie's decision—and hers—never to speak of her by name until the divorce led his family to think of her as "a young and attractive graduate student [who] pursued him, caught him at a difficult age, broke up his home and created for him such a burden of guilt that it destroyed him." She knew this was not entirely true, that Charlie was very sick, but she suspected that guilt was part of it. Above all she needed a friend who knew and valued Fenton to talk to. "I feel that if I can just find something that will make the separation less complete, it will help," Ginger said at the end of the letter. "For the first week I only asked myself why; I believe this was protection for it never led me up to the real sorrow. And it is this, his absence, that has me now. Forgive my selfishness. Please write to me."

Norman did write, and Ginger worked through the worst of her grief in their correspondence. On the first day of classes at Strasbourg, she wrote him, the professor addressed her as "mademoiselle en noir" (she was wearing a black sweater) and asked her to read. Instead she began shaking. When the request was repeated, after what seemed an eternity she heard herself shout a strangled "No." Then she began trembling and the students on each side helped her out of the room. To prevent being called on, for months Ginger went only to lectures, dropping out of all the participation classes in French. It took her a long time to understand what was going on. Finally, she angrily demanded an answer of herself, and these words came into her mind: "Because I'm terrified of being singled out by the professor." As at Duke, as by Professor Fenton.

On December 3 she wrote Pearson about Charlie's traumatic beating at Eaglebrook. Pearson immediately grasped the importance of that episode on the 14-year-old boy and the man he was to become. If Charlie could only have unburdened himself about what happened there and why, it might have

Fenton of Duke, 1959. Fenton Family Photo

made a tremendous difference, he thought. "His is almost a classic case of how an incident in boyhood can overshadow a man's life," he wrote Ginger. "I wonder sometimes when he struck out at things later in his life—physically, I mean—if he was trying to revenge himself on the brutality done to him then. It was his hidden cancer, and being hidden from others he tried to hide it from himself."

Pearson also linked the Eaglebrook incident to the brutality Fenton underwent during his confinement at Darland during the war. Ginger's letter about Eaglebrook brought that back to him, Norman said. Did she know what it was that got him arrested and imprisoned during the war? Just being AWOL? In the 1943–44 prize-winning novel, it had been the beating of men in the stockade Charlie tried to tell about. "Was it really Eaglebrook he was describing?"

More than brutality tied the two events together. In both cases, Charlie Fenton withheld the crucial piece of information: what he had done to deserve his punishment. Where his service in the RAF was concerned, he was able to speak about his *de facto* desertion with a few fellow veteran students at Yale, but unable to admit it—even in the guise of fiction—to the wide world beyond that coterie. As to what caused the beating at Eaglebrook, he simply couldn't manage to summon it from the recesses of his mind. It would certainly have been therapeutic had he been able to do so, for guilt lies heavy on those who cannot or will not release it. Malcolm Cowley told Pearson that in the novel of the war (*The Long Summer*) that Charlie was planning to rewrite, he could not negotiate between the fictional and the autobiographical. He was holding back something extremely important, Cowley believed. "If Charlie could have told that thing in the novel, he would be alive today," he said.

After long consideration Andy Fenton arrived at a similar conclusion, that his father "was deeply ashamed and guilty for having gone AWOL and having survived a war that had taken the lives of almost all of his fellow RCAF enlistees." When Andy was still a toddler, his father used to dress him up in his RCAF uniform and call him "Soldier Boy." Charlie even cut the legs off to fit his son, and the uniform jacket still had three Sergeant's chevrons on each sleeve, although he'd been busted back to the lower rank of Airman Second Class. During the war Charlie Fenton flew many dangerous missions over heavily fortified German targets and repeatedly faced terrifying bursts of anti-aircraft fire. Only then did he go on the trot, serve hard time in the stockade, and receive a misconduct discharge. But he could not bring himself to confess the details of his post-combat behavior, even to his family. They knew he'd gone AWOL, and that he'd written about a brutal internment in a story (his lost prize-winning 1944 novel, apparently) called "The Glass

House," but still, as Andy recalled, "we all thought he'd served honorably and heroically."

Charlie might have been able to work off a measure of his guilt by rewriting *The Long Summer*. In January 1960 Cowley urged him once again to undertake the job, adding that "for the book to be as good as it ought to be, you have to bite the bullet and tell what happened and to hell with everybody." William Sloane at Rutgers University Press also read the manuscript, and—like Cowley—both believed in it and had revisions to suggest. And, according to Ginger Price, he did plan to follow their suggestions by "making the hero more prominent and dramatizing more of the episodes."

As it stands, unrevised, *The Long Summer* promises—and fails to deliver—an ending that directly confronts the issue of going on the trot. The first scene in the novel takes up the issue of "desertion, which intrude[d] on all our actions during that long summer." Johnny Frome, the putative hero, is discovered to have overstayed his leave (for two days) by a London-based Scotland Yard detective. The detective tracks Frome down in South Kensington, a residential district "so remote from the conventional scenes of West End gaiety . . . that men in uniform . . . were a rarity in its quiet streets and decorous pubs." Two things are worth remarking upon here. Fenton himself, like bomber pilot Frome, took a cavalier attitude toward minor AWOL infractions: he was absent without leave twice during his training in Canada, once for three days, once for two days. And South Kensington adjoins Betty Lyon's Chelsea, the similar residential section far from the hangouts of most servicemen where Fenton lived during his seven-month period on the trot (after a month, in the RAF, it constituted desertion).

The Scotland Yard man instructs an incredulous Frome about the dangers posed by such long-term trotters. "Did you know, my lad, that there is at all times in the United Kingdom these days a constant group of deserters and absentees numbering never less than sixty thousand men?" Many of them subsist on "petty crime" or "crimes of violence," he points out, and at least a few of them were guilty of providing information to the enemy. "Ten bob here, a quid there, and the enemy knows what regiments are going overseas, what regiments are just back from Gib or India or the desert." Riding back to Cambridge, Johnny pondered the detective's remarks. "That sort of college-boy delinquency of ours," he tells the narrator, "going ayewoll for a night, or maybe a day or two, is plainly kid stuff." Johnny's pay is docked and he is given a Severe Reprimand for his dereliction, just as Fenton was for his month-long absenteeism (2–8).

By beginning his novel in this way Fenton produced an expectation that desertion would become part of the story before it ends. For most of its length the story concentrates on the details of the air war and its physical and psychological costs on the men trying to beat the percentages. The RAF Bomber Command, it is made clear, so callously placed its airmen at risk of death that they had every reason to go on the trot. Then, near the end, there is another extended scene in which the airman-narrator, on leave in London, meets a Canadian deserter. The Canadian had been caught before and sent to Aldershot, the worst of the glasshouses, and is proud of having done time there. "He enjoyed talking to an innocent flyboy about Aldershot. Aldershot was his badge. He was a tough guy. He was what they called a persistent offender against the King's Regulations" (205–08). Again, the issue of desertion is raised and then dropped. But Fenton's narrator does not overstay his nine-day leave, does not spend six months harbored and protected from the secret police by an Englishwoman, does not get caught and sent to detention. He simply returns to his squadron in Cambridge, where he finds out that Johnny Frome and ten others had died in an accident caused by mechanical failure. Another bomber lost an engine on takeoff and spun right into their aircraft (222). There the unrevised novel ends, a most unsatisfactory ending because, as Cowley realized, the reader has been led to anticipate something very different. Perhaps in revision Charlie might have added a part of the story in which he did "bite the bullet" to deal openly with desertion, and in that way expiate some of his burden of shame.

This lasting psychological wound from the war, as Pearson intuited, had a probable parallel in the beating at Eaglebrook, for that incident may have resulted from some action of Fenton's so horrific that he could not summon it from his subconscious. Then, during the spring and summer of 1960 at Duke, he was beset by additional feelings of guilt for abandoning his commitment to wife and family. Defiant challenger of authority though he certainly was, the Charlie Fenton that Pearson came to know at Yale took a conventional view of marriage. "His marriage was rocky from the beginning," Pearson wrote Doob, "yet he clung to it out of a sense of responsibility for first his stepchildren and then his own son." In fact he used to inveigh against Hemingway, Pearson recalled, for his four marriages, serially leaving "wives and issue at the side." The clacking tongues of the gossipers in Durham were bad enough. The guilt he visited upon himself—and did not want to admit to—may have been worse. The young woman he fell in love with thought of him as "noble and fine and extraordinary." Charlie could not think of himself in that way.

So, at least, one can speculate, for it is an interpretation that fits the available evidence and seems highly plausible. Still, as Alvarez observed, "no single theory will untangle an act as ambiguous and with such complex motives as suicide" (12). And it may be that Fenton was holding back traumas traceable to his earliest days. From his study of suicidal cases, Shneidman arrived at the view "that the subsoil, the root causes of being unable to withstand

. . . adult assaults lie in the deepest recesses of personality that are laid down in rather early childhood" (162–63). "We will never know what very early experiences" shaped Fenton, Tom Greening observed, "way before that beating he got in school." To illustrate the point, Greening quoted two lines from the Irish poet George William Russell (AE)—"In the lost childhood of Judas/ Christ was betrayed"—lines that gave Graham Greene the title for "The Lost Childhood," his 1947 essay. Such early experiences may well have formed the risk-taking defiant man who was Charlie Fenton, Greening proposed. "In the forgotten or remembered defeats of childhood, the doomed, vainglorious hero was made."

Without intending to, Charlie bequeathed a legacy of sorrow, regret, guilt, and anger to family and friends as they tried to come to terms with an inexplicable act. "Suicide is a death like no other," as Jamison commented, "and those who are left behind must confront a pain like no other." They are left with the unanswerable *Why*, with the silence of others too horrified or embarrassed to cobble together an expression of condolence, "with the assumption by others—and themselves—that more could have been done." Worst of all, they are left with "a hole in the heart" (292–93).

By January 1961 Ginger Price was finally able to attend participation classes at Strasbourg and really learn the language. In February she spent four days with Leonard Doob and his wife in Merano, Italy, and the healing continued. Writing to Pearson represented "the best letting go." Much better by May 1, she told him that "I felt I could write you anything, anytime, and I did that. Even though you never received most of those letters, I talked with you many, many hours." Now Ginger wanted to see Pearson, and when she came back to the States they met, talked about the man they had both known and loved, and became friends. She subsequently married, had children of her own, taught for a while, took her doctorate, and moved to New York to fashion a distinguished career in book publishing. She is by all accounts an admirable, intelligent, and attractive woman. Half a century later, Ginger Price is still beset by terrible memories of the time when she and Charlie were in love, and how it ended.

In undertaking research for this book, I tried repeatedly to arrange a meeting with Ginger. Even finding her took some doing, but eventually—after I'd located what turned out to be the wrong Ginger Price in Washington, D.C.—Reynolds Price and Lou Budd at Duke and my agent Peter Matson in New York directed me to the right one: now Virginia (Ginger) Barber, married to book editor Ed Barber, herself a successful book agent and scout, living in Charlottesville and New York City. We spoke on the telephone in an awkward conversation, and she made it clear that she was not prepared to revisit the details of a relationship that ended so traumatically. At the same time, though, she expressed a willingness to see what I was writing about the life and death of Charlie Fenton, and I duly sent her sections of the story as it got down on paper—with each submission, wondering if she might not relent and consent to a discussion of the way it was.

Ginger acknowledged each of these documents as they were sent her in e-mail attachments. Then, for about a six-week period in the late summer and early fall of 2008, we were in fairly close communication through the third-party mediation of Merrill Skaggs. Merrill's name cropped up in one of Ginger's letters to Pearson. I wrote her at Drew University about this project and so discovered a wonderful and enthusiastic ally. As his student, Merrill knew that Charlie Fenton deserved remembering, and she was one of Ginger's closest friends (they co-authored a book about parenting, *The Mother Person*, in 1977). In e-mails and phone calls Merrill declared us friends, gave me encouragement, and when questions were relayed through her, provided access to Ginger's recollections. Then Merrill died, suddenly and unexpectedly—thousands came to her memorial service—and although we had never met, I took the loss hard. Her last e-mail to me, sent less than a week before her death, outlined a number of ways in which she felt this story might be made stronger and more appealing. These were the thoughts of an experienced and highly skilled editor and writer, and in revision I've followed the path she laid out for me.

Charlie meant a lot to Merrill as a teacher and friend. He also became her "first and only ghost." She and Cal Skaggs came back to Duke in the fall of 1960 as newlyweds to finish their graduate work, and rented a small apartment with a window view of the Washington Duke hotel. The first article of furniture they purchased was "a bookcase, our only essential." They were unpacking books in the living room when Merrill looked up and saw Charlie. She was about to speak when he turned into a ladder, leaning against the bookcase. "*But he was smiling.*"

With her husband's death, the romantic life of Gwendy Fenton, only 39 at the time, effectively ended. She stayed in Madison, and was invited everywhere because people, both men and women, enjoyed her outspoken ways. Potential beaux, including Roddy Ham, came to call, but she was not interested. No one could take Charlie's place. For the rest of her life Gwendy Fenton looked in vain for the answers about what happened in Durham on the morning of 21 July 1960. After the suicide, she bought two plots in West cemetery—one for Charlie and one for herself. She brought up Andy and built a real estate business to support herself. When she died in September 2007, Gwendy was laid to rest alongside her husband. But she could never shake off the bitterness about Charlie's affair with Ginger and the separation, and expressed herself on the subject in her feisty and ungrandmotherly style.

Talking with son Richie a few days before her death, Gwendy asked him if he thought she would see her parents and her husbands in the afterworld. Richie replied that he had no idea, that like the British novelist John Mortimer he thought of that realm as "The Great Perhaps." Well, she didn't know either, Gwendy said, but if spirits survived and could speak to each other, she planned to greet Charlie Fenton by saying "You Son of a Bitch."

Wendy and Paul Nielsen honored Fenton's memory by naming their first child Charles, but Wendy still looks back in astonishment at her stepfather's final weeks. Letting Andy go without a fight? Putting Mister down? Arranging for a reconciliation and then jumping? These were not the acts of the man who had helped to guide her through girlhood and adolescence. "Charlie's death was the most complicated event of my life," Paul Nielsen recalls. At the time he felt personally abandoned, and ashamed of the provincial holier-than-thou atmosphere of Durham—his home—that had ostracized Fenton. Later he came to feel anger as well, thinking it irresponsible of Charlie to leave them all behind. In due course the Nielsens divorced, Wendy to settle on the West Coast and Paul in New York. Richie reverted to his birth father's name, and as Richard D. Grant constructed a prosperous career in Wall Street. As much as anything, he remembers Charlie Fenton for his reckless, enthusiastic, and belligerent defiance of authority and convention. Dave Fenton, the younger brother who filled the breach to arrange for Charlie's funeral and settle his affairs, continues to look back on his older sibling with enduring affection and admiration, as his hero.

For many years it was difficult for Andy (Charles Andrews Fenton, Jr.) to accept what happened in Durham. When he married, he told his wife that his father died in an automobile accident—an untruth that came to light a decade later. At one time he suspected that Charlie, an outspoken advocate of racial integration during a time of turmoil and unrest, may possibly have been the target of a fatal beating. Yet he also realized that "CAF had ample reasons to take his own life, and no one needs to make . . . excuses for him. He was a man among men, and even his death was larger than life." Andy greatly admires the man who gave him his name.

Financially, Charlie Fenton had little to convey to Andy, his "sole heir in law." He did leave $73,000 in several life insurance policies (one firm refused to pay because of the manner of his death). Otherwise, nothing was left to inherit. Fenton's 2,000-plus books were appraised at 25 cents each. His 12 boxes of research cards and 9 file drawers of research sheets—the working documents of his projected Spanish Civil War book—were judged of "no saleable value." The Hillman needed repairs, and was evaluated at $350. His share of the proceeds of the sale of the Durham house was substantially balanced by a note Gwendy's father held from financing its original purchase. Funds trickled in from Duke, and from various publishers, but by the time that administrator E. K. Powe paid all the taxes and bills, the net value of his estate had vanished.

Half a dozen posthumous publications brought Fenton's name back into sight. The last essay he wrote, about William Styron's third novel *Set This House on Fire*, appeared in the Autumn 1960 *South Atlantic Quarterly*. Styron's book had been widely disparaged, and Fenton took it upon himself to correct that misjudgment. The novel, he declared, granted the same confirmation of a major talent in 1960 that "*A Farewell to Arms* represented in 1929 and *The 42nd Parallel* in 1930 and *Tender Is the Night* in 1934" (470). In other words, Styron promised to achieve the same eminence in his generation as Hemingway and Dos Passos and Fitzgerald had in the preceding one. After linking Styron with Norman Mailer as the "primary writers" of that generation, Fenton discussed the merits of *Set This House on Fire* at length. It was "a novel of our times" (472), he said, sensitive to the great political events of the previous twenty years. Even more importantly, Styron's theme was "nothing less than the stagnation and regeneration of the spirit" (472). Fenton was strongly attracted to literary works on this theme; he'd praised MacLeish's *J. B.* in similar terms. He must have seen his own recovery from a series of youthful misadventures—most of them associated with the bottle—as a similar process of regeneration, a journey toward that "solid citizen's status" that formed part of his divided self-image. The public odium that surrounded him in his last months brought him to question—as the typewritten note he left behind, insisting on his virtuous attributes, suggests—whether that regeneration had succeeded, whether he deserved to think well of himself.

On 27 October 1960 Fenton was honored posthumously at a Yale reception marking the publication of the *Selected Letters of Stephen Vincent Benét* that he edited for the Yale University Press. More than 60 people attended, including Gwendy Fenton, Benét's widow Rosemary, Thomas C. Mendenhall, president of Smith, and Norman Holmes Pearson, associate professor of English. Chester Kerr introduced Mendenhall and Pearson, who made brief remarks about their friendship with Fenton. Mendenhall recalled with good nature that Charlie "always had something of the enlisted man's suspicion of all brass, including academic brass" like himself ("Author Fenton"). Pearson pointed out three salient points about Fenton's life and work. First, "all his books had in common the experience of war," and he "thoroughly and sensitively" examined the role of writers in warfare. Second, Fenton had "a very real understanding of literary apprenticeship as an important factor in the history of literature," much of it gleaned from his own experience in writing fiction. "He knew there were few cases of the divine amateur," Pearson said, that great writers had to learn their craft. In his books, Fenton set out to understand how Hemingway had learned, how Benét was always learning. Third, Fenton possessed "the great power for friendship" that was characteristic of Benét as well. It showed in Fenton's own letters to students, and gave him the capacity to choose the best of Benét's correspondence with rare skill. So, Pearson said, the *Selected Letters* was "a memorial of both men, and as such we greet it with joy." Like most books of letters, this one was not widely reviewed. One commentator echoed Pearson's remarks at Yale by noting how Fenton's "graceful and shrewd introduction" displayed his awareness of "the daily routine and problems of the working writer." Charlie knew that territory.

With characteristic modesty, Pearson did not acknowledge his own involvement in producing the volume of Benét's letters, and in facilitating Fenton's career. Recognizing his promise, Pearson directed Charlie's dissertation/book on Hemingway and kept him calm in the face of stormy letters emanating from Hemingway in Cuba. He guided his protégé toward Benét as a subject for a biography, introducing him as an ideal candidate for the job to the poet's widow Rosemary. He fought for Fenton during the competition for promotion at Yale, and when he left for Duke continued to serve as his advocate in the profession. When Charlie died, Norman took on the task of reading the galleys for the edition of Benét letters, correcting minor errors and supplying a few omitted names for the index.

When David Fenton brought Charlie's body back to Connecticut, he telephoned Pearson and asked him to take care of his brother's papers. The family wanted them sent to Yale for preservation. Although not officially designated as Charlie's literary executor, Pearson soon found himself performing that function. Early in October Russell Lynes, publisher of *Harper's*, sent him the manuscript of Fenton's "Down with the Trustees" article that the magazine had been considering "for an inordinate amount of time." Finally, Lynes said, *Harper's* decided against publication. There was "a fine hue and cry" in the piece, but it was full of holes too. "Maybe [Fenton] could have plugged up those holes, but if we were to do it, it would be our piece, not his piece." After reading it, Pearson agreed. The article looked like a first draft, and since it used Duke's administration as a starting point, that might make it seem like an attack from a "disgruntled" observer.

Pearson made a concerted effort to see the two books Fenton left behind into print. Unfortunately, his efforts were unsuccessful, and neither Fenton's short history of the National Institute and American Academy of Arts and Letters nor the collection he planned to call *The Writer as Professor and Other Essays* were published after his death. The first of these had actually been accepted by the Duke University Press, with a subvention agreed to by the institution's Research Council, and the second was under serious consideration at Duke as well. But Fenton was not around to do final polishing. He was no longer a fair-haired boy in the university's English department, brightening its classrooms and burnishing its national reputation. There were those on campus who preferred to forget his two-year presence there.

An additional complication was that Fenton's papers remained under lock and key in the office of E. K. Powe in Durham, a lawyer equipped to handle the disposition of Fenton's financial estate but wholly unfamiliar with literary matters. On 13 December 1960 Ashbel Brice, director of the Duke Press, wrote Pearson in some frustration that he had sent the contract for *The American Man of Letters* (the National Institute–American Academy book) to Powe weeks earlier, asking him "to sign it or send it to the proper person for signature." Powe did not respond, and Brice wondered if he'd by any chance sent the contract to Pearson. Two other matters also gave him pause, Brice added. Had Charlie secured the necessary permissions from journals where a number of the book's chapters had appeared? Did his papers contain the page of notes that was missing in the manuscript Brice had before him?

Pearson replied (as he had learned from David Fenton) that because of North Carolina law and because Charlie was legally separated at the time of his death there would be long delays in getting the papers released to Yale. The only thing to do, it seemed to Pearson, was to have some one walk into Powe's office—Brice and Powe were in the same town, after all—and ascertain why the contract had not been signed and whether the missing page was among his papers. But Norman went further, pointing out that getting permissions could be quickly taken care of and generously volunteering "to help in any editorial way, or otherwise." Charles was both his friend and protégé, he said, and he was anxious to have his publications appear.

It seemed to Pearson that the matter was more or less settled, and that the book would indeed be published. He wrote as much to Ginger in France, who was delighted by the news. She and Charlie used to joke over how much "mileage" he'd got out of his "little monograph" on the Institute and Academy: six articles and/or notes in four different journals. For whatever reason, however, Ashbel Brice decided that the manuscript needed another reading, and he sent it to novelist Glenway Wescott, who had succeeded Malcolm Cowley as president of the National Institute of Arts and Letters. Wescott's judgment arrived in April 1961, and it effectively scotched the book.

In his disputatious prose, Charlie Fenton regularly impugned the intelligence and competence of figures of authority. He did so vigorously in *The American Man of Letters*, characterizing the early leaders of the nation's most prestigious organization of Arts and Letters as foolish fuddy duddies. This was too much for Wescott. What bothered him about the manuscript, he wrote in his reader's report, was that the "tone and interpretation [were] deliberately provocative and controversial." He accused Fenton of "intemperate and disrespectful" comments and of describing events "churlishly." Wescott was of course exactly right. Fenton was not writing to please the old guard. He was busy exposing literary and artistic brass, and readers less closely aligned to the organizations under fire than Wescott would have read his lively treatment with pleasure instead of outrage.

In closing his comments, Wescott made an unveiled threat on behalf of the National Institute. "[I]f you publish this poor study in anything like its present form, our lawyers [will] be asked to read it, upon the chance of there being some basis for a libel action against Duke University Press." That disposed of the Institute-Academy book, at least for the next half century. Before his death in the summer of 2008, Matthew J. Bruccoli—who had been Fenton's worshipful student at Yale—was working toward resurrecting that volume, and planning to write an introduction to launch it anew. That may still come to pass.

Misunderstandings and, again, at least one unsympathetic reading, sidelined Fenton's *The Writer as Professor, and Other Essays.* Brice had told Charlie, when he first proposed a collection of his essays, that the only possible way to get such a book accepted "would be to get glowing recommendations from men too authoritative to be ignored." Then two such recommendations came in, one from Earl McGrath, who had served as the United States Commissioner of Education, and the other from Fenton's friend and supporter Mark Schorer. Schorer's evaluation, written less than a month after Charlie's death, was one of the most wholeheartedly favorable reader's reports ever written. Fenton's book of essays struck him as "a remarkably fine and cogent work," written with "peculiar vigor and dash." Schorer found all of the essays enlightening, most of them entertaining, and a few hilarious "in the author's incisive irony and impatience with academic and literary nonsense." The book promised to blow through the collegiate world "like a crisply fresh wind," causing a good deal of comment and winning major applause. Schorer further envisioned an audience extending beyond the academic world to professionals and intellectuals generally, for Fenton's work spoke "directly and lucidly to any person concerned with the state of the national culture." The Duke Press could anticipate selection by one of the smaller book clubs, and an invitation to reprint in paperback from Noonday or Meridian or Anchor or Grove.

Not content to leave his recommendation at that, Schorer made specific suggestions about how the essays might be reorganized and retitled for maximum impact. For a title, he had in mind *Writers and Academics: Essays on Literature, Scholarship, and Higher Education.* Should Duke turn it down, he added, he'd like to urge it upon a couple of places he was fairly confident would be delighted to publish it. As a last word, Schorer inquired who was "in charge of Fenton's affairs. His death seems to me one of the truly great losses in a world that can't afford them."

Despite this enthusiastic endorsement, Duke decided against publishing the book. Chester Kerr at Yale University Press thereupon asked Ashbel Brice to forward the script to him, and sent it to Pearson for a report. Although he thought Schorer's prediction of sales of 10,000 copies over-exuberant, Pearson recommended publication. With some editing by Cowley, Schorer, and himself, and with a preface by Cowley or Schorer, "an attractive volume" could be made from Fenton's essays, he wrote on 15 January 1961. Besides, there were "particular reasons why the Yale University Press should want to pay this tribute to one of its authors." With the support of McGrath, Schorer, and Pearson, the book went to the Yale University Press editorial board, and once again ran up against a reader who could not stomach Fenton's prose style. This was Frederick W. (Ted) Hilles, a specialist in the age of Samuel Johnson who was to edit a book of essays in honor of his colleague Frederick A. Pottle: the Boswell scholar Fenton had imprudently made sport of to his students in Daily Themes. Hilles criticized Fenton's diction and his opinions. One essay struck him as "very very smart" but written in "(Charlie forgive me) Luce-empire style." Another, "Down with the Trustees," was "very very clever, and so unfair" that Hilles found himself rooting for the trustees. The essays reminded him of "undergraduate editorials," and repeated what "all young teachers have felt." Publishing the book would bring no honor to the Press or to Charlie's memory, he concluded, and the board concurred. Kerr sent a copy of Hilles's diatribe to Pearson, and with that he retired from the field.

After reading the essays at Yale's Beinecke library, I think that Hilles was wrong and Pearson right. Fenton's essays on the state of higher education ca. 1960 continue to resonate 50 years later. Remarkably little has been done in the interim to correct or amend the practices that Charlie found objectionable. In his articles Fenton was indeed setting down what many other young teachers have felt—and continue to feel—as they learn their way around the academy, but that seems to me a virtue rather than a handicap. And he did so in a voice that was distinctly his own. As one of Fenton's students remarked, it was uncanny "how forcibly and poignantly his personality hovers in his prose." That iconoclastic, irreverent personality—transmitted to the page—offended men of good taste like Wescott and Hilles, yet at the same time enlivened Fenton's writing for the larger group of less fastidious readers. With minor editing and reorganization, Fenton's essays would still make a valuable and interesting book.

Oddly, when Brice sent *The Writer as Professor* essays to Kerr, he included *both* Schorer's rave review of that book and Wescott's withering report on the Institute-Academy volume. This led to confusion in Kerr's mind. When he consigned Fenton's collection of essays to Yale's Beinecke library for preservation in 1966, he conflated the two books and misremembered why Yale University Press had decided against publication of the essays. Wescott had written a threatening letter, Kerr noted in his letter of transmittal, and Schorer had contributed "an adverse report"!

One cannot measure with precision what was forfeited with Charlie Fenton's tragic death, but it was surely a great loss. He was only 41, about to enter his prime as a writer and scholar. He had been enormously productive during his brief tour of duty at Duke. The notes he accumulated toward *The Last Great Cause* offer abundant evidence that his book would have presented a definitive overview of the Spanish Civil War and its influence on American history and culture. *The Writer as Professor* essays would have emerged, and his irreverent account of the Institute and Academy as well. He would have reconfigured *The Long Summer* into the wonderful novel Malcolm Cowley envisioned. He would have written the academic novel, centered around his experiences at Duke, he'd been sketching out in conversations with Ginger. And there were other books ahead of him too, in which he could address twentieth century American literature and culture and history in his vigorous and distinctive voice.

The greatest loss of all, surely, is that of the students deprived of the chance to know and learn from him. "Give me the food for which you have already given me the appetite," Dante asked of Virgil, his guide (quoted in Wilder 242). But there is always a shortage of Virgils, master teachers capable of stimulating and satisfying the yearnings of students to learn. Charlie Fenton, who met classes for only a decade, was one of them. Mary Church wonders if such teachers still exist, knowing how rare it is to find someone with a gift for genuine insights and the ability to convey these to others. His "was a terrible, terrible loss," she said. Yale President A. Whitney Griswold expressed the same message in his letter of condolence to Gwendy: "I feel, now, infinitely sad for all the students who will miss his teaching."

In a letter to the editor days after the suicide, his young colleague Gale Carrithers eloquently discoursed on the kind of teacher Charlie was. He did not secrete himself in an Ivory Tower, or evade the world of responsibility. The books he read and taught and wrote provided "a platform from which he could speak the more fluently and the more resonantly on the pleasures and problems of twentieth century America" and—even more broadly—they served as "instruments for examining with ever-increasing rigor the nature of ourselves, and our world, and our duty . . . Those of us who were privileged to know him will always be different persons for his words, and for the example of his intense, humane, unselfish and even debonair commitment to his ideals." Charlie Fenton was an excellent scholar, a talented writer with a voice distinctly his own—at once amusing in its dismissal of received wisdom and serious in its advocacy of his ideals—and a charismatic and inspiring teacher. He taught students and colleagues and readers alike that American literature and its makers were important, that they had much to teach us about the nation's history and culture, and that it was foolish—even wrong—to leave their work and lives unexamined.

Those were the lessons I learned from him, even when I was not entirely conscious of them. When I left a career as a newspaper reporter and editor in 1963 to earn a doctorate at Minnesota and begin teaching and writing about American authors, I did not say to myself, *this is what Charlie Fenton did.* Still, his example was always there, in the recesses of the mind. That, and the other very different bequest of his suicide, and trying to puzzle out what caused it. At the time, I let the matter rest in the shroud of the unknown, substantially agreeing with Carrithers' elegant *ave atque vale* to Charlie Fenton in his memorial letter: "No doubt like all men he had traits and actions to think upon with regret. No doubt like all men he was capable of being severe with his fellow-men. But what sets him even farther apart among the heroic few is that he was more severe with himself than with anyone else, or that anyone else ever was with him. We can only subside into the pained murmur of the Greek chorus at the terrible sentence he passed, for whatever reason or reasons we shall never know, upon himself" (Carrithers).

Were he still alive I like to think that Charlie and I, two old guys past 90 and 80, might foregather, say, at the May meeting of the American Literature Association. Over lunch and a glass of wine, we would brag about our grandchildren, confess our mutual pleasure in choosing an occupation that paid us to talk about books, deplore the descent of the academy into the stony badlands of "theory," lament the shortage of jobs in the college-teaching market, talk about some of the twentieth-century writers we've admired: Hemingway and Fitzgerald, Steve Benét and Archie MacLeish, E. A. Robinson and Dr. Williams, John Cheever and John Updike, Bill Styron and Norman Mailer, and share anecdotes about the pitfalls of writing literary biography.

That cannot happen, because of a tremendously promising life brought crashing to earth. Tragedy is a much overused term, yet it seems no overstatement to call Charlie Fenton's death a tragic event: he had that much promise as a human being. This account was written, in good part, out of a conviction that Fenton and the times he lived through deserve to be remembered. Far more than I realized when the quest for understanding began, his life and its end throws light on the prevailing mores of the country Charlie Fenton inhabited for 40 years in the middle of the twentieth century and what it meant to grow up a man in that place, at that time. Finally, writing his story derived from a sense of obligation as well. Should a few others pick up this book and read it, and think—not of Fenton's suicide but of his career and the idealism behind it—that *I can do that*, or, even better, *I will do that*, putting these words down on paper will have found its reward.

Notes on Sources

Books and articles cited are keyed to the bibliographies—of Charles A. Fenton and of Other Works Consulted—that follow. Interviews, email, and letters sent to me are acknowledged in the notes, tracking the text of the book. Notes for the interviews, copies of emails, copies of letters privately held, and unpublished work by Fenton will be housed, along with papers accumulated for my previously published biographies, at the Earl Gregg Swem library of the College of William and Mary.

Abbreviations

CAF: Charles A. Fenton
NHP: Norman Holmes Pearson
Beinecke: Beinecke Library, Yale University

Introduction

Epigraphs: telephone interview James Stevenson, 17 December 2007, email Paul Nielsen, 17 January 2008. *Paul Harvey*: email Frank Gado, 31 October 2008; *"real drunk . . . big shot"*: telephone interview Gwendy Fenton, 14 May 2007.

First Sighting

Daily Themes: telephone interview Tom Greening, 19 March 2011; e-mail William Deresiewicz, 11 June 2007 and 21 November 2007. *Tap Day*: telephone interview Peter Matthiessen, 13 December 2007.

Bomber Boy

Whitridge letter: RCAF records; *training, to England*: CAF letters to parents, 1940–41, RCAF records; *diet, old school tie*: CAF to parents; *busted*: RCAF records; *"getting nervy"*: CAF to parents; *evading women*: CAF to parents, n.d.; *writing when AWOL*: CAF to parents, 5 September 1943; *prize-winning novel*: CAF to Ernest Hemingway, 18 September 1951; *marriage plans*: CAF and Betty Lyon to Dorothy Fenton: *suspicion of brass*: emails Richard D. Grant, 15 and 16 December 2007.

The Young Academic

Discharge: CAF to parents, March 1944, RCAF records; *Gwendy described*: funeral remarks Maxwell Grant and Richard D. Grant, 18 September 2007, telephone interview Andy Fenton, 14 December 2007, telephone interview Wendy Nielsen, 17 December 2007, email Wendy Nielsen and David W. Fenton, 27 December 2008; *drinking . . . black periods*: telephone interview David W. Fenton, 8 December 2007, letter Andy Fenton to SD, 14 December 2007, telephone interview Richard D. Grant, 15 December 2007; *plays about war*: Margery Bailey to CAF, 13 June 1947 and 24 October 1947, Stanford University Archives; *amending discharge*: RCAF records; *IQ tests*: telephone interview Marshall Coleman, 1 December 2008; *prep school performance*: Eaglebrook School and Taft School records; *Pearson lecture*: telephone interviews Malcolm Mitchell, 4 September 2008, and Tom Greening, 19 March 2011; *English 15 evaluations*: CAF papers, Beinecke; *how to teach writing*: letter Wallace Stegner to CAF, 5 December 1949, CAF papers, Beinecke; *Yale student reminiscences*: telephone interview Malcolm Mitchell, 4 September 2008, telephone interview James Stevenson, 17 December 2007, letter Stevenson to David W. Fenton, n.d., telephone interview Peter Matthiessen,13 December 2007, telephone interview Gaddis Smith, 28 November 2007, telephone interview Matthew J. Bruccoli, 2 December 2007, telephone interviews Tom Greening, 19 March 2011, 9 April 2011, and 17 April 2011; *family dynamics, drinking*: telephone interview Lewis Jones, 10 November 2007, telephone interview Peter Matthiessen 13 December 2007, telephone interview James Stevenson, 17 December 2007, telephone interviews Wendy Nielsen, 26 November 2007 and 17 December 2007, email Wendy Nielsen, 12 March 2008, telephone interview David W. Fenton, 8 December 2007, email Richard D. Grant, 20 May 2011.

Hemingway vs. Fenton

In writing this section, I relied when possible on copies of the Hemingway-Fenton letters in the Hemingway Collection at the John F. Kennedy library.

The dates of these are made clear in the text, and so are not annotated, nor are Hemingway letters to and from his sister Ursula Jepson and from his Toronto friend Dorothy Connable, also housed at the JFK library.

Letters duly annotated in the text include Hemingway-to-Fenton letters quoted in "The Hemingway-Fenton Correspondence" edited by Matthew J. Bruccoli (Bruccoli) and in Sotheby Parke Bernet's catalog of the 1977 Jonathan Goodwin collection (Sotheby), as well as Hemingway letters to others about the Fenton dispute in his *Selected Letters (Selected)*.

Another biography: letter CAF to Schorer, 23 August 1956, Schorer papers, Bancroft Library, University of California.

Carving a Career

Departmental backbiting: telephone interview Peter Matthiessen, 13 December 2007; *prospects not intoxicating* and *summer lectures*: letter CAF to Schorer, 13 December 1954 and 18 April 1955, Schorer papers, Bancroft Library, University of California; *summer lectures*: letters CAF to Cowley, 19 April 1955, 13 May 1955, 5 July 1955, 7 July 1955, and Cowley to CAF, 24 April 1955, 11 May 1955, 18 May 1955, Cowley papers, Newberry Library; *Best Stories anthology*: letters CAF to Cowley, 1 September 1955, 21 September 1955, 28 October 1955, and Cowley to CAF, 28 December 1955, Cowley papers, Newberry Library; *better off dead*: undated newspaper article "Magazine Contributor," CAF file, Yale archives; *on lookout for money*: letter Leonard W. Doob to NHP, 17 November 1960, Pearson papers, Beinecke; *most impressive volume*: letter Cowley to CAF, 15 August 1957, Cowley papers, Newberry Library; *Guggenheim application*: "Statement of Plans for Research," October 1956, Fenton papers, Beinecke Library, Yale; *glittering words . . . limp thoughts*: Cowley to CAF, 7 October 1957, Cowley papers, Newberry Library; *American Man of Letters*: letters CAF to Cowley, 14 August 1957, 27 August 1957, 30 December 1959, Cowley to CAF, 15 August 1957, 25 August 1957, 30 August 1957, Cowley papers, Newberry Library; *pedantic . . . breezy*: telephone interview Gaddis Smith, 28 November 2007; *scholarly game*: letter Leonard W. Doob to NHP, 17 November 1960, Pearson papers, Beinecke; *deciding on Duke*: telephone interview Louis J. Budd, 3 December 2007, telephone interview Richard D. Grant, 15 December 2007, telephone interview Frank Gado, 21 September 2008; *academic jungle*: letter CAF to Cowley, 25 April 1958, Cowley papers, Newberry Library; *Trotters*: letter Cowley to CAF, 12 August 1958, Cowley papers, Newberry Library.

A Different Planet

Adventurous appointment: telephone interview Louis J. Budd, 3 December 2007; *transform Duke*: unattributed note, CAF file, Yale archives; *wholesale segregation*: letter CAF to Chester Kerr, 30 August 1958, Fenton papers, Beinecke; telephone interview Wendy Nielsen, 26 November 2007; *house . . . honor system . . . teaching load . . . students*: letters CAF to Chester Kerr, 30 August 1958, 12 September 1958, 15 September 1958, 20 September 1958, Fenton papers, Beinecke; *most popular professor*: letter Gaddis Smith to David W. Fenton, 24 March 1995; *voting on promotion*: letter CAF to Chester Kerr, 17 November 1958, Fenton papers, Beinecke; *Gohdes*: telephone interview Louis J. Budd, 3 December 2007; *hand was damp*: letter CAF to "Aunt Alice" Ross, n.d., Fenton papers, Beinecke; *Mendenhall to Smith*: letter CAF to Chester Kerr, 13 November 1958, Fenton papers, Beinecke; *admiration immense*: letter Mark Schorer to CAF, 18 December 1958, Fenton papers, Beinecke; *numbers of creatures*: letter CAF to Chester Kerr, 17 November 1958, Fenton papers, Beinecke; *accosted Price*: telephone interview Reynolds Price, 26 July 2008; *shake up things*: telephone interview William W. Combs, 4 December 2007; *extra step*: telephone interview Mary Church (Williams), 16 October 2010; *greatest gift*: telephone interview Calvin Skaggs, 24 August 2008, email Calvin Skaggs, 25 August 2008; *breath of fresh air*: telephone interview Merrill Skaggs, 20 August 2008; *amazingly good*: telephone interview Michael True, 20 August 2008; *not embalmed*: telephone interview Frank Gado, 21 September 2008; *not everyone favorable*: telephone interview faculty wife, 20 November 2007, email William W. Combs, 25 April 2011; *Gwendy uprooted*: email Wendy Nielsen to David W. Fenton, 27 December 2008; *dinner invitation*: telephone interview faculty wife, 20 November 2007; *George and Martha*: telephone interview Reynolds Price, 3 December 2007; *me and the animals . . . Christmas*: CAF to Gwendy Fenton, 20 December 1958 and 25 December 1958; *good looking guy*: telephone interview Louis J. Budd, 3 December 2007; *Hillman Minx*: email Tom Greening, 31 March 2011; *secreted hormones*: telephone interview Joanne (Marshall) Mauldin, 8 December 2007; *bedazzled*: email Paul Nielsen, 17 January 2008, telephone interview Paul Nielsen, 6 February 2008; *terrific and strained*: telephone interview Richard D. Grant, 15 December 2007; *animals, golf, work, reunion Biltmore, sex, jealousy*: letters CAF to Gwendy Fenton, summer 1959; *Long Summer critique*: letter Cowley to CAF, 14 July 1959, CAF to Cowley, 17 July 1959, Cowley papers, Newberry Library; *history of Institute/Academy*: letters John Tate Lanning to Schorer, 16 November 1959 and 21 December 1959, letters CAF to Schorer, 14 December and 21 December 1959, Schorer papers, Bancroft Library, University of California, CAF to Cowley, 30 December 1959, Cowley papers, Newberry Library; *ACLS grant*: letter D.H. Daugherty (ACLS) to CAF, 6 January 1960, Fenton papers, Beinecke; *Yale Alumni Day talk*: letter A. Whitney Griswold to CAF, 20 August 1959, Fenton papers, Beinecke, letter Leonard W. Doob to NHP, 17 November 1960, Pearson papers, Beinecke; *MLA Heming-*

way: letter George Winchester Stone, Jr. to CAF, 25 May 1960, Fenton papers, Beinecke; *cesspool*: telephone interview Malcolm Mitchell, 4 September 2008; *good young critic*: letters CAF to Schorer, 20 November 1959, 3 December 1959, 14 December 1959, 10 January 1960, Schorer papers, Bancroft Library, University of California; *redshirting*: letter DeLaney Kiphuth to CAF, 3 February 1960, Fenton papers, Beinecke; *dozing conscience*: "Martin Luther King, Jr. Visit—1960," Durham (N.C.) Civil Rights Heritage Project online; *panic and alarms*: letter CAF to Cowley, 31 March 1960, Cowley papers, Newberry Library; *statesmanlike pronouncements*: note CAF to Ashbel Brice, 25 May 1960, Duke University archives; *relaxing indignation*: letter William P. Fidler to CAF, 6 May 1960, Fenton papers, Beinecke.

Sailing through Air

Nielsen wedding, courses: telephone interview Paul Nielsen, 6 February 2008; *Order of the Chair*: telephone interview Paul Nielsen, 6 February 2008; *waiting to crumble*: telephone interview Reynolds Price, 26 July 2008; *Ginger Price at Duke*: Duke University archives; *sexiest man*: email Merrill Skaggs, 23 August 2008; *breakup with Gwendy*: telephone interview Paul Nielsen, 6 February 2008, letter Reynolds Price to William Styron, 20 September 1960, Perkins Library, Duke, telephone interview Joanne (Marshall) Mauldin, 8 December 2007, telephone interview Wendy Nielsen, 17 December 2007; *Gwendy's anger, departure*: telephone interviews Andy Fenton, 17 November and 24 November 2007, letter Andy Fenton, 20 November 2007, telephone interview faculty wife, 20 November 2007, telephone interview Reynolds Price, 3 December 2007, telephone interview Frank Gado, 21 September 2008, Charles A. Fenton and Gwendolyn Fenton separation agreement, 19 April 1960; *selling house to negro*: letter CAF to Gwendy, 24 April 1960; *outings with Skaggs*: telephone interview Merrill Skaggs, 20 August 2008, telephone interview Calvin Skaggs, 24 August 2008; *explaining to mother*: letter CAF to Dorothy Fenton, 13 May 1960; *strength of ten, wonderful life*: letter Ginger Price to NHP, 1 May 1961, Pearson papers, Beinecke; letter Gale Carrithers to NHP, 13 September 1960, Pearson papers, Beinecke; *two very strong pulls*: letter NHP to Leonard W. Doob, 13 November 1960, Pearson papers, Beinecke; *money low, house in disorder*: telephone interview Andy Fenton, 14 December 2007, telephone interview Richard D. Grant, 15 December 2007; *gossip . . . chaste*: telephone interview Gaddis Smith, 28 November 2007, letter Reynolds Price to William Styron, 20 September 1960, Perkins Library, Duke, telephone interview Wendy Nielsen, 17 December 2007, email Merrill Skaggs, 22 August 2008, email William W. Combs, 7 December 2007, telephone interview faculty wife, 20 November 2007, telephone interview Louis J. Budd, 3 December 2007, letter CAF to Chester Kerr, 30 May 1960, Fenton papers, Beinecke, letter CAF to Mark Schorer, 9 June 1960, Schorer papers, Bancroft Library, University of California; *Ginger's father, CAF's mother*: telephone interview Merrill Skaggs, 20 August 2008, letter NHP to Leonard W. Doob, 13 November 1960, Pearson papers, Beinecke; *Darlington Dayton*: letter Ginger Price to NHP, 3 December 1960, Pearson papers, Beinecke, telephone interview Marshall Coleman, 1 December 2008, email Ginger Price (Barber), 31 December 2008; *bouts of depression*: letter Ginger Price to NHP, 3 December 1960, Pearson papers, Beinecke, letter NHP to Ginger Price, 11 December 1960, Pearson papers, Beinecke, email Wendy Nielsen, 16 March 2009, telephone interview Richard D. Grant, 15 December 2007; *Dr. Hart . . . how vile*: email Andy Fenton, 8 January 2008, letter CAF to Dorothy Fenton, 27 May 1960; *no furniture . . . venom*: letter CAF to Gwendy Fenton, 30 May 1960; *no raise*: NHP, notes on CAF's death, Pearson papers, Beinecke; *other positions*: letter CAF to Mark Schorer, 28 May 1960, Schorer papers, Bancroft Library, University of California, letter Chester Kerr to CAF, 13 June 1960, Fenton papers, Beinecke; *trip to Memphis*: letter Ginger Price to NHP, 3 December 1960, Pearson papers, Beinecke; *Wendy . . . Ginger*: telephone interview Wendy Nielsen, 17 December 2007; *life . . . hellish*: letter CAF to Gwendy Fenton, 30 June 1960; *$300 . . . subpoena*: letter Gale Carrithers to NHP, 13 September 1960, Pearson papers, Beinecke; *putting down Mister*: telephone interview Wendy Nielsen, 26 November 2007, telephone interview Frank Gado, 21 September 2008, telephone interview Merrill Skaggs, 20 August 2008; *Gado thesis*: telephone interview Frank Gado, 21 September 2008; *mother . . . Christmas*: letter CAF to Dorothy Fenton, 7 July 1960; *loonie*: letter Ginger Price to NHP, 3 December 1960, Pearson papers, Beinecke; *psychiatrist visit*: CAF notes on depression 1934–1941, letter Dr. Bernard Bressler to David W. Fenton, 29 July 1960, interview David W. Fenton, 26 May 2008, San Francisco, email Ginger (Price) Barber to Merrill Skaggs, 25 August 2008; *finest teacher*: letter Gale Carrithers to NHP, 8 November 1960, Pearson papers, Beinecke; *last day with Ginger, find a fiddle*: letters Ginger Price to NHP, 3 December 1960 and 25 January 1961, Pearson papers, Beinecke, email Ginger (Price) Barber to Merrill Skaggs, 25 August 2008; *bad news*: letter Ginger Price to NHP, 25 January 1961, Pearson papers, Beinecke; *I'll be back*: email Ginger (Price) Barber to Merrill Skaggs, 23 August 2008; *certain to hurt*: email Frank Gado, 31 October 2008; *calling Gwendy*: telephone interview Wendy Nielsen, 17 December 2007, telephone interview Andy Fenton, 24 November 2007; *turned in grades*: telephone interview Reynolds Price, 26 July 2008; *prescription*: telephone interview Merrill Skaggs, 20 August 2008; *all my love*: letter

Ginger Price to NHP, 3 December 1960, Pearson papers, Beinecke; *evening at Nielsens*: telephone interview Wendy Nielsen, 17 December 2007, telephone interview, Paul Nielsen, 6 February 2008; *returning book*: telephone interview Frank Gado, 4 December 2007; *ultimate horror story*: telephone interview Reynolds Price, 26 July 2008; *where they were*: letter Gaddis Smith to David W. Fenton, 24 March 1955, telephone interview Paul Nielsen, 6 February 2008, telephone interview William W. Combs, 4 December 2007, telephone interview Joanne (Marshall) Mauldin, 8 December 2007; telephone interview Mary (Church) Williams, 16 October 2010, interview David W. Fenton, San Francisco, 21 May 2008; *invalid will*: affidavits Gwendolyn Fenton Nielsen, 22 July 1960, and Jennis M. Mangum, 18 August 1960, Durham County records; *third note*: letter Reynolds Price to William Styron, 20 September 1960, Perkins Library, Duke, letter NHP to Leonard W. Doob, 13 November 1960, Pearson papers, Beinecke.

What Might Have Been

Reaching out: telephone interview Reynolds Price, 26 July 2008, letter NHP to Leonard W. Doob, 17 November 1960, Pearson papers, Beinecke; *Matthiessen clipping*: letter J. Gerald Kennedy, 25 January 2008; *Hemingway's Reaction*: letter Ernest Hemingway to Carlos Baker, 16 January 1961, Green Library, Stanford University; *Pearson/Doob correspondence*: letters Leonard W. Doob to NHP, 2 October 1960, and Norman Holmes Pearson to Leonard W. Doob 13 November 1960, Pearson papers, Beinecke; *Skagg' wedding hurtful*: letter Merrill Skaggs to NHP, 7 February 1961, Pearson papers, Beinecke; *"not to intrude"*: letter Ginger Price to NHP, 13 September 1960, Pearson papers, Beinecke; *first day of classes*: letter Ginger Price to Norman Holmes Pearson, 25 January 1961, Pearson papers, Beinecke; *hidden cancer . . . holding back*: letter NHP to Ginger Price, 11 December 1960, Pearson papers, Beinecke; *deeply ashamed*: letter Andy Fenton, 14 May 2011; *proposed revisions*: letters Malcolm Cowley to CAF, 28 January 1960, Cowley papers, Newberry Library, Ginger Price to NHP, 13 September 1960, Pearson papers, Beinecke; *rocky marriage*: letter NHP to Leonard W. Doob, 13 November 1960, Pearson papers, Beinecke; *A Mentor's Suicide*: email Tom Greening, 28 May 2011; *lost childhood*: email Tom Greening, 31 March 2011; *smiling ghost*: email Merrill Skaggs, 26 August 2008; *Gwendy romantic life*: telephone interview Wendy Nielsen, 17 December 2007; *greeting CAF in hereafter*: Richard D. Grant remarks at Gwendy's funeral. 18 September 2007; *astonishment*: telephone interview Wendy Nielsen, 17 December 2007; *most complicated event*: email Paul Nielsen, 18 January 2008; *auto accident*: telephone interview Andy Fenton, 17 November 2007; *man among men*: email Andy Fenton, 14 December 2007; *little to convey*: letter E.K. Powe to Gwendolyn R. Fenton, 18 August 1960, Final Report in the Matter of E.K. Powe, Administrator of Charles A. Fenton, Deceased, Superior Court, Durham County, 15 September 1964; *Pearson Benét Letters*: NHP, remarks at reception 27 October 1960, Pearson papers, Beinecke; *Trustees essay*: letter Russell Lynes to NHP, 6 October 1960, letter NHP to Russell Lynes, 16 October 1960, letter NHP to David W. Fenton, 16 October 1960, Pearson papers, Beinecke; *Man of Letters complications*: letters Ashbel Brice to NHP, 13 December 1960, and NHP to Ashbel Brice, 24 December 1960, Pearson papers, Beinecke; *"mileage"*: letter Ginger Price to NHP, 16 January 1961, Pearson papers, Beinecke; *Wescott report*: letter Glenway Wescott to Ashbel Brice, 3 April 1961, Fenton papers, Beinecke; *Schorer report*: letter Mark Schorer to Ashbel Brice, 10 August 1960, Fenton papers, Beinecke; *Pearson . . . Hilles reports*: letters NHP to Chester Kerr, 15 January 1961, Frederick W. Hilles to Chester Kerr, 28 January 1961, Chester Kerr to NHP, 14 February 1961, and NHP to Chester Kerr, 16 February 1961, Beinecke; *"his personality hovers"*: letter Paul J. Hurley to NHP, 9 December 1960, Pearson papers, Beinecke; *adverse report*: letter Chester Kerr to Donald C. Gallup, 8 December 1965, Fenton papers, Beinecke; *"terrible loss" . . ."infinitely sad"*: telephone interview Mary (Church) Williams, 16 October 2010, letter A. Whitney Griswold to Gwendolyn R. Fenton, 3 August 1960.

A Charles A. Fenton Bibliography

"You'll Get No Promotion" [short story], *Penguin Parade* 11 (1944): 139–55.
"It's a Story They Tell" [short story], *Adventure* 112 (January 1945): 75–77
"Another Language" [short story], *Cross Section 1947*, ed. Edwin Seaver New York: Simon and Schuster, 1947, pp. 72–79.
"'The Bell-Tower': Melville and Technology," *American Literature* 23 (May 1951): 219–32.
"Ambulance Drivers in France and Italy: 1914–1918," *American Quarterly* 3 (Winter 1951): 326–43.
"No Money for the Kingbird: Hemingway's Prizefight Stories," *American Quarterly* 4 (Winter 1952): 339–50.
"Hemingway's Kansas City Apprenticeship," *New World Writing* 2 (1952): 316–26.
"Ernest Hemingway: The Young Years," *Atlantic Monthly* 193 (March 1954): 25–34, Part I; (April 1954): 49–57, Part II; "The Paris Years": 39–44, Part III.
The Apprenticeship of Ernest Hemingway: The Early Years. New York: Farrar, Straus & Young, 1954.
"Hemingway's Apprenticeship," *Saturday Night* 70 (18 December 1954): 17–19; (25 December 1954): 14–18; (1 January 1955): 11–12; (8 January 1955): 14–18; (15 January 1955): 16–18.
"The Ivy-Covered Wild Blue Yonder," *Harper's* 211 (November 1955): 40–44.
"The Writer as Professor," *New World Writing* 7 (1955): 163–70.
"The Careful Young Men [Yale]," *Nation* 184 (9 March 1957): 202–03.
"The Writers Who Came Out of the War," *Saturday Review* 40 (3 August 1957): 5–7, 28.
The Best Short Stories of World War II: An American Anthology. New York: Viking, 1957. Introd., pp. vii–xx.
"Theatre" [Review of Archibald MacLeish's *J.B.*] *Nation* 186 (10 May 1958): 425–26.

"The Writing of *John Brown's Body*: Stephen Vincent Benét in Paris," *Atlantic Monthly* 202 (September 1958): 45–51.

Stephen Vincent Benét: The Life and Times of an American Man of Letters, 1898–1943. New Haven: Yale UP, 1958.

"The American Academy of Art and Letters vs. All Comers: Literary Rags and Riches in the 1920's," *South Atlantic Quarterly* 58 (Autumn 1959): 572–86.

"Theodore Roosevelt as an American Man of Letters," *Western Humanities Review* 13 (Autumn 1959): 369–74.

"The Founding of the National Institute of Arts and Letters in 1898." *New England Quarterly* 32 (December 1959): 435–54.

"The Care and Feeding of English Departments," *College English* 21 (January 1960): 203–07.

"The Purpose of the University," *Duke Chronicle* (10 February 1960) 2.

"Books" [Review of Henry F. May's *The End of American Innocence: A Study of the First Years of Our Time, 1912–1917*]. *South Atlantic Quarterly* 59 (Spring 1960): 284–86.

"The Lost Years of American Literature," *South Atlantic Quarterly* 59 (Summer 1960): 332–38.

"The Writer as Correspondent," *Virginia Quarterly Review* 36 (Summer 1960): 430–41.

"A Note on American Expatriation," *Western Humanities Review* 14 (Summer 1960): 323–29.

"A Literary Fracture of World War I," *American Quarterly* 12 (Summer 1960): 119–32.

"William Styron and the Age of the Slob," *South Atlantic Quarterly* 59 (Autumn 1960): 469–76.

Selected Letters of Stephen Vincent Benét. New Haven: Yale UP, 1960. Introd. vii-xxvi.

"The Sweet, Sad Song of the Devoted College Teacher," *AAUP Bulletin* 46 (December 1960): 361–64.

"The Founding of the American Academy of Arts and Letters in 1904." *Texas Studies in Literature and Language* 2 (Winter 1961): 481–91.

Unpublished Writings

You'll Get No Promotion [novel]. 1944.

But We Had Fun [novel]. 1945.

Members Only [play]. 1947.

Happy Valley [play]. 1947.

The Long Summer [227 pp. novel]. 1958–60.

The American Man of Letters in the Twentieth Century: A History of the National Institute of Arts and Letters and the American Academy of Arts and Letters. [i-ix + 242 pp.]. 1959.

"In Defense of Literary History" [10 pp. article], 1959–60.

"Publish or Perish Revisited" [10 pp. article], 1959–60.

"A Literary History of Princeton College" [14 pp. article], 1959–60.

"Graduate Schools and the Humanities" [22 pp. article], 1959–60.

"The Yale Writer as Alumnus," Yale University Alumni Day Program (20 February 1960), 11–23.

"Down with the Trustees" [15 pp. article], 1960.

"'Duke's Mixture': A Harvard for the South—Maybe" [15 pp. article], 1960.

The Writer as Professor and Other Essays [essay collection], 1952–1960. Preface (1 January 1960): v-viii.

Other Works Consulted

Aldridge, John W. "Before the Sun Began to Rise," *New York Times Book Review* (11 July 1954): 4.

"Alumni Notes," *The [Eaglebrook] Hearth* (21 February 1943): 4.

Alvarez, A. *The Savage God: A Study of Suicide.* New York: Norton, 1990 [1971].

"Author Fenton Honored Posthumously at Yale University Press Reception," *Yale Daily News* (28 October 1960): 1.

"Author Leaps to Death." First UPI dispatch (21 July 1960).

Baker, Carlos. *Ernest Hemingway: A Life Story.* New York: Scribner's, 1969.

———. "The Palmy Days of Papa," *Saturday Review* 37 (29 May 1954): 14–15.

Barkley, Dick. "Duke Prof Leaps to Death Here." *Durham Sun* (21 July 1960): 1A-2A.

Bishop, Patrick. *Bomber Boys.* London and New York: Harper Perennial, 2008.

Bly, Robert. *Iron John.* Reading, MA: Addison-Wesley, 1990.

Bullman, Tim A., and Han K. Kang, "Posttraumatic Stress Disorder and the Risk of Traumatic Deaths Among Vietnam Veterans," *Posttraumatic Stress Disorder: Acute and Long-Term Responses to Trauma and Disaster,* ed. Carol S. Fullerton and Robert J. Ursano (Washington, DC: American Psychiatric Press, 1997), pp. 175–90.

Carrithers, Gale H., Jr. "Professor Fenton" (letter to the editor), late July 1960, *Durham Sun.* Duke University Archives.

Castronovo, David. Beyond the Gray Flannel Suit: Books from the 1950s that Made American Culture. New York: Continuum, 2004.

"Charles Fenton, Writer, Killed in 12-Story Plunge from Hotel." Second UPI dispatch (21 July 1960).

Chase, C. Thurston. *Eaglebrook: The First Fifty Years, 1922–1972.* Privately printed. n.d.

———. "The Psychotherapy of the Adolescent from a Schoolmaster's Point of View." *Psychotherapy of the Adolescent,* ed. Benjamin H. Balser (New York: International Universities Press, 1957), pp. 182–246.

Cowley, Malcolm. *The Literary Situation*. New York: Viking, 1954.

Deming, John N., ed. "Fenton, Charles A.," *Yale 1941 Class Directory* (New Haven: Yale University Archives, 1956), p. 37.

Deresiewicz, William. "Love on Campus," *American Scholar* 76 (Summer 2007): 36–46.

Donaldson, Scott. "Hemingway and Suicide," *Fitzgerald and Hemingway: Works and Days* (New York: Columbia UP, 2009), pp. 455–64.

"Doubleday-Twentieth Century Fox Prize Awarded." *Publishers Weekly* 147 (9 June 1945): 2286.

Dunar, Andrew J. *America in the Fifties*. Syracuse, NY: Syracuse UP, 2006.

Engle, Lars. "The Remarkable Course Called Daily Themes," *Yale Alumni Magazine* 46 (April 1983): 16–19.

Engle, Paul. Review of Fenton's Benét biography. *Chicago Sunday Tribune Books* (26 October 1958): 2.

Fenichel, Otto. "The Counter-Phobic Attitude," *International Journal of Psycho-Analysis* 20 (July-October 1939): 263–74.

"Fenton Leaving Yale American Studies To Assume Full Professorship at Duke." *Yale Daily News* (n.d.: Spring 1958). Yale University Archives.

Freud, Sigmund. *The Interpretation of Dreams*, trans. and ed. James Strachey. New York: Basic Books, 1955.

Gass, William H. "The Doomed in Their Sinking." *The Best American Essays of the Century*, ed. Joyce Carol Oates (Boston: Houghton Mifflin, 2000), pp. 373–82.

Ham, Roswell G. *Fish Flying Through Air*. New York, Putnam, 1957.

Hastings, Max. *Bomber Command*. London: Pan, 1999 [1979].

Hemingway, Ernest. *Ernest Hemingway: Selected Letters, 1917–1961*. Ed. Carlos Baker. New York: Scribner's, 1981.

———. "The Hemingway-Fenton Correspondence," ed. Matthew J. Bruccoli, *Dictionary of Literary Biography Yearbook 2002* (Detroit: Bruccoli Clark Layman/Gale, 2003), pp. 282–99.

———. Letters to Charles Fenton, 31 August 1951–3 May 1954. "Lot 157, Catalog Jonathan Goodwin Collection." New York: Sotheby Parke Bernet, 1977.

"'Higher Education' Topic for Outstanding Debaters," Watertown (CT) newspaper, 6 February 1956.

Hoagland, Edward. "Heaven and Nature." *The Best American Essays of the Century*, ed. Joyce Carol Oates (Boston: Houghton Mifflin, 2000), pp. 507–19.

Hotchner, A.E. *Papa Hemingway*. New York: Random House, 1966.

Hyde, Louis, ed. *Rat & the Devil: Journal Letters of F.O. Matthiessen and Russell Cheney*. Hamden, CT: Archon, 1978.

Jamison, Kay Redfield. *Night Falls Fast*. New York: Vintage, 1999.

Jencks, Christopher, and David Riesman. *The Academic Revolution*. New York: Doubleday, 1968.

Kernan, Alvin B. *In Plato's Cave*. New Haven: Yale UP, 1999.

Kimbrell, Andrew. *The Masculine Mystique*. New York: Ballantine, 1995.

Kimmel, Michael S. *Manhood in America: A Cultural History*. New York: Oxford UP, 2006.

Knight, Douglas M. *Street of Dreams: The Nature and Legacy of the 1960s.*Durham, NC: Duke UP, 1989.

Kriegel, Leonard. "Hemingway's Pain," *On Men and Manhood* (New York: Hawthorn, 1979), pp. 91–112.

Leggett, John. *Ross and Tom: Two American Tragedies.* New York: Simon and Schuster, 1974.

Lockridge, Larry. *Shade of the Raintree: the Life and Death of Ross Lockridge, Jr.* New York: Viking, 1994.

Manchester, William. "Okinawa: The Bloodiest Battle of All." *The Best American Essays of the Century*, ed. Joyce Carol Oates (Boston: Houghton Mifflin, 2000), pp. 497-506,

"Matthiessen, Noted Critic, Ends His Life," AP dispatch, 1 April 1950.

Mills, C. Wright. *The Power Elite.* New York: Oxford UP, 1956.

Mizener, Arthur. *The Far Side of Paradise.* New York: Vintage, 1959.

Oates, Stephen B. *Let the Trumpet Sound: The Life of Martin Luther King, Jr.* New York: Harper & Row, 1982.

O'Brien, Tim. *The Things They Carried.* New York: Broadway Books, 1990.

Price, Reynolds. *Ardent Spirits.* New York: Scribner, 2009.

Pritchard, William H. *English Papers: A Teaching Life.* St. Paul, MN: Graywolf, 1995.

Reynolds, Michael. *Hemingway: The Final Years.* New York: Norton, 1999.

Riesman, David. *The Lonely Crowd: A Study of the Changing American Character.* New Haven, CT: Yale UP, 1950.

Safire, William. "Generation What?" *New York Times Magazine* (30 November 2008): 18.

Sauter, Edwin, Jr. "The Hand of the Master (A Memoir)." Unpublished article, 2008.

Shepherd, Elizabeth. "Three Generations of Fenton Men at Taft." Taft School publication, unpaginated, 2005.

Shneidman, Edwin S., and Norman L. Farberow. *Clues to Suicide*, foreword Karl A. Menninger. New York: McGraw-Hill, 1957.

Shneidman, Edwin S. *The Suicidal Mind.* New York: Oxford UP, 1996.

"Skydiving Legend Bill Ottley Recalls," *Drachen Foundation Journal* (Fall 2004): 19–20.

Stegner, Wallace. *The Uneasy Chair: A Biography of Bernard DeVoto.* Lincoln, NE: University of Nebraska Press, 2001.

Stiles, Bert. *Serenade to the Big Bird.* Atglen, PA: Schiffer Military History, 2001 [1947].

Stossel, Scott. "Still Crazy After All These Years" (review of Jonathan Engel's *American Therapy: The Rise of Psychotherapy in the United States)*, *New York Times Book Review* (21 December 2008): 16–17.

Strychacz, Thomas F. *Hemingway's Theaters of Masculinity.* Baton Rouge: Louisiana State UP, 2003.

Styron, William. *Darkness Visible: A Memoir of Madness.* New York: Random House, 1990.

Tabachnick, Norman. "The Crisis Treatment of Suicide," *California Medicine* 112(6) (June 1970): 1–8.

Thurber, James. "You Could Look It Up," *James Thurber Writings and Drawings*. New York: Library of America, 1996. Pp. 553–67.

Trollope, Anthony. *An Autobiography*. Introd. Bradford Booth. Berkeley and Los Angeles: University of California Press, 1947.

Whyte, William H. *The Organization Man*. New York: Simon and Schuster, 1956.

Wilder, Thornton. *Theophilus North*. New York: HarperCollins Perennial, 2003 [1973].

Wilkinson, Alec. "Remembering William Maxwell," *American Scholar* 73 (Winter 2004): 39–46.

Wilson, Sloan. *The Man in the Gray Flannel Suit*. New York: Simon and Schuster, 1955.

Winks, Robin W. *Cloak & Gown: Scholars in the Secret War, 1939–1961*. New York: Morrow, 1987.

INDEX